'A worthy new book, filling up large blanks in the hegemonic Anglo-American view of World War Two, part of a necessary excavation of suppressed and ignored histories'

PANKAJ MISHRA, New York Times

'A gorgeously written, heart-breaking book'

VEDICA KANT, Business Standard

'Karnad is battling the passage of time, and the passing of generations, but his work is a stunning work of recovery and commemoration'

MATTHEW PRICE, The National

'Equal parts genealogy, political history, and literary storytelling'

NEHA SHARMA, L.A. Review of Books

'Karnad's skilful achievement is to take us on an epic journey, while subtly revising our perspective on the Second World War ... The Afterword is worth the price of the book itself'

ANDREW DUFF, Military History Monthly

RAGHU KARNAD is an award-winning writer and journalist who lives between Bangalore and New Delhi, India. His essay detailing the origins of this book was described by Simon Schama as 'nothing short of brilliant'. *Farthest Field* is his first book.

Praise for *Farthest Field*:

'Karnad has a quite astonishing talent. He is a master of the sublime, writing poetically about a chain of battlefields he has never seen. I found myself wanting to reread almost every paragraph in a book so carefully arranged that at times the purity of its prose very nearly obscures the importance of the tragedy it is recounting. The precision is offered in equal measure to matters simple and profound'   SIMON WINCHESTER, *New Statesman*

'There is a very English control of irony that can suggest Forster ... at his best, but there is nothing remotely Bloomsbury or comfortingly English about the imaginative power, intelligence and descriptive richness of a narrative that, again and again, startles by its originality before convincing by its utter fitness'

DAVID CRANE, *Spectator*

'I wanted to savour his prose. That this is Karnad's first book just goes to show that well-crafted writing needs no authorial pedigree ... Karnad illuminates brilliantly the "so much owed by so many"'   JOHN KEAY, *Literary Review*

'One of those rare and extraordinary books which bring people alive again ... Written with imagination and engrossing to read'

SIR MICHAEL HOLROYD

'A bravura feat of literary-historical imagination – the kind that one would normally associate with a novelist ... Like a superior commander himself, Karnad marshals and orders a huge range of materials, locations and actions with apparently effortless skill, making everything cohere not only through a galloping and affecting narrative but, crucially, through a passionate moral core that repeatedly exposes the numerous ways in which Indians were treated as fodder by the Empire'

NEEL MUKHERJEE, *Financial Times*

'A dashing mixture of fact and imagination, *Farthest Field* tells a grim and epic tale, but it is also full of charm and playfulness, for Raghu Karnad is as alive to the incongruities of war as to its horrors. He gives equal value to the respect and even affection as well as to the resentments and inequalities between the British and the Indians in what everyone could see were the last days of the Raj. The book is an audacious achievement for a first book, and one more welcome sign that the years of oblivion are coming to an end'

FERDINAND MOUNT, *Telegraph of Calcutta*

'In *Farthest Field*, the distinguished journalist Raghu Karnad's spectacular first book, he describes how as a child he grew up familiar with the faces of three young men contained within three silver-framed sepia photographs, but never asked their names ... Prose that verges at times on poetry'

JULIET NICOLSON, *Daily Telegraph*

'Few books ... better communicate to outsiders the dilemmas of modern Parsi life; few conventional histories so effectively convey the personal trauma of war'

DAVID ARNOLD, *Times Literary Supplement*

Farthest Field

An Indian Story of the Second World War

Raghu Karnad

WILLIAM COLLINS

William Collins
An imprint of HarperCollins Publishers
1 London Bridge Street
London SE1 9GF
www.WilliamCollinsBooks.com

First published in Great Britain by William Collins in 2015
This paperback edition published in 2016

1

A catalogue record for this book is
available from the British Library.

ISBN 978-0-00-811573-9

Maps by John Gilkes

Printed and bound in Great Britain by
Clays Ltd, St Ives plc

MIX
Paper from
responsible sources
FSC
www.fsc.org   FSC™ C007454

For my mother,
who didn't let me forget

Contents

PART THREE: East

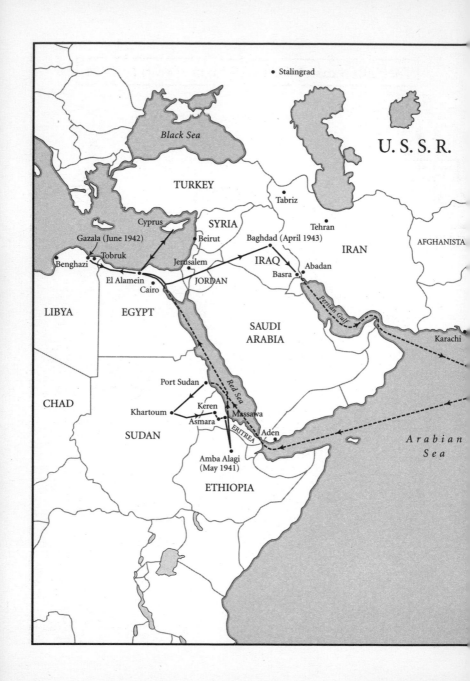

The Fifth Indian Infantry Division at War: 1940–44

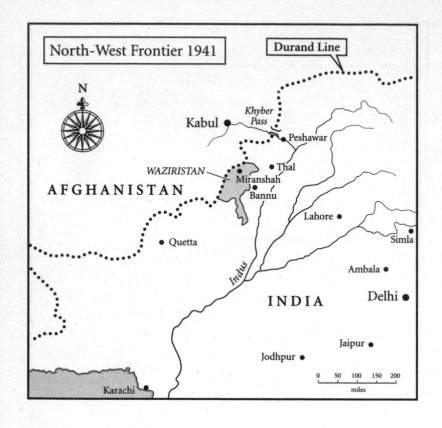

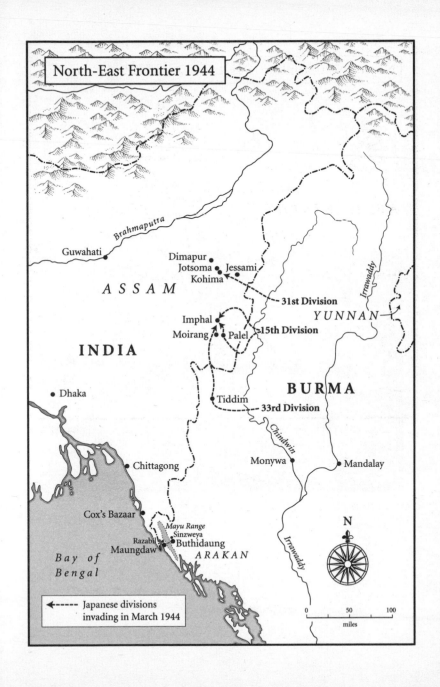

Prologue

I had known their faces my whole life, but never asked their names till it was too late. Their portrait-style photographs, full of grain and shadow, were not in albums – that would have placed them somewhere in the train of family history, and when the albums were opened, we'd have asked, 'And who's that?' Instead they were isolated in dull silver frames on table tops around the house in Madras; beheld but not noticed, as angels are in a frieze full of mortal strugglers. I never even noticed that I looked like one of them.

I still can't believe I was so late. By the time I asked, not only were those men long gone, but my grandmother was too, and her sisters, and most of their generation. Nugs, my grandmother, could have told me everything, though she might have refused. I think she had banished her youth from her mind by the time she died, though I don't actually know. I never asked. I was a child, curious about anything but family. All I'd wanted from her was the hoard of gold which I believed was hidden under a clicking tile in her bedroom. She told me I could have it after she died. So, after she died, I knew precisely where to look for what had never existed. And what had existed – her story and the stories of those young men in the photo frames – I had to search for without her.

There was an injustice in it, which I sensed as it dawned on my mother how little she knew of their stories either – though one of the men was her own father, and the others her two uncles. She and my grandmother were always close, as I'd imagined a single child and bereaved parent had to be. Half a lifetime they had spent together, but neither one asked or told about what happened. My grandmother, a doctor, had sutured that past shut. Eventually they were both doctors, and when my mother moved away to work in New York for nearly twenty years she wrote back every week, and in the house in Madras I found every one of the thousand letters, bound up into bricks that could build a playhouse. Everything my grandmother could save of my mother's, she had. But of the men, there was almost nothing.

Still my mother did know the names of those who, in the late hours of their lives, held onto strands of the story. With visit after visit, we followed the thinning thread of those lives, right up to the point where it frayed, came apart, and came to an end.

What I learned first, before I even learned their proper names, was that they had been in the Second World War. That was surprising. It was almost outlandish, because Indians never figured in my idea of the war, or the war in my idea of India, and I thought I had a good idea about both. There was certainly no public notion of it; nothing we were taught in school or regaled with from the silver screen, even though the Indian Army in the Second World War was the largest volunteer force the world had ever known. Personally, I hadn't thought Madras could even be mentioned in the same book as Pearl Harbor; I was accustomed to thinking of the war as Western Front, Eastern Front and Pacific. When I looked through the eyes of Indian soldiers, however, the globe turned, revealing new continents.

The larger story was the key to retrieving what I could of their private stories. From the start, to learn what happened to my grandfather and grand-uncles was to discover the lost epic of India's Second World War, as well as the reasons we chose to discard it. I started with names. To the family, they were Bobby, Manek and Ganny; their proper names, which I'd never seen in writing, I confirmed from a registry of Commonwealth soldiers. The registry also listed the units to which they belonged. With luck, I found those units' diaries. This meant that in my desperate pursuit, even at times when I lost sight of them, I still knew the road they had taken.

Graham Greene describes Henry James as once saying that a writer with sufficient talent need only look in through the mess-room window of a Guards' barracks in order to write a novel about the brigade. James didn't say anything about non-fiction, but the challenge of this book felt similar. Could one write a true story on the basis of only glimpses into the lives of forgotten men?

I might have tried to write a novel, but I knew there was nothing I could invent that would outdo the true, brief course of their lives. Instead I approached this book through what I think of as forensic non-fiction: I started out with three unknown, dead men on my hands. Who were they? How did they die, and where, and what took them there? The result is my best shot on the case of the three brothers-in-law turned brothers-in-arms. To deal with their interior lives, which I was determined to do, I took a sort of forensic licence, using fragmented evidence and testimony to build an account of their thoughts and beliefs. This was a compromise, but one that helped me confront the paradox, which only grew in magnitude, of becoming familiar with forgotten men. That apart, I have limited all incidents, anecdotes, speech, and details of movements, operations, environment and milieu to what I learned from interviews or records, or could generally establish as fact.[1]

Even what I have categorised as facts are often themselves a kind of fiction, reshaped and revised during their long storage as personal and institutional memories. Nothing drove this home like my face-to-face interviews with Indian veterans of the war Most were in their nineties. Many remembered their twenties as well as I do mine, but their answers, especially to the question of why they joined a colonial army, seemed to have been mentally corrected over their much longer service in the army of free India. In general, their memories, like all memories, were smoothed and polished by time, as pebbles in a stream. Many of the claims of Army histories and memoirs may be just as unreliable: shaped by agenda, nostalgia and pride.

So this story is imperfect, live flesh drawn over skeletons rebuilt from scattered bones. But it is one in which the lives of a few might stand in for many others. One of the felicities of these men's lives was how they captured, in reflection, the hidden landscape of India's Second World War. But whether or not any single book could document India's engagement, this book does not. It is not a scholar's history, no more than it is a traditional biography. Rather it is an exercise in reaching into darkness and considering what is retrieved.

I have not strained to depict events too far outside the circumference of the characters' lives – especially not those which are best remembered, such as the explosion of the freighter *Fort Stikine* in Bombay harbour, or the battles of the Italian campaign. This book is less about the devastation of total warfare than about private apocalypse reaching people in places very far away from the war as we have come to imagine it. The limits of documentation mean that many elements of their personal lives are missing, such as relationships within their units, especially with orderlies, jemadars or other ranks. These would have been powerful bonds, but were recorded nowhere that I could find. This is a story about being lost in the middle, and one way that this appears is that its characters are from a middle class. It was a class better informed and generally more politicised than Indians of the ranks; it was the class that staffed the leadership of the Freedom movement as well as of the Indian Civil Service. Their legend is not one of heroic conviction and unity, but of ambivalence and division, which only grew deeper over the course of the war.

When the war was over, the Indian Army – and the more than two million men and women who served in it – found that they had spent the past six years on the wrong side of history. Ever since, having fought for free India would be the price of admission into national memory. Those who survived still had a chance to earn that coin, and many did, in the new wars that began almost at once. But those who died would be left to lie, in silent cemeteries where words carved in marble insisted to nobody: 'Their Name Liveth For Evermore'. Their faces were lit by the candlelight of private memory, till even that dwindled and was gone.

People have two deaths: the first at the end of their lives, when they go away, and the second at the end of the memory of their lives, when all who remember them are gone. Then a person quits the world completely.

War brings the two deaths close, because it chooses young people most deliberately to die. If he died at twenty-five, those who loved him still had long journeys to make, with little of his to carry with them. He had barely begun to live in the first place. Their lives had barely begun either. Eventually he is kept more as a photograph than a name, and even the photo sinks under the layers of their life's increase. People can have two burials.

Countries keep alive the memory of the war dead: their own and their enemies'. Usually the war dead are remembered best of all, killed more easily than they are forgotten. But sometimes even countries try to forget their wars, and the second death, of the idea of you, closes in.

Death is a field from which no one returns. The second death is the farthest field of all. That was where I found Bobby, trying to cross.

Bobby and Nurgesh
Mugaseth in Calicut

Bobby

Ganny

John Wright

Bobby and classmates at
Guindy College

Nugs (second
left) in Calicut

PART ONE

Home

1

Everybody's Friend
Calicut, 1936–39

It is said that the news of the world war reached Calicut along with the morning eggs. Perhaps that isn't true at all. Perhaps it's only true that the price of eggs was the first the Calicut Parsis saw of the costs of war; the first of many. Maybe they remembered what happened to the price of eggs, even years and years later, because they wanted to forget what happened to the boys.

If, however, it is true, then it must have begun with a commotion at the Marshall house, nearest the pier. The noise would have been swallowed by the rowdy waves of dawn, on a sea swollen by the late monsoon. If Bobby had been in Calicut, he would have been there in an instant. Rounding the corner to the beach road, he would have spotted the egg boy cowering behind his bicycle; then the Marshalls' cook, aggrieved, wiping his neck with the tail of his checked-cotton mundu; then Keki Marshall, hollering as though he meant to argue the sun back into its bed. He would bloody well not pay four annas a dozen. Not for eggs. Whatever conspiracy of grocers, hoarders and bastards thought they could double the price of eggs overnight, they were going to learn differently from him, war or no war.

But did someone say war?

The egg boy may have been told that rationing and shortages were expected, and eggs would be priced up as a precaution. But he couldn't have explained about the Panzers in Poland, the craven declaration from London, or the Viceroy in Delhi already committing India and Indians to the fray. Instead the egg boy fled. He wobbled his bicycle a safe distance from the gate and rested a moment, calming himself down. Ahead of him was a full street of Parsi homes. He knew precisely how many eggs they took. He knew he was going to catch hell at each doorstep. He couldn't imagine the hell he was going to leave there.

News, like almost everything, travelled slowly to Calicut, though it was the largest town in Malabar. The province lay in the narrow lap of the western coast, with its head leaned up against the high range of the Western Ghats, and its feet dipped in the Indian Ocean. The town was a minor entrepôt for timber, pepper and cashew coming down to the sea, and fish, petrol, shop goods, and the post going back up. Once it had mattered more. It had been the seat of the Zamorin of Malabar, whose rule extended south as far as Cochin, and it was here that Europe first trod on India's soil, when Vasco Da Gama scraped up on the beach at Kappad.

The centuries since had left Calicut to turn in its own slow eddy of trade.[1] Its provincialism concealed the scale of its wealth and commerce, and the rhythms of the town played like a drowsy accompanist behind the full-lunged score of the sea. Arab dhows rode at anchor, waiting to unload sacks of dried fruit from Yemen, then raised their sails and blew away like kites on the horizon's glittering string. Coconut trees crowded the shore, and further inland all was covered in layers of matted green. Pink lotus wilted in the temple pond, and in the courtyards stood elephants, black and mottled and as brilliantly daubed as the lingam within. At the market, Maplah wives in long-sleeved blouses and headscarves mingled with bare-breasted Ezhava women selling clams and jackfruit. The town had no garrison, no real port. So Calicut concerned nobody but the sahibs who owned plantations on the Wynaad Plateau, the many local castes and creeds, and the Parsis.

The Parsis: pale as scalps, mad as coots, noses like commas on the page. They were devoutly civilised, consummately lawful, and still abided by the spirit of the first contract they made in India,[2] as refugees shin-deep in the surf. *Parsi*: it meant from Persia, and the label never peeled away; the centuries only stiffened their pose, polite and helpful, as India's permanent houseguests.

They were friends to all, up to the King and down to the cobbler, and while they could be silly buggers, there was always a politesse, acceptance of the King's law, distaste for conversion or preaching aloud. They were sporting in business, and business-like at sport. What Gurkhas were in the Army, Parsis were in civilian life – the exemplary race, making the best of British command without any desire to usurp it. So they retained the state of public grace that best served private wealth. *Humata, hukhta, huvrastha*: Good thoughts, good words, good deeds.

Bombay was their metropole, Karachi too; further south they got a bit native. In Malabar the men all spoke Malayalam, could gallop it in their mouths, but the women were not exposed too much, for the sake of their complexion, and their accents remained. Women wore saris but the men wore shoes indoors. Like Anglo-Indians, they were attentive to cutlery; unlike Anglo-Indians, they were content – a creed of Oneness had chased them out of Persia, and a creed of Innumerables had received them, and they had prospered, most major of minorities. At the beginning of the new war they were as numerous as they would ever be, and that was only 100,000, a homeopathic dose for India: a thimble of sweet milk set down beside its vats of steaming oils and syrups.

Away from the pier, near the Heerjees' soda factory, was the house in which Bobby Mugaseth grew up with his three sisters. The pier was where Bobby staged one of his classic pranks: going down at dawn, when the boats knocked against it like toddy-drunks clutching at a rail, and dropping into the water for a swim, against his father's rules. Afterward he splashed up the beach to circle the Marshall house, tapping at the louvred windows until Bacha Aunty suffered him coming in to bathe.

Bobby, properly Godrej Khodadad Mugaseth, did believe himself a good Parsi. If his hand was easily turned to mischief, that was not necessarily un-Parsi-like – only unlike the paragons of Parsi merit who occupied the nearer branches of his family tree.

His grandfather Dhanjibhoy had arrived in Malabar in the 1850s, and quickly transformed from a sunken-cheeked box-wallah into the very Moses of Parsi society there. On the broad Beypore he had built Malabar's first steam-powered sawmill, turning its estuary into one of the busiest timber yards in the world, and himself into the patron of Calicut's industrial and civic life.

Bobby was relieved to have never known him, and to encounter him principally through the clipping books in which his obituaries were preserved. He was a 'sincere admirer of British rule and British institutions' (the *Statesman*) 'held in high esteem among a very wide circle of European friends and admirers'. He was 'the Grand Old Man of Calicut' (the *Spectator*). Yet the most captivating image of his grandfather was from the story, gleaned from these admiring reports, of a single spectacular failure.

The coffee-planters of Wynaad had long struggled with transport between plantation and coast. Dhanjibhoy had an inspired solution: a camel caravan. He purchased a herd from the Rann of Kutch, had it transported by boat and equipped in Calicut. But there his animals perished, unable to tolerate the tropical climate. Nothing could displace the picture in Bobby's mind of a silver-bearded prophet, brow shining with sweat, struggling up the slick incline to the promised plateau, followed by a train of damp, doomed camels.

Young eyes primed for slights, Bobby noticed that every obituary tipped its hat to Dhanjibhoy's older surviving son, his Uncle Kobad. None bothered to name the younger son, Bobby's father Khodadad. Kobad, a doctor, had both retained 'a large practice among the European community' and 'nobly maintained the traditional charity of his honoured and esteemed father'. He was in a big book called *Who's Who*, and was the sole Indian member of the Whites-only Malabar Club. Nothing persuaded the British to embrace an Indian as warmly as when the Indian could treat a baby that had squalled through the night.

Kobad served the Empire directly, too. The Great War had ended the year before Bobby was born. In Europe they said there'd be no war ever again, but in Asia it started at once: in the Arab states, in Afghanistan, and eventually in Malabar. The Maplah Muslims, many of them soldiers demobilised after 1918, rose in rebellion and took the districts around Calicut hostage. Thousands were killed, even British soldiers, before order was restored. Afterwards, hundreds of Maplahs were sent to penal settlements in the Andaman Islands. When an Indian delegation was sent to check on their welfare, Kobad was asked to join. The other delegates reported that the convicts were half-dead, but Kobad authored a minority report, insisting that 'the Maplah had proved himself to be an ideal colonist and pioneer'. For this – for recognising the humane intentions of the Maplah Colonisation Scheme – he was specially thanked by the Excellency-in-Council in Madras.

Britain was their good master. Dhanjibhoy's early career had been testament to how the colonial economy rewarded enterprise, and his later life showed how the government rewarded loyalty. The family firm was given a monopoly contract to supply salt to all of Malabar. They had, even in a literal sense, accepted the salt of the Raj.[3]

They were happily out of the salt trade by 1930, when Gandhi rallied against the monopoly, leading his long march to lift a clump of slimy salt at Dandi.[4] Inspired, the local Congressmen planned their own salt *satyagraha*, to start out on the Calicut beach and end up at Payyanur. But the police let them have it, right there in front of the Cosmopolitan Club. Bobby could hear the cries from his house, and drew a picture of the thin men being knocked one way and the other by the arcing *lathis* and the curl of the morning waves. Some left on stretchers.

School reopened, and while the Civil Disobedience Movement ran its course, eleven-year-old Bobby led a thrilling double life. The Congress was demanding *purna swaraj*, complete independence. He was swept up in the boys' talk of boycott and bonfires, and their ardent horror at the convulsions in the furthest reaches of the country: revolt in Chittagong and massacre in Peshawar. At home there was only contempt for Gandhi and his eruptions; Bobby's father was no less loyal to the British order than his father before him.

Khodadad had always been bright, but had achieved nothing to the hurricane lamp of his brother's success. What made it worse was that when a certain kind of Calicut conversation came up about Uncle Kobad, it drifted into a vague and unnecessary reproach of Bobby's father. Khodadad ran the firm, chased shipments at the Harbour Works, and managed the increase of a venture that was already big. He built up accounting successes that interested nobody. His disappointment did not move him to draw his family closer. Instead he pressed his affections like flowers between the pages of two books: his Avesta and his accounts ledger.

He began to assume a pious scrutiny of the community: a prerogative recognised mainly by himself. During Sunday service at the *dharamsala*, a building built by his father, Khodadad would clear his throat if the *dastur* misspoke a prayer, to embarrass him into repeating it. When Khodadad came down the street, kids scattered, abandoning their game. By the time they were teenagers, Khodadad only seemed to notice his children when he carried the *aferghaniyu*, swinging it on its thin, squeaking chains and puffing sweet smoke into every room of the house. He'd present it to each child, and watch from behind a veil of smoke as each one added a piece of frankincense to earn its benediction.

While the country fought for freedom, it was his sisters who first showed Bobby what that might mean. There were four children – one every four years, like clockwork. Bobby was third; the only boy. The oldest, Subur, was eight when Bobby was born and featured in his life mainly as an exemplar of good schoolwork, which never struck him as much of an identity. Subur was a regular bluestocking, and her academic career was for a while the light of Khodadad's eyes.

Nurgesh, the next sister, was clever too, but her nature was tempered by her strident and overbroad compassion. 'Nugs' was the one who sighed and worried about the ribbed creatures, man or horse, that pulled the family around Calicut on rickshaws and tongas. To the world she turned a bright and stubborn face, though on her own she was prayerful and nervous about the hard work it took to be a woman, and furthermore, a doctor, which was her intention. Khorshed – 'Kosh' – four years younger than Bobby, was spoilt and a baby. She had looted the family's share of good looks, with an oval face and delicate nose, and without the wide mouth that made them look so Parsi. People said she looked like a movie star – like Ingrid Bergman, they would say later on. Bobby said that was ridiculous.

When Khodadad had a photographer come to take family portraits (always at home, never with backdrops, though it pleased him to have a mat printed with a lion at his feet), the girls behaved but their faces gave much away. Subur wore the faint beginning of a smirk, Nugs alone would be smiling; Kosh had her cheek and her neck turned just so. Bobby's expression was the most elusive. His face was a good one, with large, somnolent eyes under dark brows, smooth cheeks, and a bundle of dark hair with the slightest widow's peak. He could easily make himself look both handsome and sincere, which was useful for a young man so capricious. But in every photograph his expression was slightly translucent, as if he meant to defy the picture, or anyone looking at it, to record what he really was.

The house belonged to the women. Every room was a warehouse of lace and muslin, light *sadras* and blouse pieces and petticoats, nighties and Chinese borders and vials of rose water. It was the girls who paid the real price of Khodadad's piety, however. Trapped at home, confined for five or six days each month to a dim room that held nothing but an iron bedstead, and kept from going to the cinema – even when the Crown and Coronation showed pictures that would be the summer's sole conversation.

Their freedom movement began with Subur, who won a scholarship to Oxford in 1932, before Khodadad knew women could even go to Oxford. Yet off she went, past the horizon of his control, to dilate on the poetry of the contemporaries of Alexander Pope. For four years she was reduced to a monthly telegram that reported her successes in exams and Society. Then Subur cabled from Marseilles, to say she was about to board the HMS *Strathaird* and come home. She was not returning alone, but with a man she planned to marry: Gopalaswami Parthasarathi. The Iyengar name hit Khodadad like a lead weight, and left the rest of the boy's identity (... a double blue at Wadham, son of a distinguished civil servant ...) barely ringing in his ears.

It was betrayal. The pure blood in their veins had been poured carefully from the cup of one generation into the cup of the next through centuries, without admitting a drop of pollution. Subur was allowing a Hindu's spit in it. A Parsi woman who married a non-Parsi lost her religion and her community. She could never enter a fire temple, not even for her parents' last rites. That Khodadad, whose distinction in Calicut was his religious excellence, had to watch his favourite daughter stray from the faith was vandalism – not only of her soul but of his. A carriage came to the gate one evening and Subur was in it. Her parents had not seen her in four years, and now they would not. Khodadad sat by the door, curled and tense and hard as a scorpion to see that she wasn't let in. Out front, Nugs and Subur hugged each other's heads through the carriage window and sobbed.

Those were hot months, mingling too many tears in the sweat of the coastal summer. Bobby watched from the sidelines, ready to run away into the street and ripen his Malayalam in the sun. The house weighed less heavily on him, except that he was the only boy. He must inherit the town's most eminent trading concern, to manage in his turn. Sons turn into their fathers, Bobby knew, but an end so inevitable could only be treated as impossible: same as death. The picture playing on the screen in

Bobby's head was different. Its action would not be caught in the stifling funnel of the southern coasts, between that seaward gate of the Calicut customs office and the cargo bay of the Madras docks. His story would take him further, though he could not yet imagine how far.

He went hunting with the Heerjee boys and daydreamed down his barrel. Out on the estuary were the only decent summer game — fat, mean muggers lying still and inconspicuous by the water's edge, looking like sunbaked cowpats unless one had its jaws open. As long as they were sunbathing, the advantage was yours. Once the crocodiles entered the water, it was theirs. You had to get a mugger at the base of its neck, where the scales weren't armour-hard. If you missed, they were in the water in an instant. They could overturn a boat and slide a child down their throats as if it were a prawn. Or so he'd been told, when he was a child. In the bellies of the oldest muggers there was royal treasure, silver nose-rings and anklets, intact long after the princesses who wore them had been digested.

The moss-mirror surface of the Beypore gave him no foreboding of what lay ahead; bridges on the Ganga, pontoons on the Euphrates or the ferry across the boiling waters of the Manipur. The decade already hastened towards war, but it was someone else's war, very far away. Bobby never imagined, any more than the egg boy, how the war would rise up around India, or how it would divide the country, divide the army that enlisted him, and even divide Bobby against himself. Or that he, his sisters and new-found brothers, his countrymen and men from all over the Empire, would be drawn out onto roads that led very far from home, and did not all lead back.

If he had known, he might not have been in such a hurry to leave. But nothing was changing yet in Calicut. Every year on his birthday, his family bathed him in milk and rose petals. Every year he protested, letting only his mother Tehmina do it, and every year his sisters would break in, shrieking, to fling the petals at him before he even had his pants on. In his teens, his long face revealed a strong jawline, to balance the effect of the sweet mouth and eyes. As soon as he could, he wore the sharp moustache that was in fashion, like Errol Flynn's — two sabres crossed on his lip. He was seventeen. It was time to get moving.

2

Hukm Hai

Madras, 1939–40

Time to get moving.

Bobby's eyes opened and passed over the area. No room for error now – this was where it got dangerous. He surveyed obstacles and alternative escapes, in the event that the exit was blocked. To his left, the elderly owner of the Irani café dozed at his desk, his head drooping forward and jerking back. His son, the manager, thick-armed but mild, hid behind a rustling headline: 'KEEP THE ENEMY AWAY FROM INDIA: Contribute again to the Governor's War Fund'. A Tamil bus boy moved between tables, clattering thick china plates and steel forks into a tub.

Bobby pinched the last saffron streaks from the plate, licked his fingers, and moved into action. He stretched out wide, wincing with satisfaction. As his left arm reached into the air, his right hand danced the plate across the table, ringing out the signal he was finished. Smooth as a top, the bus boy turned toward him, and Bobby rose and strolled to the desk.

'What you had, beta?'

'Two plates dhansak, uncle,' he answered, beaming. 'But I don't have any money to pay.'

'*Suu*? What?' The drooping spectacles marched up the length of nose.

14

Bobby pursed his lips, contrite. The idea was to keep the volume down.

'Bloody bugger!' the old man shouted, rising to his feet. So much for the volume. 'Who the hell are you that I should feed you for nothing? Heh?'

'Uncle, what can I say. I'm a Parsi.'

'What Parsi! Who's a Parsi! I never saw a Parsi giving ... to not pay for his food! What behaviour? You rascal, you don't ... You are not a Parsi!'

Bobby stumbled backward into a chair, aghast. A soda fell over and fizzed in somebody's rice. His expression wobbled from the wound, and he turned his palms out to the wrathful Irani. 'Me, not a Parsi? Uncle, say anything, but don't question my ancestry ...'

'You are never a Parsi!'

Bobby swung his head in fierce reproach. The son was now trotting across the shop, wagging his index fingers to call for peace, but Bobby had changed gear. His fingers flew down the buttons of his shirt, and pulled it open. Clutching his white undershirt like a loose cotton skin of his heart, he said, 'Sadra!' Without lifting his eyes from the Irani's refracted glare, he reached back for a chair, and clambered onto it to stand above the room.

All eyes were pinned on him.

'Daddy, for God's sake what –' said the son.

Bobby chanted:

> *Yatha ahuvariyo*
> *Atha ratush ashat chit hacha,*
> *Vangheush dazda manangho –*

> ('As the Lord is chosen,
> So is judgement chosen
> In accordance with truth –')

15

'Get out!' the old Irani screamed. 'You – just get out right now!'

Bobby dropped off the chair and was out the door. As he ran down the street, he squeezed his trouser pocket, checking for the change he would need to get back to Guindy, the suburb down the shore from Madras. His leather soles clapped against the asphalt, applauding his daring and his escape.

Madras was a city that, if not on the boil, was at least kept simmering. Its skyline bubbled with domes, each bunch marking a grand institution beneath: a court, a college, a church of any faith. The older domes were Gothic fruit, and the newer domes raised in this century were called Saracenic: white hemispheres with brims like sola topis, sly effigies of the White men who built them. They had some opposition from the baroque gopurams of the city temples, and the rustling ficus trees. But Madras was the founding British city in India, the first to be lit up by the bulbs of modernity, and it was the domes that drew young men and women from a hundred peninsular towns, especially at the start of an academic year.

To say that Bobby arrived here, in 1936, to go to college would be misleading. He did attend the Loyola College, a new Jesuit institute at the edge of the city, and did matriculate in two years. But he was enrolled more seriously in a programme of unlearning than of learning; specifically, unlearning the habits of his upbringing. One new friend, Sankaran Nair, had the pleasure of walking into Bobby's room and finding him on his bed stark naked, knees splayed out, trimming his toenails with his teeth. The joke became that Bobby, 'while at his pedicure', had gone wide and 'made himself a Muslim'. If anyone asked, he said, sure, he could prove it.

He had a good length of leash in his head, and sometimes he would just run to its end, to see how far he went. He stood outside his chemistry lecture hall once, poised until he had thrown a brick through the window – just to see if his arm had the nerves to do it, to let fly – and then he appeared in the doorway, while the curses and the clear solutions were still rolling off the table tops, and the lecturer's eyes fell on him as though Bobby had sacked a temple, and Bobby said, 'Spot of fun ...'

You didn't forget a guy like that. Nair would later write about his two Parsi friends, Bobby Mugascth and Manek Dadabhoy, 'There is a belief that Parsis are weirdos in some way, perhaps due to inbreeding. These two did exhibit some craziness occasionally. It only added to their charm.'[1] Bobby looked up to Manek: he was the type of Parsi brimming with dash and confidence, which came from growing up in the big city. He was shorter than Bobby and broader – square in the shoulders, square in the jaw, with a heavy brow, and he looked you square in the eye. Nobody called Manek lovely, or cooed over his features as they did to Bobby, but girls did call out when they saw him on the street.

He had 'a craze for suicidal speeding', Nair found, on the day he borrowed his uncle's brand-new motorbike, a 350cc Ariel Red Hunter. Manek swiped it whenever he could. They rode it out along the sweltering Cooum river, or idled by the gates of the Women's Christian College, gunning the engine for looks. On the sweep of College Road the boys did stunts, opening up the throttle and trying to pull a 180-degree turn without crashing. Only Manek could. In fact, he could pull out of an awful, squealing, imminent catastrophe, rebalance, and ride back with his hands off the handlebars, patting his pockets for his Hohner harmonica and puffing out a tune just as he sliced back through the group.

For their generation, raised in the doldrums of the Depression, the motorcycle was a promise of a new decade of speed. For

Manek it was more: a simulation of his real dream, which was to join India's new air force. In the Hunter's skid and turn, he played at dives and spins and open sky. In the college canteen he was a one-man recruitment centre, reading IAF ads aloud from the papers. 'Be a Leader Among Men,' he hollered. 'High up in the sky, you are in independent command, monarch of all you survey!'

Parsi boys were mad about flying, anyway: the gadgetry, the gallantry, the gymnastic possibilities of the open sky.[2] Even Manek's little brother, Edul, was itching to sign up. The Indian Air Force was a new thing in the world, budding and flexible and deadly glamorous. But military aviation relied on advanced technology, and there was scepticism, especially within the RAF, of Indians' ability to handle it. That scepticism was a headwind, creating both impedance and lift. It made the IAF a service for daredevils. Manek would go.

Organised in alphabetical order, Bobby Mugaseth's room-mate at college was P. Mukundan, whose family was from Calicut too. The Mukundans were Thiyyas, a caste deliberately advanced by the British to counter the strength of Brahmins and Maplahs. They were loyal in return, and around the Cannanore Cantonment, they had grown noticeably lighter-skinned, the wages of their hospitality to British soldiers. Mukundan taught Bobby bits of political doggerel – 'Gandhi *sanyasi*, India *maanthi punn'aki* ...' – 'Gandhi the *sanyasi* tears at India and opens its sores' – with which they mocked the Congresswalas, boys who rose early in the mornings to struggle with cotton tufts and turning spindles.

It was nothing personal, and in any case, things had been pretty quiet since Bobby had arrived in Madras. A new constitution had been introduced in 1935, and nationalist parties had agreed to join elections to form provincial governments. The Congress had done very well, and in 1937 it formed a ministry in Madras under the moderate premier Rajagopalachari, who was fondly called 'Rajaji'. A few protests took place, but it was less easy to protest the government now that they were part of it.

In the spring of '38, Bobby and his friends finished at Loyola, and prepared to go their separate ways. It turned out that none of the ways led very far from Madras. Through most of the 1930s, a middle-class young man could expect to finish his education and find nothing to do, only irritating his family, squandering his eligibility and beating the air with superfluous certificates. Bobby and Mukundan enrolled together in the College of Engineering in Guindy, and Bobby saw plenty of Manek; in fact, he had to keep an eye on him.

Manek's magnetism had an opposite pole: Bobby's sister, Khorshed Mugaseth, who had arrived in Madras in her turn. As with any risky manoeuvre, Manek was a dab hand at courtship. He found a sudden passion for the opera, and then the boys were over listening to *La Traviata*, and Kosh came along.

Bobby had a theory that he had put to Nugs and Subur: that after Calicut, they had studied literature and medicine as the two most direct ways to learn about men. Kosh went and got herself a real one. Manek would pick her up at the hostel, and she ran out to the gates while her girlfriends catcalled from the verandah. Queen Mary's College sat plumb on Marina Beach, so if he didn't have the motorcycle they walked, eating puffed rice, and her *pallu* billowed in the breeze to run over his hands and face.

At the end of her first year Kosh dropped out of college, and she and Manek were married. Kosh was young and out of turn, and should have let Nugs marry first. But Manek was a Parsi, and after Subur's elopement the couple was harassed by the blessings of priests and parents. Their wedding day was a profound vindication for Khodadad, fitting with his new opinion on the proper schedule of education and matrimony for young women. Often he looked over at Nurgesh, expecting her confirmation that all was in order in the family, and nothing would happen again to upset him so dreadfully. But Nugs was not herself. To the guests who noticed, she explained that she was harried by all the organising, which they took to mean that she was dismayed at her much younger sister beating her to the altar. Bobby knew better.

It was in Subur's home that Bobby first saw him, apparently trying to hide beneath a towel. He sat on a chair with his head between his knees. The towel hung off his rounded back and fell like a curtain to his toes.

Bobby knew that Gopalaswami Parthasarathi – GP – had a lot of socialist friends from London, and that even now he and Subur sometimes harboured young Tamil communists while they hid from the police. For a moment, Bobby wondered if that might be what this man was doing. But of course it wasn't.

'You're ... Ganapathy?' Bobby asked the mound. It straightened, and the towel was pulled aside. Ganapathy's face emerged with a puff of steam, like a conjuror's trick. A bucket of just-boiled water was between his feet, and his face was glazed with condensation. 'Yes,' he wheezed, 'Hullo. Sorry about ...' and wiped his forehead with the towel. 'It's my asthma. Your sister has been ...' he wheezed.

'Don't talk, then,' Bobby said, and sat.

The man nodded. He touched his chest and said, 'Ganny'.

Looking him over, Bobby must have thought: *typical*. Nugs would always choose the sick puppy. Sick, though really quite well built and evidently well treated by life. His face had a residual roundness, and a tidy moustache held within the bound of his lips made the curve of his cheek look fuller. A face like that made a person look trusting, even without its being steamed pink. Nugs obviously trusted it in return. Something between them made them allies against the rough tendencies of the world. The truth was the reverse, though. It was their alliance that would make the world cruel.

Bobby had heard through collegiate chatter how much time his sister spent in 'joint revisions' with a fellow, *not* a Parsi, as his name made clear. Kodandera Ganapathy was a Kodava, of the arrogant tribe from the densely timbered, isolated hills north-east of Malabar. Those hills had bred a martial race, not one recognised by the Army, but definitely by their neighbours in Canara and Mangalore, who considered them dagger-bearing, boar-spearing, maiden-stealing terrors; worshippers of rifles, or of ancestors to whom they made offerings in arrack. Which was fairly accurate.

By the twentieth century, however, the Kodavas had been tamed by the Raj, and their wealthier clans sent sons into the police and forest services. Ganny's father had been Deputy Conservator of Forests, so Ganny was raised in civilised postings across the Presidency. Fourth in a household that had six children and zero privacy, he had grown into a shy, asthmatic young man, reluctant to make easy friendships but devoted to the ones he had.

Nugs and Ganny were in love, and for four years they had found no way of ending it. The Kodavas took endogamy seriously, and were even better than Parsis at enforcing it. One distant aunt had promised to set herself on fire if her son married a Telugu girl; when he went ahead, she did too. Ganny's family was above that, he knew, which only meant that it was the family that would face the ire of the clan. He would be long gone: a limb infected by romantic insolence, so cut off.

Thanks to Subur, Nugs had seen what she was in for if she married Ganny. The scales could never settle when she weighed young love against the old bond of family. To marry Ganny would mean a fugitive existence, and already, at least until they finished medical school, it meant lying low. They spent their summers apart, pretending the other didn't exist. He carried a fountain pen in his breast pocket, and in its cap, in a tight scroll, he kept her photograph.

Their lives in Madras were their own, however, and the Mugaseth siblings met the new additions with happiness and curiosity. Soon they saw less of Subur and GP, whose lives were helter-skelter between a new baby and his job at the national newspaper, *The Hindu*, and their trips to Kashmir, where his father was Dewan to the Maharaja. When they did meet, they only quarrelled with Manek about the war.

It was the other five who learned to laugh at and tease one another, the way Kosh teased Ganny about the mole – the chic 'beauty spot' he had on his lip. She pretended to pinch it off and place it on her own.

'Can't I have it, Ganny?' she said.

'You're pretty enough already,' he replied. 'But you can have it if Nugs says so.'

Like children in a treehouse, out of reach of their parents, they formed a new unit in Madras, with new rules of membership. Through his sisters, Bobby was bound to new brothers, and they built themselves, half-unawares, a new family. It was his sisters who poured the milk and roses down his neck on his twentieth birthday. The boys dressed their hair after Ganny's instruction, with rich pomade and many pulls of the combs they kept in their pockets, whisking the hair grown long on top into victory rolls. They learned new dances and how to drive, had brandy evenings and gramophone nights. They let their days slip from the clutch of memory into the quickening stream of the decade.

A month after Kosh's wedding, far away in the west, the war began. Hitler's Germany invaded Poland, and from Whitehall, a morose Neville Chamberlain informed the world that he had waited until a quarter past eleven, giving Hitler an extra fifteen minutes, but was compelled at last to declare war. The next day, the Viceroy Lord Linlithgow declared for India.

Indians, who had spent two decades entering the river of nationalist sentiment, now found its flow violently reversed or eddying in confusion. The freedom struggle was a diversion from the fight against fascism, or vice versa. The word 'freedom' pulled one way and then the other. It meant freedom for the men of Europe. It meant freedom *from* the men of Europe. Likewise 'victory': frowning black Vs appeared amidst the newsprint and on walls, everywhere, demanding that the populace believe the war their own.

Beneath the turbulence of ideology, the tow of opportunity pulled as hard and also in many directions. Khodadad, like most Parsis, supported the war. It was almost tradition that, when the Empire got into fights, the Parsis were entitled to what spilled from its pockets. War in Europe and Africa would mean a tidal rise in industrial orders, without any risk to Indian property. As leaders of Indian capitalism, the Parsis could appreciate how the economy would be fattened up by military salaries and rising commodity prices. Where Congress ministries had failed to bring about import substitution, German U-boats would succeed. Europe's combustion was a genuine concern, but also an opportunity.

The princes were similarly aligned. They raised funds and regiments, and freed up land for new airfields: favours they hoped to redeem whenever decisions were made about the fate of the princely states in free India. The Muslim League, the Hindu

Mahasabha and other parties of the right were happy, too, to trade global support for domestic credit.

The communists and socialists called Nazi tyranny no different from British tyranny and disdained the war effort. In the main recruitment districts in Punjab, they chanted, 'Na ek pai! Na ek bhai!' – Not one penny, not one man. Before long, however, Germany would invade the Soviet Union, and the tow would reverse. The survival of the communist hope was more important than India's transition to bourgeois self-rule. The college comrades then rose from their picket lines to line up instead at the recruitment centres. At the same time, the insurgent Bengalis of the Forward Bloc, friends with whoever opposed the British Empire, gave rapturous speeches comparing Hitler to Lord Vishnu, and spread implausible tales about Panzer tanks in France flying the Kapi Dhwaj, the standard of the chariot of the mythic hero Arjuna.[3]

It was the Congress, the party that would speak for the nation, which remained perplexed. Through the thirties it had opposed fascist aggression: much more so than the British government. 'In India there are no fascists,' Gandhi's protégé, Nehru, told a Czech journalist in 1938. 'We are very well aware of what Berlin, Rome and Tokyo want but we shall never allow the forces of our national anti-imperialist movement to be harnessed to their carriage ... They want to drown the world in blood.'

With the war begun, however, Nehru could not accept that Indian soldiers would die for the freedom of a nation which denied that very freedom to India; or that Indian taxes would pay to maintain those troops. Above all, the Congress leaders were appalled by the arrogance with which the Viceroy had committed India to war, without even consulting them.[4] Linlithgow had met Gandhi, whose first reaction was keen anguish at what violence lay ahead. Gandhi expressed his sympathy for Britain's heavy task. During the Great War he had personally recruited ambulance teams for the British side. Afterwards he had felt betrayed, as Britain would not repay India's sacrifices with freedom. Now he would write letters to Hitler imploring him to 'shun the method of war'. But he could not endorse a violent reply to the blitzkrieg.

Nehru, though an ardent Anglophile and anti-fascist, took a stronger position. If some Indians saw their private opportunity in supporting the war, Nehru saw all of India's best chance in opposing it. After meeting in council, the Congress leaders offered support for the war effort in exchange for Indian independence at the war's end. It was declined. In October 1939 all the Congress's provincial ministries resigned. They had governed since 1937 and grown complacent with petty powers. Now the movement could be re-energised as a true opposition, though its first agitations did not strike much of a chord.

The war was far away. There was no chance of dissuading new Indian volunteers. Their rural homes in Garhwal and Rajputana were as removed from the havoc as they would have been at the top of Kanchenjunga. It was still the year of the 'phoney war', when Britain only scowled at the fascists from across the English Channel. Around the world, the belligerent states chewed on their new possessions – Eastern Europe and Manchuria – in their respective backyards. India was safe, and its confident army sailed abroad to distant campaigns.

No place felt further from the action than Guindy. The college was a handsome one, the oldest school in India for training engineers, a monumental pile of pink brick and granite crowned by another sola-topi dome, and skirted by a cool arcade. Students sat in the archways, cross-legged over diagrams, the Brahmins tugging at top-knots which would be gone by their third year.

On the morning before his lunch escapade, Bobby had burst into the room where Verghese Kurien was spreading textbooks open on a mat on the floor. 'Kurien!' Bobby implored, pushing pinched fingers into Kurien's face. 'One rupee. One rupee. One rupee ... Please?'

He got the rupee.

'Thank you! Thank you thank you thank you —' and he was gone. His day was in motion. The ticket at the New Elphinstone, nine annas; a cool drink at the soda fountain, one. Nobody would bring him back to Guindy for less than four annas, so his lunch had needed to be free.

That evening, he went searching for Kurien again. He found him at the Non-Veg Mess (D),[5] where they were both invariably drawn by sizzle of pepper and coconut oil. Bobby wasn't about to pay Kurien back yet, only to reassure him how well his rupee had been spent. Kurien was from Calicut too; in fact, he had been brought into the world by Kobad's hands, and for that service, Bobby thought, it was fair to still be charging twenty years later.

Some alarm entered Kurien's eyes as he listened to Bobby breathlessly brag about his complimentary lunch. He finally told him: 'Mugaseth — I think you had better join the Army.'

Bobby thought so, too.

At Guindy, both boys were enrolled in the University Training Corps, the voluntary training unit for potential army officers. Early every Saturday, before the sun poured its jellied heat over Madras, they lined up at the Allen Grounds, occasionally for some riflery but mainly for endless parade. Kurien was hopeless. Ordered to shoulder arms, he'd get his rifle stuck in the next man's shirt-cuff, and drop it onto the ground. '*Pick up your damned rifle, you butter-fingered idiot!*' a sergeant shouted down the line, in some terrifying English Midlands accent. Bobby, with callous lack of effort, made the top student rank. He could out-shoot some of the NCOs at the rifle butts. Though the discipline never pleased him, every week his officers clapped him on his shoulder, and told him to put some stripes on it.

The Indian Army was the world's largest mercenary organisation; though it did not regard itself as such, its critics did not hesitate to. It was a force of paid soldiers who upheld the foreign occupation of their own land, and other people's lands as well. The Army was older than the Raj itself, and it had filled with the silt of centuries, out of which grew all its pomp and folly.

But the period between the wars had stirred that sediment. The first principle of the Indian Army had always been European command. The officer's commission, a King's Commission, was the privilege of White men. It brought moral order to the quarrelling castes and creeds in the other ranks, the natives whom Kipling had depicted in 'Her Majesty's Servants' as a conference of mules, bullocks, horse and elephant, united only by the animal grunt of *'Hukm hai!'* – It is an order! – *'Hukm hai!'*

After the Great War, so many British men lay in the ground that the government began to wonder how in the future it could staff its armies in Britain as well as in the colonies. The Congress, too, was insisting on a plan of 'Indianisation' of state personnel, including military brass. The year Bobby was born, native officers were cautiously commissioned into seven Indianised battalions. By 1932, an Indian Military Academy was opened at Dehra Dun, and established the right of Indians to join the army command. The numbers admitted were small, and the men selected were practically, and often literally, princelings.

Facing a new world war, with its allies under German occupation, Britain needed the strength of its colonies and dominions. It needed to expand their armies and – an unnerving thought for leaders like Churchill – their corps of native officers. A gate that had creaked open an inch in two decades suddenly flew wide. In came the newest martial caste of the British Raj: the Indian middle class. With an Emergency Commission, an Indian would be trained and paid on a par with White officers, and would receive his pips in just six months, instead of thirty. On college grounds across India, young men traded one uniform for the other, khadi for khaki.

This new war would not be like the Great War. In 1914, it was said the mud in Ypres was only brown because so many Indian jawans lay in it. While they had filed into the trenches of an alien continent, to die of gangrene, disease or the cold, the Army had sententiously debated whether it was alright for black Indians to kill White Germans, or even to have their wounds treated by White nurses. But Indians were not for crawling any more. They would not rank with dumb animals, only good for taking orders. They would be the *sahibs* now, saluted by subordinates of every race.

As for the mud, by the end of 1940, no war front remained on the continent. They would sail out to the far fields of the Empire, into the *jang-e-azam*, the war of the world, to perform deeds that would never be forgotten.

Savages of the Stone Age
Miranshah, November 1941

It was all very well for Manek, up there. But did he know what they did to a Tommy on the ground, if they caught him alive? Tortured to death, and that's just the start of it. If he was carrying his kit, they knew to look for the mess tin with its folding handle, and they used that pretty handle to gouge his eyes out. Then he's scalped, and they have his brains out, and fill the cavity with dust and stones and straw. They cut his privates off and stitch 'em into his mouth, and put burning cigarette ends up his nose.

Mind you, that's just his head ...

The sergeant trailed Manek through the circuit of the aircraft, making final checks. He was on his second tour in the North-West Frontier, he said; the last time had been with the Army, so close to the ground he could smell the fakir's sulphur smoking off the hills. He thought it only right, and some small pleasure, as a man who had felt flint-chips dance down his shirt when bullets struck his sangar walls, that he should inform the young Indian pilot-officer of the true nature of the foe. Air force men never saw much of them. But no one's initiation to Miranshah was complete without him getting a picture of how he would look after a Pashtun beauty treatment.

An hour later, Manek was cocooned in the cockpit of his Hawker Audax, 2,500 feet above the mineral sea of Waziristan. The slopes below him graded from the rule of brown to disobedient shades of purple, ferrous orange and powder blue, and the outcrops cast flat black sails of shadow, pointing east, east and east in the afternoon light. Here and there, notched into the hills, was a small white 'Y': the Frontier pickets signalling 'We have nothing for you. All is well.' Manek was now at the outermost point of British-Indian power, beyond the last garrison, wheeling through the furthest, coldest orbit of what was called India. The hills beyond them had been ceded to the control of the Afghan king. As if they were anyone's to cede, or to control. Manek thought of the recruitment ad in the newspaper: *Monarch of all you survey*. Kings ruled the air here, but not the land.

From this elevation, the Tochi river was a twist of green silk scarf, tied to conceal the beige blisters rising from the ground beside it. Those were the villages of Waziri Pashtuns, who grew rice and apricot trees on the riverbanks. Higher up the hills, they grazed sheep in the shade of the juniper and pine. In between, they lay among the stones, invisible, nibbling at sugary balls of *channa-gud* from their pockets, and waiting for the Empire's men to enter rifle range.

Once a week, on road-opening day, supply trains of armoured trucks ventured out to the Scouts' post at Datta Khel, the camp nearest the Afghan border. Up in the folded hills, the Army manned pickets to watch the valley road, while down at the river, stockades secured the larger villages at Boya and Kharmakar. At the base of the valley was Miranshah, knuckle of the Empire, home to several battalions of the Indian Army and the headquarters of the Tochi Scouts, tribesmen paid to control tribesmen in the most hostile sector of the Frontier. Yet control, bought at whatever price, never lasted long. When they grew restive, the

Pashtuns were stone-sprung terrors. At the end of road-opening day, when the pickets were called in to join the rearguard, seasoned soldiers came running like children from the dark. This was why the Army shared its base in Miranshah with the Indian Air Force and the RAF.

Other forts in the Frontier were crowded by hilltops, from which the Pashtuns sometimes took potshots into the kitchen lines and hockey fields. Miranshah, however, sat some distance from the nearest hills, a clay battleship in a flat, stony bay. At night, all life retreated into its thirty-foot hull. With its crenels and watchtowers silhouetted by the stars, the fort could belong in any century. But at dawn the gates opened and a modern air force was wheeled out onto the plain. Bomb racks and fuel tankers scrawled on the dust, and the Audaxes of No. 2 Squadron rolled into the haze, ready for the fight.

It was sixty years almost since the Forward Policy had advanced British control, not just to the base of the mountains beyond Punjab, but into their heights. Those passes had been the gates for the invasion of India since Alexander, and for as long as Britain had ruled the Punjab it had maintained a grizzled guard against threats from the west. Mud forts were built and garrisoned in monastic isolation, exposed to the elements and to trigger-happy tribesmen, and service in 'the Grim' became a rite of passage for young officers and regiments. By the turn of the century, once the wounds of the Mutiny had closed, the imperial imagination filled instead with exploits on the Frontier.[1]

The implacable Pashtun was inscribed in tradition, with a tsarist agent and a 'Mad Mullah' whispering in either ear. This grudge was not released even in 1941, when Germany invaded the Soviet Union and Britain's sullen, opportunistic nemesis was transformed into its valiant ally. The foreign shadow over the Hindu Kush did not disappear – it simply became a fascist one.

The figure of the Mad Mullah, too, was still intact in 1941. The mullah of the present was the Fakir of Ipi, Mirza Ali Khan, who in 1936 had stoked the Waziri and Mahsud *khels* into full armed rebellion. It took three years and half the strength of the Indian Army,[2] supported by the RAF, to suppress them, but the fakir remained at large. Using guile, or sorcery, he escaped every British grasp: whenever Gurkha units captured a cave being used as an insurgent hideout – killing, say, thirteen men – they invariably found fourteen beds inside. One person had simply been spirited away.

The Italians had been the first of the Axis powers to make contact with the fakir, using agents sent out of Kabul disguised as Pashtun tribesmen. They had made gifts of arms and equipment, including machine guns and a wireless set, and sought the financial terms on which the fakir would agree to create trouble.

Soon, German agents, with larger funds to dispense, tried to take over the negotiations with the Fakir of Ipi, the figure they codenamed '*Feuerfresser*', 'Fire-Eater'. Spies, some posing as scientists collecting specimens of butterflies, attempted to reach the fakir and foment a full-scale uprising in September. The Axis aim was to break the Soviet line at Stalingrad and the British at the Nile, and blitz across Central Asia. Through these passes, India could be invaded again, by a force of traitors and terrors: Nazis, Indian mutineers, and Pashtuns berserk under the spell of the Mad Mullah.

So it was that dragon's teeth grew in the ancient gums of the Khyber Pass – concrete pyramids to snag and slow the German Panzers. And so it was that in 1941, in the middle of a world war, Flying Officer Manek Dadabhoy patrolled the Frontier on duties a century old.

Manek was now at the tip of the lance of British-Indian power, raised against threats from the west. As he flew on, his mind travelled back along the taper of the lance: to Miranshah, the forward operating base, then Bannu, the supply station, and Kohat, where the No. 2 Squadron had its headquarters. Further back was Peshawar, the last real city of India, filled with commerce and political clamour. Beyond Peshawar the land descended to the busy fields of Punjab; to Lahore and Ambala, where he had learned to fly, and then Delhi, capital of the Raj and general headquarters of its army, the shoulder that raised the lance and set him here in the sky. Finally, at the end of an endless country stippled with shrines and laddered with railway track, where at last the land became water: Madras, where his family and his sweet wife awaited him.

Manek's family had never been as scrupulous as the Mugaseths, but like any Parsi home, theirs was printed at regular intervals with the icon of the winged-disc Farohar. The figure was sewn in cross-stitch and hung by the kitchen door; it was embossed onto the front of brass pen stands and printed on the warped paper stickers that someone once applied to the corner of each bedroom's mirror. The general effect was as if Farohar spent all day fluttering around the house, alighting on any old thing, spreading consecration like bees spread pollen.

The first impression Manek ever had of his faith was that it centred on a man riding a winged device. His tribe had spent 4,000 years admiring an angel who set an example impossible to follow – until now. Not to say that Manek felt divinely enjoined to be a pilot, but he did sense that in flight he might approach a lofty state that he never achieved on the ground. When he won his wings, the silver badge of a pilot officer, he thought of them as the pug mark of Farohar on his khaki breast.

After his appointment as an officer-cadet, Manek had taken a long train ride from Madras to Lahore for preliminary training at

Walton airfield. His months there were an already misted memory of drill, physical education, riflery and lectures; theory of flight, theory of weapons, assembly and disassembly. Half of his fellow cadets were cocky young men from Bombay and Karachi, members since their teens of the flying clubs there, and with more flying hours than some instructors. The other half were Khalsa schoolboys who had never set eyes on an aeroplane, let alone flown one. They struggled with every sentence spoken by the sergeants in their regional brogues. 'Brother, what are "goons"?' one whispered, at the end of a demonstration. 'He keeps saying "*goons*".'

'Guns,' Manek replied.

The Cranwell accents of the RAF officers could be equally elusive. 'Fahpah, what is *fahpah*?'

'*Firepower*,' Manek hissed.

He made the first selection and went on to Jodhpur, for flying instruction on the fine airfield of Maharaja Randhir Singh. They were billeted in tents, but they messed like rough-necked royalty in the Maharaja's guest house. They learned the luxury of living with bearers – magical chaps who could despatch you from your tent with gleaming shoes and your training schedule, and be waiting at the mess when you arrived there, setting out your bacon and eggs.

Manek learned to fly at last, in the Tiger Moth, a plane forgiving of beginners' errors. The Moth took care of him. To put it into a spin, you pulled the nose up until the plane stalled, and let it begin to drop, with one rudder held down. The plane corkscrewed towards the ground. He neutralised the rudder, and the Moth recovered on its own. It made the cadets cocky: they placed bets on who could pull off the longest spins. Manek's body stopped fearing the sensations of flight in the fabric vessel: the restless bob of the fuselage over the wheels as the props began to turn, its brief careening sway as it moved down the tarmac, and the effortless, almost absent, moment when flight began and the horizon dipped away. Back on the ground, he could feel a throb of racial rivalry among his fellows. But for him there was only one superior race: the flyers – all those who summitted their alp of air, and did effortlessly what their fathers in their youths would never have thought possible.

At Ambala he learned to attack the ground, dropping dummy bombs and strafing on the range. He learned to fly at night, high above the cancelled earth, flashing code down into the darkness and fighting panic until the 'glim' lamps were uncovered along the airstrip, one by one, a faerie road to bed. At last, in the summer of 1941, Manek returned to Madras carrying a scroll of rich parchment – his letter of commission. It began in lettering so thick with tendrils and curlicues that the words themselves seemed borne on a bank of clouds:

George VI by the Grace of God, of Britain, Ireland and the British Dominions beyond the Seas, King, Defender of the Faith, Emperor of India &c …

And then, in a tighter calligraphy:

To our Trusty and well-beloved *Manek Hormusji Dadabhoy* Greetings; We reposing, especial Trust and Confidence in your Loyalty, Courage, and good Conduct, do by these Presents Constitute and Appoint you to be an Officer in our Indian Air Force …

The letter was signed by His Excellency's Command, the Viceroy Lord Linlithgow. It was a splendid thing. It rustled with honour and authority.

Newly winged, Manek left for Peshawar to join the No. 2 Squadron. 'The Winged Arrows' had been raised on 1 April, but had spent months waiting for its aircraft, the dregs of the RAF fleet. The Westland Wapiti, popularly called the 'What-A-Pity', was a biplane that had actually been out of production since 1932. To start its propellers, a team of airmen threw a length of rope around a blade and yanked it into motion, as if hand-cranking a car. Still, the Wapiti was endemic to the skies above Waziristan: brown, spindly and locust-like, with bright RAF roundels for eyespots and tappets beating as visibly as an insect's heart.

Far more exciting than the planes Manek could expect to fly were the men who flew them – and the most exciting of them all was his squadron leader, Aspy Engineer. Manek had been too young to remember when Lindbergh crossed the Atlantic, but the Parsis had their own flying ace, and Aspy was it. He and his three brothers, all in the air force, were an Indian sensation.

Aspy was from Karachi, and grew up with the whine of biplanes rising from the great RAF depot at Drigh Road. While he was still a boy, his father used the family savings to buy a Tiger Moth so that his sons would learn to fly. By the time Aspy was seventeen, and the Aga Khan offered a prize to the first Indian to fly solo between Britain and India, Aspy was able to take his Moth and, without a radio or much else by way of instruments, win it. Two years later he was at the RAF College in Cranwell, one of the first dozen cadets selected for the Indian Air Force. At Cranwell he won the Grove Prize for best cadet of the year; jumped from a burning plane and survived – and made it back to India just in time to take a commission with 'A' Flight, the very first squadron of the Indian Air Force.

At the start of the war Aspy and 'A' Flight were on duty in Karachi, watching for enemy bombers in the sky and U-boat shadows in the water. By 1941, however, they had returned to the Frontier, where the Waziris were being roused by the Faqir of Ipi once again. In March, Aspy led a nocturnal rescue mission to Boya Fort, flying out in the black of night and returning mid-morning on wings tattooed with eighteen bullet holes. That operation would win him the Distinguished Flying Cross.

In June, only days before Manek reached there, Aspy had arrived in Peshawar to take command of No. 2 Squadron. He was only thirty, and not at all the grinning daredevil Manek had imagined and prepared to impress. At their first meeting, the new CO was reserved and oddly focused on protocol. He left Manek with a single, modest piece of advice that would become his own credo. 'Remember,' Aspy said, 'good flying means doing the right thing at the right time.'

Where Aspy was concerned, this meant leaving immediately to fly the duty wing out to Miranshah to get his new squadron blooded. The Waziris now threatened the post at Datta Khel, and four army battalions were sent to meet them, with a train of a thousand mules, trucks and guns. On 7 July, the Winged Arrows dispersed a gang of over two hundred hostiles who blocked the column's march.

It was from Miranshah that the RAF had led its first entirely independent campaign, in 1925, when GHQ India invited air staff to test their own solution to endless Mahsud raids. Three squadrons of Bristol and de Havilland biplanes rose from Miranshah to make continuous day-and-night attacks on the Mahsud villages; in less than two months, at the cost of only two British lives, the rebels surrendered.

The creation of India's own air force, in 1932, had made a bold statement: that an imperial armed service could be staffed by Indians alone. Unlike the Army or navy, the IAF was a service of the twentieth century, and in its miniature but modern establishment it reflected new expectations of the country itself. It did not prefer martial races for recruitment, and it scorned the segregation of faiths and castes, the cornerstone of order in the Army. The motto of its first squadron mixed Urdu and Hindi to pointed effect: *Ittehad mein shakti hain* – 'In unity there is strength'. But the proud, precocious start of the IAF belied the ancient duty it was made to perform: aiding the RAF in suppressing the Pashtuns. As it grew from a token force during the war, it still upheld the first principle of aerial bombing: that it was used to pay out to Black people the wages of opposition to White rule.

In October of 1941, a hundred *badmashes* attacked a picket at Asad Khel and were holding back a relief force across a rivulet called the Khaisora. The duty wing was scrambled to the fight, now flying Hawker Audaxes, better than Wapitis, though still canvas biplanes, towed out of their hangars like oxen.[3] They were above Asad Khel in twenty minutes. The pilots and observers peered down as bright white runes formed against the barren ground. Below them, signallers rolled out strips of cloth that spelled 'X–V–T' followed by cloth discs indicating the distance to the enemy positions. The pilots lined up and dived, squeezing their triggers and tearing up the ground in front of them, while the observers swung their Lewis guns, firing into the blur. The Waziri fighters fired back from wedges in the rock. The formation arced back into the sky, and came back through again and again, giving the infantry a chance to rush forward each time.

After the third pass, one Audax of the IAF climbed out but then sank in a nauseating drop. It recovered, lurched again for height, and buzzed down heavily into the gap between the Army and Pashtun positions. What happened was described by the pilot, Flying Officer Arjan Singh, while he was having his nose stitched up back at the base. His Audax landed hard on the bed of the Khaisora, smashing his face against the instrument panel. His gunner, Ghulam Ali, was so thoroughly disoriented by the shock that he got to his feet and fled – but in the wrong direction. He leapt out of the gully and ran right at the tribesmen, whose bullets popped at the ground by his feet. Arjan Singh, hand over nose, sprinted out in pursuit and finally caught him, fifty yards further up, and turned him around. Both men lay low in a deep cut of the stream bed, listening to the bullets blow past overhead, until they were rescued by the jawans.[4]

M anek was then still stuck in Peshawar, living out an endless yawn. In the mess, much of the conversation turned on the question of why they policed the Pashtuns at all. Some of the Indian pilots, the more political sort, believed that the Frontier was kept deliberately tense, and that the tribal *khels* were clay pigeons periodically set off to give them target practice. To Manek this seemed idle talk, the froth of idle hours.

Their cantonment was as mannered as every cantonment in India, and the walled city was out of bounds. In Peshawar the bloody chivalry of the Pathans overlapped with the mass politics of Gandhi's Congress, giving rise to something the Congress could barely control any more than the government.[5]

Manek was delirious with impatience before his turn came to join the duty wing. But he was there, in November, on a day that the telephone rang in the office of the Miranshah station commander, and a captain took the handset, listened for a moment and set it back in its cradle. Then he lifted it again to dial a number.

Aspy appeared in the door. 'XX?' he asked.

That was the code for an emergency flight. The captain shook his head. 'Just proscription.'

Years of regular imperial air control had culminated in the proscription bombing policy, with warnings delivered ahead of time, to minimise civilian casualties. One plane would go out and drop pamphlets over the target area, ordering the evacuation of women and children from certain villages; the next day, anything or anyone that remained – people, livestock, buildings – became a sanctioned target.[6]

Manek and the other pilots had until late morning to gather for the briefing, around a table covered with indexed maps and catalogued photographs. Soon they would go over their grid references, approaches, ordnance and the colours of the day with Aspy, but first they were addressed by the political agent, a quiet man Manek had seen flitting in and out of Miranshah wearing a captain's pips and speaking mainly to his driver in fluent Pashto. He began by describing the high pastoral villages and cave dwellings of the target area. Four days of bombing would be sufficient to bring their leaders to the *jirga*, where he would negotiate their compliance, confiscate arms and 'make sure they understand the good intentions of the government'. He didn't say with what the tribesmen were being asked to comply. In the stick-and-carrot strategy of India's government, they were the stick; their concern was only where to strike and how hard.

Manek wrote to Kosh of his excitement, and told her he'd be carrying her photo in his pocket. It was folded up with his blood chit, which the pilots called a 'goolie chit' because it promised in three languages a reward to anyone who helped an injured pilot return to base with all his bits intact. Kosh wasn't to worry, though: the Pashtun weapons were mostly old Lee-Enfields and Italian Martinis, and rifles built on British patterns in their own workshops. The pilots were never in range. He'd be in no danger.

He hadn't promised not to freeze to death, though, Manek thought as he pulled the Audax into the air. It was a slow plane but its cockpits were open. It was winter now: the snow caps had grown on the further peaks of the Hindu Kush, and the Audax swam through their icy breath. Manek and his observer wore hooded, fur-lined jackets, inverted-leather boots and gloves, with fur on the inner lining. He felt like a yak flipped inside out.

All about him the aircraft's Kestrel IIB engines throbbed and the atmosphere hummed tunes in the plane's wires. They were navigating by the line of a valley, centred on a pink vein of soft river bed. Before the days of the air force, this mission would have required at least a battalion on the march, a long, exposed train of followers, mules, field ambulance and remount staff trudging up the valley. The sergeant had told Manek how such missions went. How there came an echoing report from high above and disorder spread in the column, noses slamming into the packs in front of them. A man falls, or two, with panting screams. Machine guns are pulled off the mules and sections form up, some covering the hilltops as others climb, hot acid in their legs. A hundred yards from the top, they fix bayonets, pump their calf muscles with their hands, and charge. On top of the hill they find nothing but sky. In the next valley the rifles sing out again, more men fall; again the hill is bare. So, again and again, until the regiment reaches some settlement of goats and grandmothers, and smashes it until their rage and the village are levelled.

That was the punitive strategy of the previous century, referred to as 'Butcher and Bolt'. Now the Audax served the same end in a matter of hours, and they called it 'Watch and Ward'.

Manek straightened in his pilot's seat and raised his face into the slipstream. The formation slowed in the air and climbed down to pinpoint their target. He signalled bombardier mode to the cockpit behind him, and his navigator sank onto his knees, to stretch out prone beneath Manek's seat and access a hatch and a bombsight in the floor. The flight passed over and banked. Manek was the last to go, and he watched as one by one the other planes dropped low, and he saw the rips of light open and close, doing invisible damage among the dirt houses. Tiny figures scattered out beyond the village wall.

His mind passed over Arjan Singh's crash. It passed over his parachute harness. It passed over the photograph in his pocket. He pushed down the stick, read the ground and target as if they were part of his instrument deck, and felt his engine sigh at the load's release. Behind him, the shaggy head of the explosions rose from the ground. Above, the other aircraft dallied, innocent as doves. He rejoined them and turned back to Miranshah, at a loss for feeling.

His fight had begun at last. Against whom, he wasn't certain.

4

The Centre
of the World
Madras, February 1942

The defence of India – or the first visible sign of it in Guindy – was a fence raised by a gang of workers using a batch of defective propeller blades as fence posts. It was at the back of the Guindy campus, against the fields, where the army had built a new R&R centre for troops behind a sign that read 'Holiday Homes'. British soldiers had already moved in, and soon they were crowding the edge of the college football field, smoking cigarettes and hailing nervous students to come play a game.

The war was headed to India, and not from the direction anybody had anticipated. There was meant to be fighting in Europe, fighting in Africa, and war on and under the sea. Indian divisions were splayed out from the North-West Frontier through Iraq and up to Libya, holding back an enemy in the west. But nobody was prepared for war to reach Madras, and from Japan.

Only when the time came to start cramming did Bobby realise how loud the noises of war had grown. They weren't the noises he had expected. The suburban soundtrack of a distant hammer knocking became ten hammers sounding all around the students' heads. Glass panes came out of all the windows and were piled into sea-green slabs as the college handymen boarded the holes over with ply. Air-raid precautions had been ordered, and the campus juddered with construction: a pair of concrete tanks was sunk to store water for fire-fighting; a block of congested rooms was built to house air force mechanics on emergency training. Contractors yelled at men high up on scaffolding. Cement mixers gargled gravel through the night, drowning the murmur of the waves all the way from Elliot's Beach.

Nobody could study. Nobody tried. It was urgent and necessary to talk all the time, assuring each other that they too could not focus, and acknowledging that their entire class was doomed in its exams. It was their final year, and of course there had never been a class that finished at Guindy without sensing, in that end, the end of all things. The previous year, the college had set an accelerated three-year syllabus to produce more engineers for the Army; the year before that, it had admitted women.[1] But arguably, with the advent of a world war, Bobby's year had the winning hand.

That the new belligerence came from Japan was not in itself a surprise. The nation had spent decades bridling inside a thicket of European colonies and seething over the dilemma of a late-modernising power: for its population and imperial reach to grow, Japan needed food, oil and resources, but to gain those resources, it needed to expand its empire.[2] In 1936 the military government had seized some territory from the crumbling state in China. It was instantly condemned by Western countries that had themselves spent a century exploiting China, and the USA began to supply the Chinese resistance with goods and weapons, routed through India and Burma.

It wasn't until the West fell back into war, however, that Japan saw its destiny unclouded. By late 1941, European powers had spent more than two years at each other's throats. In the last world war, Japan had protected British shipping from the Germans. Now it was willing to try the reverse. On 8 December, hours before its navy bombed the US fleet in Pearl Harbor, Japan landed an army at Kota Bahru, at the northern end of British Malaya. Two days later, off the Malayan coast, its air force sank HMS *Prince of Wales* and HMS *Repulse*, the proudest battleships of the Royal Navy. With appalling suddenness, as the United States was lamed in the Pacific, Britannia ceased to rule the waves in the Indian Ocean. Japan lunged at the colonial sprawl. Its troops crossed from French Indo-China into British Malaya, captured the island of Hong Kong, took the Dutch East Indies and the American-controlled Philippines, and advanced on the fortress of Singapore. If it could hold back the West just long enough to exploit those colonies – of their oil, rubber, timber, grain, minerals and men – it could supply its own defence against the West's inevitable retaliation. Calling itself the liberator of each new colony, it accumulated, in haste, one of history's largest empires.

Each advance through Asia was announced with a bombardment, and refugees arrived in India each day to describe it. In Penang, naive crowds had filled the market rows, waving at the Mitsubishis passing high above the town. The formations passed again and again, inscrutable, until they flew low and shredded the crowds with their machine guns. Fire spread in the native town, and European residents received quiet orders to evacuate; at the docks, while they poured into ships for Singapore, armed volunteers held back the terrified Asians. The city was surrendered without any effort at defence.

The bombers reached Burma as early as December 1941. In Rangoon, 150 aircraft appeared all at once in the clear winter sky. Incendiary bombs began to fall in the labour settlements; built from cheap materials, they burned like tinder. It was Indians, most of them Tamils, who made up the labour in the town and the rubber plantations of Burma. They had been the first to migrate and work beneath the scaffold of the British Empire, taking orders from Malayali contractors a few rungs up, who took theirs from the White men at the top. The Japanese army blew through that scaffold like a gale; the British ruling class was the first to abandon it, and the Indian labourers were the most exposed as the structure collapsed. Migrant Chinese, whose anti-Japanese activism had been recorded by spies, were at great risk of reprisals, but their civic organisations supported them through escape or occupation. The Indians scattered and flew, blown like chaff before the brewing storm.

As in Penang, they poured into the streets, and the Mitsubishi Zeros flew in low to maul them. Two thousand were killed in Rangoon the first day, and the homes left standing were festooned with human gristle. Hundreds of thousands prepared to flee from the southern provinces toward Mandalay and the ports on the Bay of Bengal, obstructing (as the Japanese intended) Army traffic and government logistics.

The good news was that Manek's squadron had been ordered back from the Frontier, scrambled to the defence of the Indian coast. For a few weeks, the Winged Arrows held to their old routine, dropping their bombs at one end of India while they listened for the sound of bombs falling at the other. Manek sat by the radio, rapt, contemplating for the first time an opponent who had aeroplanes too, and more of them, and better.

The aerial defence of south India was tissue-thin. The country still relied on a volunteer reserve to patrol the coast, and the Public Works Department had only just thrown itself into building airfields in the south: sixteen in the Madras Presidency alone. The No. 1 Squadron was already in Rangoon, and now, at last, the No. 2 returned from the Frontier. The groundcrew caught the train at Peshawar: Indian officers swaggering into the first-class carriages, behaving like overgrown schoolboys, the sullen British NCOs in second, and the native NCOs in third. After watching them pull away, each group scowling at the one ahead of it, Manek was glad to sail back in exquisite solitude, high above the human fray.

By the end of February, he was in Secunderabad, in the Madras Presidency, and any time Kosh heard a plane drone past overhead, she ran into the garden waving both her hands and shouting, 'It's Manek, come to see me!' The war, now rising on both sides of them, still seemed a mirage, difficult to believe. But they felt like heroes already.

In Guindy, on another morning, Bobby passed a crew of painters at work in the halls, putting up fat yellow letters on the building's pink brick – 'E4, LCE3, E3, LCE2' – each followed by a dripping yellow arrow. What the cipher meant was clear, but even so his professor began class by reading out from a circular about how, in the event of an aerial attack, students should proceed to the slit trenches being dug around the college grounds. 'Please commit to memory,' he droned, 'ahead of time, the assigned portion of trench according to your course and year.'

He was interrupted by the head of the department, Dr S. Paul, who commanded the engineers' company of the local University Training Corps, and had been put in charge of Guindy's air-raid precautions. After glowering at the students for a minute, Dr Paul began once again to inform them that Guindy College would very probably be a bombing target. In the absence of any plausible defences, their lives would depend on their taking ARP seriously.

'And so,' he said, 'if there is going to be an air raid, you are sure to know what to do?'

'Yes sir,' the class mumbled, not at all sure.

'You, Mugaseth – you know what to do?'

'Yes, sir!' Bobby sang.

'So what will you do if they come?'

'This,' said Bobby, and he sprang to his feet, moved lightly to the window of the ground-floor classroom, and leapt out of it. He ran out into the campus, shouting 'Boom!' at every classmate he passed, and he didn't stop running till he was back at his room.

'*Boom!*' he yelled at Mukundan, as he burst through the door. 'Everybody take cover!'

Then he got under the covers and took a long nap.

At lunchtime, Bobby walked onto the grounds to watch the trenches being dug: zigzag gutters, each ten feet long, two wide and three deep. The hard soil thrown up on the sides was already dancing, grain by grain, back down to its bed. A group of radical students stood nearby, under the lone Indian beech that was called the Unity Tree.

They were seething, Bobby could tell, at the pathetic sight: the whole college preparing to crawl into its own shallow grave, to await the blows of an imperialist war that had already set three continents on fire. He heard them arguing, their rage newly stoked. He wondered if they meant to rush the trenches themselves. Perhaps he'd be expected to resist them, here on the orange grounds of Guindy, a new front of the world war; driving the points of their setsquares into each other's eyes.

One after the other, the great Eastern metropolises filled with fire and emptied of Europeans. Native staff were left to save themselves, and native officials to organise basic services and manage their surrender. In Malaya, soldiers were ordered to enact the 'policy of denial', a scorched-earth retreat, which meant demolishing ports, power plants and oil facilities, tearing out railroad and telegraph lines; leaving in ruins every modern installation the Empire had built and held up as the proof of its greatness.

In the jungle the Japanese were like muggers in the water. They scissored through terrain the British had considered impassable, their squadrons moving by bicycle, and patrols on elephant-back. A garrison remained in Malaya to oppose them: British, Australians and Indians. The Indians outnumbered the other two combined, but they belonged to an army still held in the amber of another era, of pack mules and breech-loading rifles. Most had never seen a tank, and now were scattered before Japan's armoured advance. The Rajputs and Pathans of the 45th Indian Brigade, just trained for desert fighting, were turned mid-passage and unloaded on the jungled peninsula. They were outflanked, outfought, bewildered by the failures of their command and the sheer superiority of the enemy. They began a fighting retreat, over ten miles each day for two months, toward Singapore, the bastion of the eastern defence. The 22nd Indian Brigade – numbering more than 3,000 men – was hewn down to sixty-three fleeing survivors. As they fought their desperate rearguard battles, military lorries rolled south rescuing golf clubs and porch furniture.

A pincer movement half the span of the planet was closing in around India. The grand strategy was laid plain in February by George Orwell, then working for the BBC: 'The general plan is for the Germans to break through by land so as to reach the Persian Gulf, while the Japanese gain mastery of the Indian Ocean … The Germans and Japanese have evidently staked everything on this manoeuvre, in the confidence that if they can bring it off, it will have won them the war … If Singapore is lost, India becomes for the time being the centre of the war, one might say the centre of the world.'[3]

Nugs knew someone in Singapore, Lakshmi Swaminathan, a friend from college. The Swaminathans were from Malabar too, where they were thought of as radicals. As a result, the girls never met until Nugs arrived at Queen Mary's, where Lakshmi was two years ahead. She wasn't a banshee wearing a homespun sari hitched up above her knees, as Nugs might have expected, just a sort of prettier, communist version of Nugs herself, neither of which was as offensive as Nugs might have expected. A girl had to have both delicacy and grit, Nugs knew, but she had never seen those virtues twinned quite this way. Lakshmi, unimpeachably gentle in college, could go to marches and return all bruised by men's elbows. She preceded Nugs to medical school, where she married a man from a different caste, with no fuss.[4] In 1940, Lakshmi left Madras to start a practice in Singapore.

She was still there on 15 February 1942, when Singapore was lost – and not only lost, but abjectly surrendered. Nugs tried not to wonder if Lakshmi was alive or dead. Hearing the stories of what the Japanese did to women, she didn't know which was worse. Along with the city, nearly 70,000 Indian troops concentrated there – a third of the entire strength of the pre-war Indian Army – were handed over as prisoners, along with 15,000 British and Australians. One entire division had marched down onto the docks just in time to be made captive. Never in its history had the British Empire surrendered so many troops en masse: troops who were still needed to defend Burma, or if Burma fell, to defend their own homeland.

India had felt numb pains of distant war creeping up its limb, but with the loss of Rangoon, they burst open as a weeping wound. Until 1935, India and Burma had been a single colonial state, and for long Burma was seen as a green field of opportunity for Indians of all classes: Tamil plantation labour, Anglo-Indian railwaymen, Oriya stevedores, Muslim petty traders, Bihari landlords with whole indentured villages in train. In Rangoon, more than half the population was Indian. When the Japanese invasion began, not only was the Empire unable to defend them, it had no plan to help them escape.

The city was invaded first by rats and bombs; then by fire, as the air-raid defences collapsed. Weeks before the Japanese marched in, parts of the city were in anarchy. Looters, even White soldiers, sacked the shops along the boulevards. Officials had recognised the impossibility of defending Rangoon at least a month earlier, but its residents were given only forty-eight hours' notice, after which, they were told, neither trains nor petrol would be available. The last boats left the docks at Taungyup and Akyab, and those left behind were stripped of any choice but one: to cross the remaining length of the country, and reach India on foot.

The retreating Army crossed over in good order, with few deaths, though stricken with malaria and harassed by Burmese bandits. For them it was merely 'the Dunkirk of the East'. Behind the Army was a river of pathetic civilians, straggling down the open road. And behind them came the Mitsubishis, some ploughing the column with cannon fire; some filling the air with thousands of fluttering leaflets. These were propaganda cartoons, gaudy and shocking, depicting starving Indians ground under the heels of fat imperialists, or turbaned jawans being kicked out of evacuation lorries by blond-haired Tommies. In Hindustani or in Urdu, they said, 'The Englishmen are just not bothered about you. You will see this scene wherever you look.'[5]

The centre of ancient Mandalay became an immense refugee camp, until the bombers reduced it to acres of ash and cinders. The refugees moved on, into northern Burma, where the British roads gave way to hill tracks, and the tracks gave way to long smears of mud, monsoon downpour and human waste. Cholera spread through the camps and contaminated nearby water sources. On the most exposed segment, the 130 miles between Monywa and Palel on the border, the roadside was littered with families too drained to walk. Sometimes a parent or child was still able to move on all fours, to reach a nearby water body and find it, invariably, already fouled.

Six hundred thousand attempted the gruesome march: at the time, the largest human migration in history. Eighty thousand died, in the transit camps and in the undergrowth by the sides of the route. Many left parents or children to die. At Palel and Imphal, there were field hospitals and well-stocked camps, and Army convoys to the railhead. But even there the planes came, above the fluttering Red Cross flags, to draw the harrow over them one last time.

Never before had the Empire, and the men who commanded it, been so disgraced. In the First World War, Indians on the Western Front had first seen the forbidden sight of White men afraid, wailing, soiled, like regular men. But that was on a distant continent. In 1942 the humiliation took place in India's backyard, and its evidence streamed through Assam and Bengal and all the way to Madras.

At Madras Medical College, where Nugs and Ganny were now house officers, ward after ward filled with refugees. Many had been stretched to their last fibres by starvation, and exposure, malaria, dysentery. Nearly all had cholera. Blue-white faeces gushed out of them. The staff cut holes in the ward bedding, and stitched sleeves of waxed fabric between the holes and buckets on the floor. Nugs and Ganny monitored how much liquid the patients lost every hour, then the ward boys collected the buckets and sloshed the 'rice water' into the gutter.

Few survivors carried anything, except for anguished tales of their abandonment by the Raj. Lying in their cholera beds, they told of Anglo-Indian families whose darker-skinned daughters were turned away from camps for Europeans; of columns of Indian refugees held back until Europeans had passed, so the roads would be less begrimed; of elephants struggling up the slopes, hind legs quivering, as they carried mahogany desks out over the bodies of children. The most despised rumour, which travelled well in India, was that the Army enforced separate 'White' and 'Black' routes: so little did Indian lives count in the end.

Nugs and Ganny heard their stories in the wards, and a different kind of appeal outside. Officers of the Indian Medical Service had besieged the campus, bidding to recruit the senior students. Much of it was familiar, but a new enticement had sent a murmur of amazement through the class: final-year students who signed up to join the Army would receive a monthly stipend of a hundred rupees, starting right away.

Try as he might, Ganny couldn't get the offer out of his mind. It meant he would start his life with Nugs with some savings, instead of empty pockets, as well as an assured job. Every civil department had suspended hiring at the start of the war, and in their place, graduates were invited to apply for military commissions, and promised priority in civil appointments after the victory. War service would count double for seniority. The Army Medical Corps needed thousands of doctors – one for each new fighting company, and more down the chain of evacuation: in field ambulances, at staging sections, casualty clearing stations, ambulance trains and barges, base hospitals and convalescent depots. The government was doing all it could to make it seem a sound professional decision, rather than professional suicide.

Or actual suicide, which was how Nugs saw it. There was a terrific row. To Nugs, the war was a pathological madness, undoing a thousandfold all the efforts of all the doctors in the world. She knew that Ganny thought the same. They had nationalist friends, like Lakshmi Swaminathan – who they imagined was a captive, at best, of the Japanese – and they had come to agree with them on the lunacy of the war effort. How could Ganny even think about throwing his life into that fire, for the bribe of a commission?

The newspapers said that President Roosevelt had called for a new name for the war which would 'briefly describe it as a war for the preservation of the smaller people of the democracies of the world'. What he meant was that Europe was in peril of losing the freedom it had long denied to all other races. Churchill gave sermons about a war for freedom, but Orwell provided a sharp retort: 'The unspoken clause is always: Not counting niggers.'[6]

Ganny did not argue further, but Nugs could sense his decision hardening. The prospect of a commission was something, more than just the stipend that cooled his anxiety about their future. At the very least it was a plan. If she dared confess it, the relief it gave him helped her too. And there was something else, besides. A bravery had come over him. So she helped prepare the world's gentlest mercenary to join its greatest war.

5

Madras Must Not Burn
April 1942

April came, and every morning as the sun pulled itself from the waves, the humidity marched off the sea and into Madras like an invading force. By afternoon, the city was a hydrothermal vent. Once or twice a day, Bobby wasted a cigarette as he tilted his head down to light it and his sweat landed fatly on the paper. Sweat ran into his eyes and it burned.

There hadn't been a war in Madras in nearly two centuries. The city sweated doubly; from the heat, as every year, and from the fear, as never before. Labourers sweated as they flung earth out of trenches around the ports and the City Hall. Families sweated into threadbare *lungis* as they lined up at recruitment centres, stroking the hands of gaunt and downcast sons, hoping for reassurance about what was going to happen to them. Sweat ran down the Governor's neck as he waited in his mansion for instructions from Delhi. At the Carnatic and Buckingham Mills, workers sweated in their picket lines as they agitated for an evacuation allowance. Their union leaders swapped street rumours: aircraft were being organised to evacuate Europeans ... The Tatas were in secret talks with the Japs, to spare the steelworks in Jamshedpur from bombing ... At a village fair, up north, a Japanese paratrooper descended into a crowd, spoke to them in their own tongue, and then used his parachute to jet back into the sky ... Wavell had been killed.[1]

Families packed trunks, and the wealthiest ones had already sent servants ahead to bungalows in the Nilgiri Hills, to get things ready, just in case. The Burmese refugees who had streamed into Madras sweated in their hotel rooms and relatives' homes, watching as Madras prepared to stream out.

One exception in this sticky immobility was GP, who shot around town with an energy that suggested he was personally choreographing national events. Though he wasn't yet thirty, GP was now the chief editor on foreign affairs at *The Hindu*. It was no more than was expected of him. The Iyengar Brahmins were past masters at reincarnating ancient privilege in the form of modern success; a balancing act in which they rarely put a foot wrong. After Oxford, while GP waited for Subur to finish, he had somehow managed to train at *The Times* of London, to qualify as a barrister, to play first-class cricket, and even to grow familiar with the World Socialist Movement and various Indian nationalists in London.

In the current crisis too, he was as artfully moderate as ever – quite like Rajaji, the Congress apostle in Madras and another Iyengar. With Manek away on duty, and Bobby and his sisters too hot to say much, GP used the dinner table to rehearse his editorials without interruption.

Any day now, he'd say, a new sun could rise on the horizon beyond Marina Beach. The bayonet that had drilled through all of Asia was now pointed directly at Madras. Japanese messages were coming in on the shortwave, offering friendship to Indians, but warning that if they did not surrender, it was 'inevitable that India will receive the ravages of war'. The Commander-in-Chief in Delhi cabled Whitehall: 'India cannot repeat cannot be held against the likely scale and method of Japanese attack.' Brooding

over the prospect, the Congress leaders had taken a hard decision: the price of their cooperation would be political freedom
first.

If the war was going to be fought on Indian soil, there appeared
to be two examples of how it could go. As a British colony, the
example was Burma and Malaya: futile defence, whole divisions
squandered, cities abandoned to the mercy of the Japanese. As a
free country, the example was the Soviet Union, whose Red
Army had made a heroic retreat, fighting to the last breath,
scorching its own homeland, in what was rightfully being called
the Great Patriotic War.

But Whitehall had different ideas. By now Neville Chamberlain
had been forced to resign, handing over the government to
Winston Churchill, an implacable opponent of Indian independence. To Churchill, the war was a call to redeem the imperial
bond, not to dissolve it. India would need to be the principal
base for Britain's war against the Japanese, not to mention the
United States' campaign to aid China. The prime minister
expected Indians to 'kindle again the spark of hope in the breasts
of hundreds of millions of downtrodden or despairing men and
women throughout Europe'. Churchill despised the Congress,
but knew that popular support would be essential to fight the
Japanese back from India. He despatched a minister in his War
Cabinet, Sir Stafford Cripps, a Labour man with sympathy for the
nationalists, to obtain that support.

At the start of April 1942, GP moved Subur and their young
son up to Delhi, to ensure their safety and to allow him to follow
the negotiations under way there. In Delhi, Cripps was urging
the Congress to accept a promise of Dominion status after the
war. The Congress objected. Why not now? 'The leaders of the
people should be enabled honestly to shout to the masses,' Rajaji
pressed, 'that this war is the people's war.' A genuine national

government, in charge of its own defence, would give soldiers the morale of patriots, instead of the motives of mercenaries.

Cripps and the Indian leaders competed to raise the stakes of a solution. 'Today India is the crux of the war,' Nehru announced, at a press conference that ran to three hours. 'The only other really important theatre is the Russian theatre ... Very little else counts for the present. Every country in the world realises this, of course, except for the big people in New Delhi and Whitehall.'[2] The disagreement became a deadlock.

Deprived of their personal dinner broadcast, Bobby and the others struggled to keep up with political news. *The Hindu* reprinted a *Punch* cartoon, *Arms for the East*, which had Cripps in dock worker's overalls waiting to load a wooden crate onto a steamer. His one hand holds the winch ropes and the other steadies the crate, which is labelled 'Dominion Status for India' and stamped 'Not to be Sent Till After the War'. Watching the reaction of his baleful supervisor – Churchill – Cripps asks: 'How about shipping this thing now?' On the picture pages, with each day that passed, Cripps and the Congressmen stood further apart; the Japanese drew closer.

The script for their invasion was written and only awaited its performance: the defence of Chetpet; the rout at Thambaram; amphibian landing craft crunching into the corners of the beach temples at Mahabalipuram; the carnage and the coconut groves in flames. All that would be only the beginning of a 'Cross-India expedition',[3] a rapid advance to reach the west coast and seal the port of Bombay.

Around them, Madras prepared however it could. Twenty-two miles of trench were dug around the city. The ivory buildings of Queen Mary's, a beachside beacon to enemy bombers, were painted over in dark grey. The college lecturers, who had taught all the Mugaseth girls, were issued with timetables and tin helmets, and patrolled the rooftops after dusk listening for the sounds of bombers. Below them, the campus was under blackout. Students walked into railings and tumbled down stairs.

The ribbon of land between Fort St George and the sea supported a shoddy façade of air defence. The beach, usually crowded with catamarans and drying nets, was bare and fringed with anti-aircraft guns, though only one gun in ten was real. The others were coconut trunks, tarred black, one solid and balanced on another split down the middle. The Madras Guard dug into positions between them. The higher ground was a decoy airstrip; 'dummy' fighter planes and bombers squatted on it, and a lone flight of actual Wapitis circled out and back continuously to try and maintain the illusion. The port was closed to commercial cargo, and an anti-submarine boom pushed out across the mouth of the harbour. Undermanned, the Madras Coast Battery recruited young women to run phones and the Fire Direction Tables.

At the Secretariat, the Commissioner of the City, O. Pulla Reddy, learned one morning that Governor Hope and the majority of his staff were about to depart for the Nilgiri Hills. Reddy was able to put in a call to Sir George Boag, First Adviser to the Governor, requesting instructions. 'You can do what you like,' Boag replied. 'I have no time to discuss details. I have to catch the Blue Mountain Express in a few minutes.' So it was left to Reddy, and the Commissioner of Police, Sir Lionel Gasson, to evacuate the penitentiary – and thereafter, the caged predators in Madras Zoo. To Reddy's horror, Gasson sent in a platoon of Malabar Special Police to shoot dead the lions, tigers and panthers, as well as a single polar bear, which may alone have been grateful for it.

In the newspapers, insurance companies put out notices assuring Indian clients that 'risks to their lives arising from enemy military operations, whether by land, sea or air, are fully covered'. Chambers of commerce demanded official guarantees that there would be no scorched-earth campaign in Madras, as was being executed in eastern Bengal, at the Burmese border. An advert for Parle Biscuits advised that the ½lb cartons were airtight and the best for emergency rations. Scanning through the new movies, between ads for Laurel and Hardy in *Great Guns* and Gary Cooper in *Sergeant York*, Bobby encountered strange surprises:

SUPPOSE:

The Enemy Raiders approach our Shores
What do you expect to happen to Madras?

THE ANSWER:

To this burning question of the hour
is thrillingly picturized in a new film

'MADRAS MUST NOT BURN'
Another William J. Moylan Production

See Real Enemy Planes Rain Bombs on MADRAS
and see the Madras A.R.P. as Civil Defenders

Saturday, April 4 at the NEW GLOBE,
Mount Road, Madras

The headline a few days later: 'JAP NAVAL UNITS IN THE BAY'. Admiral Nagumo had taken the Indian Ocean like a lion rampant red on a field of blue. Five of his six carriers had been in the fleet which struck Pearl Harbor, and they meant to strike as hard at the British fleet in Ceylon.

On 5 April, two Wapitis of the IAF Volunteer Reserve, puttering out over the sea, found themselves watching as a Japanese force of one battleship, one carrier, a cruiser and two destroyers pounded a merchant vessel into the sea. The same morning, Japanese planes appeared over the coast of Ceylon, and on reaching the Colombo harbour sank 80,000 tons of British merchant shipping, along with the cruisers *Dorsetshire* and *Cornwall*.

The next morning, they attacked the Indian ports of Vizag and Cocanada, further up the coast from Madras. Silhouetted against the sun, the Mitsubishis banked, bombed the docked ships and machine-gunned the vessels in the port channels. On 9 April, they returned to Ceylon to raid Trincomalee, the base of the British East Indies Naval Squadron. The antique aircraft carrier HMS *Hermes* escaped the harbour, but Nagumo's planes found it and tore it to pieces on the deep. The British navy scattered and fled. It abandoned its bases on the Andaman Islands, handing Japan an effective base to stage landings in Ceylon and South India. This was, for Churchill, 'the most dangerous moment in the war, and the one that caused me greatest alarm … The capture of Ceylon, the consequent control of the Indian Ocean, and the possibility at the same time of a German conquest of Egypt would have closed the ring, and the future would have been black.'[4]

From the government came more and more rules for hiding: vehicles must have their headlights shaded; no lights visible outside any building, from any angle. Rather than suffocating behind heavy drapes and blackened glass, Nugs simply left the electric lights off. Like a sinking ocean liner, the city descended into gloomy darkness, and thieves came out into the street. Hundreds of wells had been dug around the city for fire-fighting, and had curdled with larvae. Mosquitoes poured out thick as gas.

The air-raid sirens struck up their song in the evenings. They were signalling practice drills, which meant blackout without stoppage of civilian traffic. There was a siren chart to memorise, so you knew which combination of steady note and modulated wailing meant a real air raid, but Nugs's mind went blank each time the sirens started.

Ganny arrived every day before sundown. As the light left through the window, they lit the kerosene lamp and slipped under their bed net together. The days were enervating, but at night their senses grew large, from the narcotic mix of heat, dark and dread. When the sirens fell silent, their hearts drummed in their ears. The skin hummed, and sweat ran down their necks with touch as sure as fingertips. At any moment, the world might go up in flames, and Nugs and Ganny made the most of that possibility.

As one of those nights turned to morning, they were woken at a quarter to five by the siren crying out a real air raid. The sound that had baptised half the world into war washed over them. They didn't move, and Nugs, in secret, felt more at peace than she had in years. For as long as she'd been with Ganny, they'd both felt a ruining anxiety about leaving their homes and losing their families. Suddenly that feeling was universal. Everybody was afraid of losing everything. It was wonderful. It made their vulnerability seem less like the cost of a private passion, and more like the rule of a new age. Henceforth, all homes are forfeit, everyone will be afraid.

No bombs fell that morning, though. The city trembled, awaiting words of instruction. Nothing came until 13 April, when the message issued by Southern Command repeated on the radio: 'The Government have reason to believe that the danger to Madras is now more serious and would advise all whose presence in the City is not essential, to leave within the next few days ...'

The phrasing was as formal and elliptical and British as ever, but the message was as clear as a gunshot: Run.

Rajaji, no longer premier but still a towering figure in Madras, was called to the municipal headquarters at the Ripon Building to urge essential staff not to leave their posts. 'Our calmness,' he announced, 'is our best weapon against both death and the Japanese.'[5] The general public demurred. Madras took flight for government camps and ancestral villages inland. The highways were choked with carts and carriages, and at night, on the pitch-dark platforms of Central Station, men hoisted up wives and daughters and pushed them through carriage windows before the trains had even come to a halt. Within forty-eight hours, Madras was emptied of 300,000; within a week, half a million of its 900,000 residents had fled.

The domes remained, over silent halls. The civil government was gone, to Ooty and Chitoor. Burma Shell had pulled back to Salem, followed there by the Board of Revenue. The atmosphere reminded Nugs of standing at the gate at the Guzdars' house in Calicut, frozen still, as their Alsatians padded up, growling, and drove their cold, wet noses against her skin: the agony of waiting for the bite. A bite that never did come. Already, on the other side of the world, a posse of American warships was chasing across the Pacific. Nagumo's fleet turned back, and the two groups met in the middle of the Pacific. Japan's navy would never fully recover from that battle, and could never return to dominate the Indian Ocean.

Day by day, the threat of invasion shrank back, until it concerned only Assam and Bengal on the Burmese frontier. For a while Madras stayed motionless, like a man who hears a gunshot and thinks himself dead. Then, shocked but untouched, it swayed back to its feet. Managers dragged their workers back to factories and mills, and an embarrassed Governor Hope returned to his lodge. On the beach, the catamarans lowered their dry prows and nuzzled back into the surf.

Bobby returned to Calicut, and the weird prospect of a holiday. The silence in Calicut was so deep that he almost missed the panic. His parents took him to ticketed recitals where kids scraped at violins and *veenas* to raise funds for the war. All the young men were gone: Nanoo and Rusi Heerjee were off with the Jats and the Ordnance Corps, leaving just little Bomi, who stayed busy helping his mother knit mufflers for the troops; Mukundan had applied for his commission, and Kurien had already received his, though Kurien's mother, just widowed, was so upset by the thought of her son warfaring that she tore the letter to pieces before he saw it.

Khodadad would not see, either. He could only see that Bobby had the family firm to inherit, and to carry on, perhaps after a few years of instructive civil practice. 'Don't try to be heroes,' he'd say – but it would not matter, because he had already taught his children to disobey him, and it was Bobby's turn now. He would not be left out while the others went off to the fight. The war wasn't a political problem any more: it was an existential one. It was not the war Manek or Ganny had signed up for, but they were in it. It was just like *Beau Geste*, and Bobby could hear the call to a Frontier rendezvous. Ganny had orders to a hospital beyond Peshawar, and Manek's squadron ought to be returning there soon. It seemed likely that Bobby and his brothers-in-law would end up posted not far apart.

These reveries carried Bobby through the day, and each day passed quietly till sundown, when he took a book and cigarettes back to the beach, and gazed out towards other continents. The Arabian Sea looked soft, well ploughed. He watched the pier, skulking in the tide, and he imagined its short thrust extending westward, its timbers multiplying and flying out over the water, building him a bridge to the war.

6

Things Sacred Between Us

Mhow, August 1942

550 Medical Wing
OTS Mhow
17-8-1942

My dear little sister,
I was so happy to get your letter and all its news about home. It is very strange that the two people I had the least to do with, or quarrelled the most with, should be the only people to write to me — I mean Dadi and you. I suppose there is some truth in the fact that each time we knock against each other we stick together firmer.

I shall tell you all the news — if it can be called news. First, about my marriage. Yes, I was married on 4 August at Kohat. I don't know how you will feel for me after this, but in your case also if it is the end of our relationship, I cannot help but accept it. My heart breaks to think that because I want to marry a girl I have loved for six years my people curse the union and cause me my life's greatest sorrow — disinheriting me. Had there been any other way to have had my parents' blessings I would have done anything, but I knew there never was.

Meens, I wonder if you sometimes think why & what I see in Nurgesh. You are fair in spite of your prejudice so let me tell you. Someday, if you ever get to know Nurgesh, you will love her so very much. Her affectionate nature, her kindness & sympathy to all poor, her understanding & patience, draw one to her. From outside she appears as a carefree, light spirit but there are oceans of deep thought in that woman's mind. Any man would wish for a wife like that.

When I first had asthma, both in college and at her sister's place, she has been both a nurse and a sister to me. The things she has done when I have had fever & gone to her place, only I know & I cannot ever forget. Can I forget her intimacies for over five years and let a trusting woman down?

The war broke out and gave us our commissions. I am 27 and she is just ten months older. If we have to wait for this war to end, I may be 30 for all I know and who wants a home then & children (I love them) so late? The beauty of life is lost by then and for so many other things sacred between us, we wanted to marry.

So, when she came to Delhi she was very upset about my health and she came back to Thal with me where she stayed with Capt Banerjee's family. It was God's hand in that Meenu, because two days after she came, I had to go to an outpost at 10pm. The nervous tension and the ducking I got afterwards brought on acute bronchitis. Nurgesh sat up with me whole days, doing the sweeper's work even, as I did not go into hospital. In four days my fever came down and on the fifth day came my order to report to Mhow for training (special). I didn't want to miss the chance as permanent comm depends on all this. My OC wouldn't let me go in my state, but I left for Mhow against both his and Nurgesh's objections. On the way at Kohat I got married.

Poor Nurgesh had to go back and I always write to her to say that I am quite well. I am far from well. I have once again become a thin shadow of my past self. I beg you not to tell her this because just at present I don't want her to worry about anything. She has had too much of mental worry about something and the poor girl pretends to look happy. I am trying my best to cut short the attack but the agony of mind & suffering I have been through has left a permanent mark which I can never again wipe out.

I am at heart a home-bird, Meens. Even this IMS I joined because I wanted money. As I wrote to Papa, if I knew that I would have his backing when & if I married Nugs, I should have loved to go on to Calcutta Tropical Medicine School. Here we lose touch with our work and gain no benefit. I have just had [a] letter from Mummy. It is very sad and it really tears at my heart-strings to read her words — 'pay the girl some money if you are in trouble' etc. — And 'you will be the cause of my death', etc. Someday, if you get to know Nurgesh well, you will realise how good a girl she is. Poor Mums won't understand.

I had a letter from Papa saying that he was proceeding legally to disown me. Oh god, Meens. I don't think I will ever bear up with this torture of mind. What is my future without my father & his guidance? I risked it, no doubt, but I prayed so hard to try to make him understand that we must marry. My youth of life is cut & now I exist with one determination — I shall never let Nurgesh feel the pangs of sorrow & shall try my best to keep our home happy. Over it will be Mum's blessings and someday I shall win my parents.

Nurgesh writes that she sees you often, but since you ignore her, she ignores you. I suppose I couldn't ask you to try to make things easier for me. When I go off overseas, my little baby will come and I would worry less if I knew one sister was looking after my wife. Perhaps I ask too much — then forgive me and please forget it.

I hope you can write to me sometimes & tell me about home. I shall be dying to know as I can never again know for myself. Pass on those drops of water to my scorched soul. Pray for me sometimes. Look after yourself and God bless you with all luck & help & happiness.

I remain ever your affec. brother,

Papu

Ganny set down the pen, then picked it up again and dated the last page of the letter, two days later than when he started it.

He shuffled the sheets together, folded them and slipped them into the envelope. The stationery was Indian Medical Service, printed with the regimental ensign, a crown mounted above the staff of Asclepius. It was framed by a motto that meant more to him now than ever. '*Honi soit qui mal y pense*' — Shamed be he who thinks evil of it.

7

Do or Die

Thal, August–October 1942

Monsoon brought India its usual relief, but another kind as well: it grounded the Japanese. In the north of Burma they had succeeded in cutting the road by which the United States sent aid to the Chinese. With the land route closed, the Americans dreamt up a scheme of impossible derring-do: to airlift goods from Bengal to Yunnan right over the Hump of the eastern Himalayas. To the north-west, the Japanese had come as far as the river Chindwin, just before the kingdom of Manipur, where they hunkered down in the rain.[1]

The relief did not extend to Nugs and Ganny's lives, and they almost missed April, when together they had been a spot of calm amid the city's turmoil. Now they were back to spinning in the rapids, without much by way of a paddle. Ganny was an unlikely candidate for a soldier, but he was a Kodava, a qualification of sorts. They were prominent among the earliest wave of Indian officers: the ones trained at Sandhurst, the King's Commissioned Indian Officers. The adjutant of the Madras Battalion had been a Kodava, replacing another Kodava. Both were from Ganny's own clan, the Kodanderas. Both had faced an establishment that was wary, often hostile, to native officers.

K. M. Cariappa, for instance, was the highest-ranked Indian in the Army, but after seventeen years with the Rajputs he was still a major. His successor in Madras, 'Timmy' Thimayya, had arrived as adjutant, and even then was refused housing among White officers inside Fort St George. When the war broke out, Timmy returned to his regiment in Peshawar, where his new CO summoned him only to snarl about a point of etiquette Timmy had overlooked. 'If you have the temerity to think that you and other Indians can be good officers, you're sadly mistaken,' the colonel said. 'Your behaviour proves otherwise. You people just don't have it in you.'[2]

The Indian Medical Service had its own reputation for racial pettiness. Now, however, the Army was desperate for medical staff of every sort, from surgeons to stretcher-bearers.[3] Few Indians were keen to join a party to which they had only been invited once the fun was over. Just that month, a lobby of Indian doctors in the IMS had made a formal complaint about Europeans being shielded from war postings. 'The head of the IMS may tell you that the government do not now make any racial discrimination between Europeans and Indians,' said their memo in the papers. 'It is in reality a myth.'[4]

The application was still a nuisance. Ganny and Nugs had just finished their medical exams, and now there were more tests, though this time they were the ones being studied. He had provided proof of his degrees, reports of his personality and academic record, certificates of his moral character, and finally he had to get a physical from a captain of the Royal Army Medical Corps.

Ganny was weak from a bout of malaria, but the captain wasn't concerned. Half the Indian Army had malaria, he said. He ticked his way down the list of conditions that Ganny was 'not at present suffering from, or previously affected with':

a) Tuberculosis

b) Insanity or Mental Disease

c) Venereal Disease

d) Disease of the heart or lungs

He raised his eyes, then looked back at the form and kept going. More interviews followed, and a final one in Delhi, before a selection board of senior IMS staff.

While Ganny was gone, Nugs visited a doctor for some tests of her own, and then went back to have them repeated. When the results confirmed that she was carrying a child, the questions that had paralysed them for years all disappeared. She and Ganny had the clear and stark answer that they had desired and dreaded. They would have to be married, very soon. Then they would have to tell their families. But Ganny already had service orders which could not be ignored and he left in July for the Frontier, for the Combined Military Hospital in Thal.

Khade-Makh, 'the Beautiful Face', was showing its beauty. The season of rain cooled the days and scattered colour over the ramped mud, washed the pine and deodar cedars, sprung melons from the sandhills at the riverbank. Shepherds led their flocks higher uphill to reach the new grass, and the face of Khade-Makh, the mountain which overlooked the fort of Thal, was softened by its brief fertility. But it would harden again at the first sign of winter, and Ganny prepared to do the same.

Thal, on the banks of the Kurram river, was one of the last British outposts before the mountain passes. It was a permanent fort built of mud, with a moat and bastions for mountain guns. This was as far as the Afghan army had advanced in 1919, when it dared to cross the Durand Line.[5] Beyond Thal was only

Miranshah to the south and Parachinar to the north, and the nervous pickets clutching the sides of the Safed Koh range. Ganny wondered if there was anywhere in the Empire a hospital more remote.

In Thal, senior officers lived in apartments with their families, while the lower ranks were each other's. Ganny had neither; his only remaining family was Nugs. But the homesickness passed quickly, because soon he was due back in Delhi, where Nugs would be waiting.

At the opposite end of the country, Nugs stepped onto her train to Delhi, right foot first for luck. She settled into her compartment and a pair of coolies entered behind her, hauling a tin basin which held a block of ice. As the train started moving the fan on the ceiling began to turn, blowing air down onto the ice and back up into her face. Nugs turned her cheek into the drape of her sari. She hoped it would be cool.

Three days later, she was sitting beside Ganny on her way from Delhi to Thal, swept unexpected from the teeming coast to the arid roof of the world. At Peshawar they switched to the light, sapper-built railway which went on past Kohat and up the Miranzai valley. In her life the only pass Nugs had ever seen was the Palghat Gap, where the Madras railway crossed the Ghats into Malabar, and temples were piled on top of each sweating mount. Now they climbed through awesome passes, earth ramping into the stratosphere, over ground where any bump might be the grave of an Englishman.

Where the railway ended, beneath the walls of Thal, was another planet. Nugs was not Ganny's wife, so would have to be the guest of an understanding higher officer, Captain Banerjee. Her own life, of sweltering commutes, obstetrics manuals and Malayali nursing sisters, had never felt so distant or so dear as in her first days in the alien fortress, which she spent trying to improve Ganny's dreary quarters, or avoiding Mrs Banerjee whose eyes were perpetually wandering over the slight swell inside Nugs's sari. Ganny was on duty all the time, at least until the morning that Nugs found him bowed over in bed, coughing to tear his lungs out. At least she was there to nurse him, to clean up and talk him through the pain, and to administer a course of M&B 693,[6] which slowly undid the infection. But right away there was another letter, directing him to the OTS at Mhow, and Ganny got out of bed only to begin packing again.

They travelled together as far as Kohat, and it was here, on 4 August, that they broke their journey to be wed by Sheikh Mahbub Ali Khan, OBE, the District Registrar of Marriages. As they held each other, he stroked her belly in enduring surprise. She listened at his chest out of habit. Then she stepped onto her train back south, and departed on her own.

By the time the engine found its pace, Nugs was so frightened about leaving Ganny that her heart was kicking like a racehorse. She couldn't make it stop, or rein in her disbelief that they were married, having waited for it for so long, and were already forced apart. She had left him sick and alone, wheeling through the furthest, coldest orbit of what was called India. And she was alone, too, surrounded by cold material, refused any reassurance by the vulcanised rubber berth under her hands, the twisted-iron window bars, or the cold steel rails on which she slid away from her husband. She held her belly instead, and warm tears came to her relief. For a long while she slept.

When she awoke, her panic seemed to have infected the air. The monsoon pitched a silver-seamed tent of grey over the country and rain drummed nervously on the carriage's metal roof. Passengers emptied out at their stations and no one replaced them. Beyond the Punjab, there were soldiers on every platform – Gurkhas mainly, short men with impassive eyes. At some stations, the train did not stop but sped up, passing through blurs of pale dusty *kurtas* and fighting voices.

On the fourth day, the ticket collector came in and asked if she had people at any of the stops along the way? She thought he was being polite because she looked lonely. But he was suggesting she get off. It was on the radio, he said, the news from the Congress session in Bombay. There could be trouble, and trains were most dangerous: they were the easiest targets. Troops could not be spared to patrol all the lines. There had already been some derailings, rumours of Anglo-Indian engine drivers set alight on the footplate. Up and down the country, even where the terrorists were not yet at work, subversives were pulling the stop chains, creating chaos on the network. At night, Nugs lay in her vulcanised berth, sleepless as her carriage moaned to a halt again and again.

In Bombay, the Congress, which had never done more than tug at the tablecloth of Empire and rattle its silver, had suddenly raised an axe over the whole affair. It was an ultimatum. Britain had allowed a war to reach India's doorstep without strengthening India to fight it. After the failure of the Cripps Mission, the squandering of Indian lives at Singapore and Tobruk, Gandhi was done waiting. A free India would ably and willingly join the war effort, but an India that remained subjugated would be unable and unwilling, as Gandhi intended to prove: 'I want freedom immediately, this very night – before dawn if it can be had. Freedom cannot wait for the realisation of communal unity ... Here is a mantra, a short one I give you,' he said. 'Do or die. Take a pledge with God and your own conscience as witness, that you will no longer rest till freedom is achieved and will be prepared to lay down your lives to achieve it.'

An instruction followed: if their leaders were unavailable, every man 'must be his own guide, urging him along the hard road where there is no resting place'. By the next evening, the Congress leadership was indeed unavailable, jailed to a man.

An uprising began in the mood of anarchy licensed by Gandhi's words. With its national leadership under arrest, the rank and file were mobbing the machinery of the wartime colony. In the west, factories and steel mills were crippled by labour strikes. In Ahmedabad, Gandhi's bastion, some mill owners paid their own striking workers to help sustain them. In Bombay, terrorists set off more than 400 bombs. In the east, entire towns and districts were plucked from state authority. Radicals there had been emboldened when they saw, with their own eyes, the battered 17th Division coming out of Burma. The Empire had collapsed, like a row of rotten tenements, up to India's doorstep. One good kick should bring it down in India as well.

The government was enraged by this turn to treachery, just when its fortunes were at their lowest in the war. It pulled troops off their embarkation schedule and marched them into bazaars, chowks and train stations across the country. Fifty-seven Army battalions were redirected to give 'aid to the civil power'.

At Arakkonam airfield, Manek's squadron was busy enacting coastal invasion scenarios. No. 1 Squadron was 'India'; the Winged Arrows were 'Enemy' and conducted sorties to 'bomb' the Madras aerodrome. Their exercise, codenamed Clive, was conducted in deadly earnest: when a pilot from No. 2 Squadron landed in Madras to pick up routine information about unserviceable aircraft, he was arrested at the point of a bayonet.

Naturally there was some confusion when a local army commander approached the leader of No. 1 Squadron, S. N. Goyal, to engage an actual target. Some stubborn nationalists had blocked a military train by lying on the tracks. 'Would you ...

fly low over those bastards? Just frighten them to hell, so they get out of the way and the train can move on?' the army man asked. 'If it's necessary, you can fire on the side of the tracks. But don't go about hurting anybody.'

Goyal, a typical IAF maverick, thought about it.

'Would you do that in England?' he asked. 'If it happened there?'

The commander drooped. 'Well, no,' he replied, 'no ... That's okay, then,' and saw himself out.

The picture elsewhere was less benign. By 15 August, 'machine-gunning from the air' was authorised by the Viceroy for the first time anywhere in India beyond the North-West Frontier. RAF planes fired into crowds in Bhagalpur and Monghyr in Bihar, in Nadia and Tamluk in Bengal, and in Talcher in Orissa. One plane crashed and a mob burned the British pilot alive. The uprising in the towns was repressed, pushing mutinous factions out into the country. Entire villages rebelled, many of them villages where land had been seized to build airfields. Revolutionary districts in the east sank into an inferno of public floggings, private torture, and villages put to flames. The Japanese had not come, but it was like war all the same.

In Madras, the radicals were better behaved. The unions of the South Indian Railway were run by closet communists, who had been on board with the war effort ever since Germany attacked the Soviet Union. Rajaji too had opposed the Bombay resolution, calling its outcome 'nothing but pure violence'.[7] The worst of the trouble was around Coimbatore, where one gang vandalising garages on the Sulur airfield mistakenly burned three drivers alive.[8]

Nugs arrived in the city to find everyone talking about Lakshmi Swaminathan. Lakshmi's voice had crackled up briefly on Radio Syonon, which transmitted from occupied Singapore, saying that she was safe, that Indians were being treated well, and then suddenly to urge her countrymen to sabotage the British war effort. Here was new trouble: a force of Indian soldiers who had surrendered at Singapore had been turned and mustered to fight alongside the Japanese. Lakshmi had volunteered, and been made an officer. Nugs should have guessed.

Similarly, in Berlin, a man was beguiling Indian prisoners of war into a regiment under German command, the Legion Freies Indien. Subhas Chandra Bose had been a misfit in the Congress movement, growing ever more impatient with Gandhi, and fascinated with Britain's enemies. 'If at that time India had been anything like Italy or Germany,' a close associate, his brother's secretary, said about him, 'Subhas Bose would have been the counterpart of Mussolini or Hitler.'[9] Bose had escaped house arrest in Calcutta, and now popped up in the German capital aiming to meet Hitler and forge an alliance between Germans and incipient free Indians, of whom the closest at hand were POWs captured in the Libyan desert. The fifth column, which the British had spent so long fearing, was at last materialising, at home and on both fronts.

Nugs went back to work, waiting for letters. Mhow was the worst officer training school, Ganny said, lacking the climate or the good trim of Bangalore or Belgaum, and the medical wing especially was the least of anyone's concern. Cadets talked a lot about the war bulletins, realising they would be at the front lines soon. Germany and Japan were winning everywhere. They should both be glad he was stuck out in Thal.

She wrote back, about Calicut, and about watching their news splash into her parents' faces. It had been slightly surreal, but she had seen it all before. Subur had had it worse: she had faced disbelief, where Nugs was believed too well. Subur had had it better: her fiancé was a Brahmin, from a distinguished family. Kodavas were tribals who prayed over rifles. The Parsis were the most civilian of communities, even if its young men made eager soldiers; the Kodavas the most martial, even though Ganny was only a soldier under duress. Nothing made any difference. Nugs cried only when she faced her mother, before she left, and Tehmina refused to bless her. So be it. She would go, and have her own home, and once she did she would never force anyone to leave it.

Though he didn't say it, she knew that it was even harder on Ganny. She could feel his anxiety – about her, on her own, and their child, and about himself, too – and his despair at his family's rejection. There were two wars in his life now. The smaller one was more frightening; every shot in it was fired at the heart.

Outside her window, the younger generation still marched, and Nugs could hear them, blocking traffic on the Poonamallee High Road. A slogan rose and crashed back into the general din, something about unity and readiness for freedom. As the words crested, again and again, she heard in their demand something in common with her own: to no longer fear an old, contemptuous system that expected obedience and order; to govern yourself, and follow your own will, even if it led to your own ruin. Never turn your back on it – they chanted through her window – however hard the fight, however weak you are at the end of it, and at the beginning of your freedom.

O ctober came, and back in Thal, Khade-Makh shed its thin upholstery. The work at the hospital was routine: the Fakir of Ipi had lately gone underground, and it was rare that Ganny treated a combat wound, unless the patient was a Pashtun. They often were admitted at the Combined Military Hospital as payment for a clan's good behaviour. Inside Thal, they were diffident, slow to speak and keen to leave; not unlike Ganny himself.

Ganny did not want to be there a minute longer, in a mud fort teetering at the world's edge. Thal frightened him, and Pashtuns had nothing to do with it. The fort was meant to be solid and withstanding, but to Ganny it seemed perilous, like a construction of planks over a dark drop, where any step could be off the edge. To keep him from falling, all he had were the provisions of the Army, which seemed to obey the principles of the land here: to be stern, dry and denying.

Just a few years earlier, the Indian battalions stationed in Thal had found their barracks being wired for electricity. This turned out to be the result of an administrative error, so the work was left unfinished, the curls of wire sprung from the mud walls. After waiting a few weeks, the soldiers conferred and decided they ought to buy bulbs themselves, pay their own meter charges and light up the gloom. Their request reached the garrison engineer, who apologised for the mistake and explained that Indian troops were 'not entitled to electricity'. An appeal went to the Assistant Director of Medical Services. Within two weeks, workmen arrived and stripped the errant wiring out of the walls. The men went on with kerosene and wicks. Above them the windows of the officers' quarters shone in bright, deep shapes.

The night air was crushed glass now, and in the mornings Ganny broke a skin of ice in his basin. His ward roster tilted from summer maladies – malaria, Delhi belly, septic sores – toward influenza and pneumonia. It was open season on lungs. Winter's winds had come in from the north, and with them came knocking that doctor's nightmare – of becoming the patient, the one in the bed instead of at the bedside. At sundown, as shadows spread and chilled the walls, Ganny stopped work to take deep breaths, and listen to the string quartet tuning up in his chest.

8

The King's Own
Roorkee, August–December 1942

The great tent, already thick with the smoke and crackle of lit torches, now filled with silent hillmen and the rustle of their loose raiment. The lieutenant with the 41 Bengal Lancers sat in a chair before a table, and his comrade stood behind him, with the stone hand of an Afridi guard on his shoulder and a rifle nosing into his ribs. Strips of sharpened bamboo were laid on the table top, awaiting the chieftain. The tent flap flew open, and Mohammed Khan entered, resplendent as a rajah in an embroidered silk gown and a plumed turban set with a stunning diamond. The lieutenant breathed fearfully. The Khan was as sanguine as only a Pashtun could be while preparing the tools of torture. Fingering the point of a bamboo stake, he said: '*We have ways of making men talk ...*'

A gust of wind came and blew the Khan and the lieutenant up and sideways, folding their bodies into a billow of white and grey. The regiment broke out in howls and hoots, and a figure ran over to the fabric screen and grabbed at the guy rope flying loose. The corner of the screen billowed up again, and for a second Bobby could see the men on the other side, laughing at the sudden intermission, their white teeth and undershirts visible though their dark skins merged with their prickly brown blankets.

This was the cinema at the Roorkee Cantonment – a weighted sheet raised on poles in the drill ground, with British men watching from one side of the screen, and Indians on the other.

So it was, up and down through every level of the British Indian Army: there were lines, and central to the decorum and discipline of being in the Army was knowing on which side you stood, to keep things in balance. The constitution of the Army of India was all precise ethnic formulae, designed to hold its groups and identities in balance.[1] By design, the men of its ranks only served in regiments with others of their own faith and province, which allowed 'that Sikh might fire into Hindu; Gurkha into either, without any scruple in case of need'.[2]

This evening's picture was a new cantonment favourite, *Lives of a Bengal Lancer*, with Gary Cooper at his best and Douglas Dumbrille as the Khan.[3] Plenty of the men in the audience, NCOs especially, had served in the Grim. Some had returned the worse for wear. But any time 'the hall' played one of Hollywood's Frontier daydreams, they all showed up, British and Indian, to cheer and slouch and criticise in many languages.

Since his arrival, Bobby had watched all the pictures, especially the ones that helped his Urdu, the official lingua franca of the Indian Army. *The Lives of a Bengal Lancer* didn't have much Urdu, but he watched it with a degree of serious inquiry about service in the North-West Frontier. The movie it had elbowed out of top billing, *Gunga Din*, was just the running babble of Douglas Fairbanks and Cary Grant as they fought a cult of Frontier Thuggees – led by a crazed fakir, of course, inside a temple of gold. Bobby sifted even that delirious nonsense for glints of reality.

Throughout his officer training, he hoped that hints to the adjutant might quickly land him with a company on the Frontier: Manek's base, then Ganny's, with every chance that Manek would return, and that Bobby would join them. They would share the Grim passage, and afterward tell stories about wild Waziris and phantom fakirs, as told by officers of the Indian Army for a hundred years. But that was before. Now he couldn't stand to watch, and he got to his feet and slipped away in the half-light.

Bobby had arrived here in August, a cadet enrolled at the training school for engineer-officers.[4] Roorkee was located where the dusty floor of north India hit the staircase into the Himalayas, where the air was hot but the water of the Ganga still cold. The town was dominated by its cantonment: the home and headquarters of his new regiment. Its acres of bungalow and grounds were bisected by ruler-straight roads and whitewashed kerbs, punctuated by boxes of pastel blooms and stubby cere-monial cannon. Everything was there, and had its place, as in a tidy, toy world arranged by a child.

At once, Bobby felt the passive, perspiring air of the previous decade lifting. Great events rose before him: blurred in detail but exalted, like the parade of the Himalayas seen from the hills nearby, their lower slopes cloaked in sky blue but their white cavalry helmets shining. On his shoulders Bobby wore two grey chevrons which sent a charge across his ribs, buzzing in his ster-num. This current of belonging he had never felt before, but he felt it connecting him, as far up as the King in his jewels, and down to the sapper recruit, and outward to his brothers, Manek and Ganny. All nodes on a humming grid that held India together – but which might also, they now learned, be fused, any day, by rebellion and mutiny.

It had been easy, during the first civil disobedience, for eleven-year-old Bobby to cheer both sides. In 1942, it was impossible.

Gandhi had fallen to blackmail, and the Congress had kicked Britain in the teeth at its weakest moment in the war. In the same month, Bobby began his officer training and felt a new and lucid sense of duty to the bedevilled Empire coming over him. The British order was an order of responsibility. This was what Bobby realised, as he prepared for the responsibility of command – and this was what the Congress could never stomach, that their right to govern India must follow from their ability to do so.

Britain was in his germ plasm, as much as Persia and as much as Malabar. For the first time Bobby understood the tradition of loyalty that reached him from his father; and from his uncle Kobad, the MBE, the Kaiser-e-Hind; even from the icon of his grandfather Dhanjibhoy, who received a Certificate of Honour on Queen Victoria's Diamond Jubilee. Soon, Bobby thought, he would like to win a medal of his own. But he began by putting officer's pips on his shoulder, and becoming one of King George V's Own Bengal Sappers.

While the August *kranti* – revolution – raged, to be an Indian officer-cadet was to be marked as a potential threat. The twin shadows of treachery, cast by Subhas Bose abroad and the vandals at home, fell as a double-umbra on Indian subalterns. Engineers especially. The skills they learned, like the use of dynamite, were the skills the terrorists needed to seed anarchy in Bihar and Bengal. The fact was that most new Indian officers were nationalists: patient nationalists, unmoved by the Congress mania. In the mood of general distrust, however, all offences levelled out: nationalism, insubordination and sabotage; defection at the front with dropping your fork at the dinner table. If a cadet went AWOL it was assumed that he was headed east to blow up a rail bridge.[5]

Old troubles resurfaced. British NCOs refused to salute Indian cadets, feigning distraction, as they used to in the days of the 'Indianised battalions'. The attitude was taken up by some White cadets, typically the ones who grew up in India: young masters from the tea estates, most resistant to seeing Indians as anything but a servant class. Parsis were exempt, of course, so Bobby was privy to the insinuations about the Wogs. 'Why's a brigade need two native battalions and one British?' was popular: 'So the Indians advance and don't run away.'

For two decades before the war, native officers had faced hostility and disdain from their colleagues, especially off duty. Their appearance in the officers' mess was a sort of miscegenation, blackening the pure-White complexion of command. It was a deep cut to be turned away at the door of an officers' club, when lamps glowed and music tootled inside, and outside only the wind danced through the campus of a Frontier fort. Still, for twenty years they were stoical and silent, stitching up their psychic injuries and doing their duty.

Their solid deportment smoothed the path for the thousands of Indian subalterns who tumbled in at the start of the war. The integration of the Emergency Commissioned Officers was also a priority for the Commander-in-Chief of India, General Sir Claude Auchinleck. He went as far as banning black-tie occasions, where Indians were regularly embarrassed. It took a person like 'the Auk' to put it out that: 'No Indian officer must be regarded as suspect and disloyal merely because he is what is called a "Nationalist" or in other words, a good Indian.'[6]

A new sort of story began to circulate, like the one about the five subalterns drinking at a club in Bombay. Interrupted by the club secretary, who regretted that one of them – an Indian – would have to leave, all five rose and marched out together – after flinging their high-balls into the mirror behind the bar.[7] The officers' mess, once a place to avoid, full of bland meats and pungent rebukes, grew comfortable for Indians as well as Englishmen.

Of course Gandhi would spoil it. Luckily for Bobby, the atmosphere had lifted by November, and his induction to the officers' mess was in the same spirit as those before him: drunken harassment. 'Doing Pooja' meant rough and gymnastic games, and a racket that swelled until the ancient silver and regimental bric-a-brac trembled on their shelves. It ended around the billiards table, where Bobby, his arms pinioned and body rigid, was inserted through the bottle racks fixed beneath the table's edge. Hanging thus, with his legs sticking out at one end and head and shoulders at the other, he was walloped with billiard cues and rolled-up newspapers until he had to blink and beat back sudden, stupid tears.

From the start, Bobby sensed that the Army at home might be out of touch with the emergency abroad. On their first day attached to the regiment, the subalterns had lectures. First was 'A History of the Corps of Indian Engineers', which gave the impression that the Bengal Sappers had spent longer fighting *in* India than it had fighting foreign enemies (which was in fact the case) and the second, curiously, was 'How to Buy a Persian Rug'. That was meant to be a bit of fun, Bobby supposed. But there was a war on, and he was already late to it.

In the evenings, washed and dressed, he retreated into the musty cool of the mess, where ancient rites prevailed. Bobby wore coat and tie to dinner, and stood at the table until senior officers were seated. Old soldiers, Sandhurst-trained, never permitted a word about politics, religion or women, although the subalterns cared about little else. Still, it was in the stiffly colonial and oddly familiar world of the mess that Bobby felt most at home. Young officers played sports together and rode, but to Bobby's mind, the real officers' game was billiards in the mess. The click of the cue ball, as it conveyed its force into red, matched the sharp tattoo of boots when his orders conveyed their force into the recruits. Order and precision – rare qualities in India, but the best qualities of its Army.

The single incident that disturbed that order was one Bobby heard of, a story that echoed in regiments throughout the Army. One evening, an Indian subaltern, or was it a group of them, settled into the empty officers' mess. The radio was droning out news of the war, or was it London swing, and one of the Indians rose to fiddle with the dial until he found a station playing film songs from Bombay. In short order, they were joined by a band of British subalterns, who tuned it back to London, commenting aloud that an officers' mess was no place for native drumming and wailing. The Indian rose and tuned it back again.

Depending on which mess, which regiment, or which soldier recounted it, there are hot words or hands on throats. A fist fight begins; fellow officers either pitch in or pull it apart, and the radio set is either broken or flung at the Brit, and either the Indian or Briton is marched before the adjutant to be either re-assured or cashiered. The truth of the event was lost, and the story itself was re-tuned this way or that, giving voices to the muted frequencies of anger that hummed in the colonial army.

With no deployment orders, Bobby stayed put, slack-sailed in the doldrums of Roorkee Cantonment. If he had walked in with his eyes shut, he might have guessed he was in a farming village or a boarding school, not the depot of an army at war. Morning reveille was bugled through the lanes by boy-soldiers on bicycles. At the polo ground he heard the panicky rumble of horses' hooves, and from inside the officers' bunga-lows, the creak of punkahs heaving the warm afternoon air. Beyond the drill grounds, the wind carried the chink of pickaxes striking gravel, and the scrape of shovels accepting their scoops,

while jemadars called out, 'Ready! Raise! Strike! Break! Rake!'
At the canal, ropes squealed and timbers splashed through wet-bridging exercises. As evening lifted, the crunch of bicycle bells began again; the high-pitched hubbub of boys' voices from the hockey fields; the snipping of shears at the grass and the snap of flags on the mast.

Beneath the cantonment's surface stillness, however, was a groundswell of new manpower: enough to fight, and not just to lose, this war.

At the end of the First World War, the Army had retrenched, shunting thousands of soldiers back into the wretched market for work. Old, proud regiments were decommissioned en masse. Most secure on the Army rolls were regiments of the 'enlisted classes', the supposed martial races of the north and west – Rajputs, Gujjars, Jats, Sikhs, Pathans, Marathas and Ahirs[8] – men whose fields had been sprinkled for centuries with the blood of invaders. Castes that had put in decades of service to British masters, but did not belong to the imagined natural garrison of India, were abruptly shut out.[9]

Once the new war began, and as the worldwide scale of India's commitments became apparent, the Army was forced to forget its cherished principles of selection. The Indian Army, the most pure-bred institution of the Raj, would have to take rough transfusions of untested blood. Recruitment officers learned to roam into new territory. They learnt new skills – such as how to fix the delicate spring balance in a weighing machine bumped over rural tracks, or how to weigh candidates in a balance used for grain and forest produce. They learned to time their efforts around plantings and harvests, around Ramzan or the months most favoured for Hindu marriage, around seasonal epidemics of plague, cholera and malaria that cut into the enlistment yield.[10]

In January 1942, when Bobby was still at Guindy, the Defence Services Exhibition Train pulled up at Madras Central Station and rested there a few days. A quarter of a mile long, its six coaches were a rolling museum of the war, exhibiting uniforms, rifles and artillery shells, photographs from the recent battles of Keren. There were models of a Grant tank and a dreadnought-class battleship. In the middle coach, stripped of its wings, was the sleek fuselage of a Hawker Hurricane fighter. The admission price of four annas made it clear that this was all for the benefit of the middle class, to stoke their enthusiasm and sell them war bonds. Out in the villages the displays were more bluntly transactional and included piles of 'model rupees' communicating Army scales of pay.

By the time Bobby arrived at Roorkee, the Army was enlisting 50,000 new volunteers a month.[11] The three services opened their arms to all the runt races formerly deemed unfit to serve.[12] Once again they enlisted the Mahars, Bengalis and Kodavas, but also Lingayats from the Deccan, Assamese from the north-east frontier, Mahsuds from the north-west. Roman Catholic missionaries in Bihar urged their tribal wards, Santhals and Mundas, to join up. Oriyas went to the Pioneer Corps; Anglo-Indian girls to the Women's Auxiliary Corps (Indian). The spine-cracking encyclopaedia of Indian castes was ironed flat onto a single khaki page.[13]

They did not serve out of love of the King-Emperor. Their allegiance was to the *pulton* – the regiment, to its *izzat* – its honour, and to the sahibs in its command. And the factor that most aided recruitment was hunger. At the end of a tour of Indian recruit depots, one officer of the Department of Hygiene recorded that 'the great majority of these recruits are poor material from the point of view of physique ... Almost all were thin, some almost to the point of emaciation by European standards.'[14]

Upon enlisting, every sepoy was entitled to a full service ration, beginning with the *bada khana* (grand dinner) they received on arrival. Within five months of enlistment, the body weight of most soldiers had increased by twenty per cent.

Hundreds of thousands of famished men were now flooding into regimental properties and units where, for decades, exclusivity had been the foundation of *pulton ki ghairath*, regimental honour. Even as the officer class changed to represent more Indians, so did the other ranks: to represent for the first time India altogether.

Around the world, mobilisation and slaughter meant rapid change in who was being brought to the front. In India it meant harvesting from new fields, almost literally – nations unknown to soldiering, as unlike as rice to wheat. Who was the Indian soldier today? A question mark. Why had he enlisted? A question mark.

It was like the poster which many years before Bobby had seen peeling off a wall – a recruitment poster from the last war. It depicted the privileges of the jawan with these images: cupped hands full of coins, a rifle with bayonet fixed, and a turbaned uniform, belt and boots, filled by an invisible figure. In bold strokes was written: *'Ye roop-e-banduq aur wardi kaun lega?'* – 'Who will assume this figure with rifle and uniform?' Beneath the invisible trooper's turban, painted out in black to form his face, was a question mark.

Bobby stared out at a line of those dark, inscrutable faces as they attempted to parade in the early winter sunshine. He scanned their shadowed eyes, their bulging cheekbones, and hadn't the faintest idea of what to do. He pulled down the brim of his pith helmet to cover for any nervousness apparent in his face. But he would still have to say something. In Malayalam,

Bobby was sure he could talk a school of fish into a marching column. In Urdu, he wasn't yet up for much more than shopping in the bazaar.

This aspect of his commission was dawning on him, that it meant giving orders to men, real men, and having them obey out of trust rather than the fear of court martial. An officer and his troops were struts that reinforced each other, producing in the unit more strength than existed in either individually. He might soon have to order them to the edge of the abyss – yet he wasn't sure he knew how to make them form up for a light morning parade.

He kept his chin high and his mouth firm, and counted the seconds until the foghorn voice of the VCO[15] blasted over his shoulder.

'*Atthara-chaubees* party, *sa'ab! Ek aadmi ghairhazir hai!*' (Eighteen twenty-four party, sir! One man is missing.)

Bobby nodded hard, and murmured, '*Theek, theek hai.*'

Now, under Bobby's supervision, the day's training could begin – and there was no shortage of things a sapper needed to learn. The sapper was the first to enter, and the last to leave a fight. His job was to alter the lay of land and water, and get its brigade where it needed to go. It was to build bridges, lay tracks and roads, run rafts or river ferries, clear mines and demolish obstacles using explosives. Alternatively, it was to demolish bridges, mine tracks and roads, and create obstacles using explosives. To speed or to impede. Sometimes this meant that sappers moved in advance of the main body of infantry. Sometimes they fought as combat troops. And when things were quiet, they were over-qualified *mistris*, knocking together huts for senior staff and water points for the ranks.

They had to learn to hit targets with a rifle or machine gun, on their bellies or kneeling; manage a ten-mile route march on a stomach green with diarrhoea; to work in all conditions and all terrains; to read a map, use a prismatic compass, lay three kinds of barbed wire. They learned techniques for improvising a bamboo raft, a sangar, a space heater, or a booby trap in a tobacco tin; to paint a fake shadow onto a military vehicle to conceal it from enemy recon; to lay a mule track, a timber road, a macadam road, a concrete road, a motorable mesh path over loose sand; to destroy any and all of the above with guncotton, ammonal or dynamite. Besides being trained in soldiering and sapper skills, every recruit learned a military trade – as a carpenter, blacksmith, fitter, or other.

The recruits started out as hapless as Bobby felt himself. They cut open their lips from the kick of the .303 rifles, and wore their gas masks upside down. At the end of the tool drill, a classic bumble: when the subedar said 'Ground tools!' they set down picks and shovels too far ahead of them. When he shouted 'Raise tools!' they bent, and their rifles slipped off their backs, knocking them in the head.

At sapper drills, however, they were naturals. Most were farm boys, fresh from the winter planting, manure still black under their fingernails. Farmers made good sappers because they both worked the earth. Both had to dig and carry, to work and move while keeping their bodies low. A bare six weeks' training separated their life in the millet fields from their life in the field companies. And then they would go, and Bobby would have to lead them, into the field of fire.

By and large, Roorkee remained adrift in its imperial reverie. Week after week slid by, and Bobby felt his brothers sliding away, far ahead of him. He had been drowsing for so long that he began to feel like the regimental elephant, a great sleepwalking brute that did nothing but haul timber back and forth for bridging exercises. Every day, he woke in the expectation that movement orders would be on his table. On the fifteenth day, a telegram arrived for him. But it was from Madras.

It informed him that, at the start of December, Ganny had had an attack that was too painful to ignore. The winter cold had weakened him, and he had been diagnosed with bronchitis. Nugs, large with child, had boarded a train that carried her all the way back to Thal, and found him there, bedridden. He drew breath through a fist clenched around his lungs. He paused, exhausted, measuring the seconds until he had to take in air again. He was sleeping between breaths.

For three nights Nugs was with him, trying every trick she had learned over six years to help him. Six years, and it felt like it had all been preparation for this attack: their long love, the bleary nights awake as he wheezed, the boiling water spilled on hands and bedsheets. The hours she had spent, muscles knotting in her back as she kept him sitting upright. The hours.

On the morning of 10 December the hospital staff had placed him on the dangerously ill list. In the afternoon, when he closed his eyes as if to sleep, and Nugs rose to take a breath of her own, he died while she was out of the room.

Crickets poured their apologetic dirge into Roorkee's cold air. Ganny was dead. The world was breaking up, while Bobby dragged his heels in Roorkee. There was nobody waiting for him at the Frontier now, not even an enemy on whom to take revenge. Inky night fell over Roorkee, blotting out the flat acres, and Bobby blinked into the darkness, wondering where he would go instead.

PART TWO

West

9

Second Field

Baghdad, March 1943

Here at last came the second lieutenant, solitary and un-noticed, to the Alexandra Dock in Bombay. Madras harbour seemed a duck pond in comparison. Beyond the Alexandra lay wharf after wharf, dry dock and lock: fifty berths, with ships doubled up beside most of them, while still more rode at anchor. High overhead, silver barrage balloons glinted, fish-like in the sun, and the dock cranes drifted among them angling for a bite. Carrier pigeons shuttled messages from ship to shore. A freighter blasted its horn across the docks and was answered by a bagpipe's light skirling, as they prepared to send him off to war.

Bombay was the Hellespont of the world war, the intercept of the theatres in the West and East. The elation of return mixed with the nausea of embarkation. Thousands of dockers and coolies milled around the corrals of Italian prisoners, Chinese refugees and Yankee quartermasters, and the whole crowd was meshed with Indian soldiers in their plumage, uniforms spic and span, with bright hackles and puttees. Many were buried neck deep in marigold garlands.

It was dusk when they set sail. Men were sick over the side before the ship had even reached the open sea, while flexing weeds and Bombay's grime were still visible on the surface.

Bobby had an officers' cabin, which was good, though it was a lonely way to begin a war. He'd imagined he would head west with a unit, and all that the word implied: a trusted CO, comrades from Roorkee, the sturdy VCOs and long lines of sappers who had never seen the sea, whose fears would displace his own. Instead it was just him with his kitbag and cases, and unknown regiments thumping around the ship above and below him. He was a reinforcement, travelling alone to Iraq to join the 2nd Field Company of the Bengal Sappers, under the 161st Indian Infantry Brigade and the 5th Indian Division: formations about which he'd heard much but knew nothing.

He slipped down to the lower decks, where the men of the ranks were stacked like cargo to the roof. It was hot as a circle of hell, and to make things worse, blackout rules required that the portholes stay closed through the night. British, Hindus and Muslims were each bunked in separate decks, and Bobby could tell from just the odorous air which was which. The soldiers retreated to their bunks, homesick or seasick, to drip tears and vomit onto the floor. It mixed and coursed through the vessel, stroking the decks and slipping under the collars of steel joinery. The prow of the ship counted out a white rosary against the black water.

Dawn brought the convoy to light, the troopships and their cruiser escorts axing through the Arabian Sea. The intense sunlight found a thousand points to strike among their bristling guns and masts and jigsaw hulls before it joined the million glints upon the waves. This was more like it. On deck, VCOs shouted over the haul and clatter of chains, assigning parties to man machine guns at bow and stern – extra fire against enemy aircraft – while men with field glasses kept watch for submarines. Bobby was nearly lifted off his feet with anticipation. They were taking it to the Boche at last! He still had nothing to do, though, so he stood at the rail, looking west for the view that had greeted so many Indians already.

In 1914, the Indian Army had invaded Basra; in 1941, they did so again.[1] That April, after Britain decided to ensure the cooperation of its former protectorate, an Indian division landed and fought Iraq's army back towards Baghdad, where it met the British units and the Arab Legion fighting from the west. After taking the capital, they secured the oil wells of Mosul and the pumping facility at Kirkuk, reoccupied the fractious border villages of the Kurds, then fanned out to occupy Vichy-ruled Syria, the oil refinery at Abadan, and finally the rest of Iran.

By the summer of 1942, a territory three times the size of France was held in occupation by the newly created Paiforce – the Persia and Iraq Force,[2] the bulk of which was Indian. It was said that you could visit a police station in any corner of Iraq and think you were in Bihar: men sat on *charpais*, boiling tea, nattering in Hindi. Most were not idle, though. There was a fuel-burning war in Libya to the west, and an earth-scorching war to the north, and Iraq was a hectic logistical backroom for both. The Soviets suffered the greatest ordeal alone, but not unaided: American Lend-Lease materiel kept the Red Army on its feet, and the most viable route to Stalingrad was through the Persian Gulf and overland. Iraq became the final link in a supply chain wrapped halfway around the globe. Americans held one end, valiant Soviets the other, and there in the middle were the Indians.

In Margil, the port of Basra, the freighters all flew the Stars and Stripes. Bobby came down the gangway beneath huge silhouettes in the air, hanging askew from the harbour cranes. Knobbly battle tanks, angular field guns; tyres strung together like garlands of figs, and barrels of aviation fluid like clustered grapes. Crates enclosing mortar shells, sulpha drugs, tank treads and parachute silk, made in Detroit or Buffalo. More than a million tons of materiel a year was landing at these docks, which sagged under the weight of the task.

Bobby was put in a lorry going north, through Basra and on, splitting the wishbone of the Tigris and the Euphrates. The road carried a ceaseless column of military traffic. The driver of his lorry looked like a Tamil, and Bobby tried him out, asking where the convoys were headed. The driver smiled at hearing his mother tongue:

'All to Russia, sir.'

'And who's driving them?'

'We ourselves.'

Bobby scanned the ground for scars of war, but he could see none. After twenty months of the occupation, most of Iraq had returned to its perennial rhythms. Outside Basra, the road leapt over creeks and canals and then settled into a flat run, striped with eucalyptus shadow, or hedged by state farms thick with fruit trees. New wheat was risen in mankind's oldest fields, and closer to the river huge panes of sunset covered the ground where the spring floods had swept in between the bunds.

At Latifiya Camp, south of Baghdad, Bobby found himself in a headquarters tent, too nervous to take a seat while the orderly went to wake the major from his siesta. The tent was pitched by a signals office, beneath its snarl of phone and telegraph wires. Through its window Bobby could only see an incandescent square of the sky, divided by the cables into wedges and trapezoids like countries invented at the Paris Conference. Pied crows perched on the wires, beating their wings against the shocked air and fussing with their feathers, undecided on whether to let the heat singe them black or bleach them white.

Major A. E. Scott was an old campaigner whose boots had collected the sand of seven countries by the time Bobby met him.

He had been a lieutenant with 2nd Field when it embarked for Port Sudan in 1940, and was officer-in-command of the company by the time of the Allies' stand at El Alamein that past winter. He was as brown as Bobby was green. This respite in Latifiya Camp, a dreary place for certain, was still welcome.[3] He explained that the only agenda now was to rest and to train.

Bobby's heart sank as the major outlined their duties. After this long period 'in the blue', he said, the men's turnout was slipping. The platoon needed daily vehicle maintenance parades. All equipment must be spotless, including water pumps. 'And supervise sub-section *naiks* on stacking bedrolls,' the major concluded, '... And keeping the pots and pans neat.'

With these rousing words was Bobby Mugaseth inducted to the 2nd Field Company and the giant, restless reserve that maintained the occupation of Persia and Iraq. He met the company officers: the second-in-command, Captain Williams, and Lieutenants Reid and Rayner. Mugaseth was the first Indian name ever written in 2nd Field's officer rolls. The others were English, and apart from Major Scott, all commissioned during the war. Another lieutenant, John Walker Wright, had been in a road accident, the details of which remained vague until Wright hobbled back to the company and told Bobby about it himself.

It happened like this. Only a week into their time in Iraq, Wright and Captain Williams had gone on a company errand to Baghdad. The captain had insisted on driving, as he wanted to strike a pose in his new pair of driving gloves. As they raced down a raised bund road past Baghdad airport, Wright's mind had wandered, watching a plane climbing into the sky. In one moment he was wondering what it would be like to fly, and the next he felt their jeep magically lifted into midair, with the tops of trees passing below it, before it slammed into the earth fifteen feet below the bund. Williams wandered off, presumably to get help, leaving his passenger semi-conscious in the wreckage. Before the captain could return, the locals had stripped Wright of his wallet, documents and most of his clothing. Then they carried him off to hospital themselves.

Wright was bitter but unsurprised, because the captain was a vicious nincompoop, and the Arabs were thieves – as every soldier here knew. Generations spent under occupation had given the Iraqis stealthy fingers. In Army legend, they could steal the tent you were sleeping in and leave you slumbering beneath the stars.

Recuperating at Latifiya after two months in hospital, Wright was put in charge of the rookie's orientation. His camaraderie with Bobby came naturally: Wright disliked the company of the other English officers – particularly Captain Williams – and preferred that of his Indian platoon. Bobby, though an Indian, was at much greater ease talking in English than in the Urdu of the troops. It was an easy match of half-measures, which grew into rapport as they learned more about each other. Like Bobby, Wright had grown up with sisters, in a family full of doctors and without much military tradition, though Wright's father had been in France in the Great War. Neither had any affection for army discipline and routine, and for both the lure of the *world war* was more in the first word than the second.

Prior to boarding HMS *Durban Castle* for Bombay, John Walker Wright had never been further from England than to go cycling in Brittany. He was reading Classics at Cambridge when he enlisted, in 1940, and was filliped into the almost vicious discipline of a British training battalion. His memories of Aldershot were of running down a country road in full kit, hearing a sergeant shout 'Gas!', pulling on a mask that was fogged up, and running smack into a tree. Later, he faced disciplinary action for taking a piss while on guard duty – all because his fellow sentry had left splash marks on the wall.

After recruit training, Wright was commissioned as an officer-cadet. Finishing at the top of his class at Ripon, the colonial armies were gems in the palm of his hand, glinting for the privilege of his preference. He could see the world, and polish his status and career, anywhere from Jamaica to Hong Kong, though no army commission was more esteemed than India's. Wright arrived in Roorkee in January of 1942, and found that life there suited him nicely. The air was chilly and crisp. Havildars and *khidmatgars* and orderlies were constantly at hand, and bearers and sweepers and *bhistis* under foot, doing things so he didn't have to. He had his own polo pony. Bobby and Wright reminisced about Roorkee: about the funny old elephant, and the town's small but essential female population of nurses and 'grass widows', wives of officers gone overseas. Last summer, Wright said, he and some others took the ladies on a midnight picnic to the banks of the Ganga. Wright accompanied one particularly pretty grass widow, unaware that the Roorkee commandant was keeping an eye on her personally. That he found out the next day, when he received orders for Egypt.

Wright had light, winking eyes, a dimpled smile, and a high forehead covered with a fall of lank hair. He spoke in a soft, bantering voice that was great for telling stories, and it eased the process of introducing Bobby to the other personnel. Together they toured the lines and separate kitchens of the three platoons, and met the non-coms, including the hero of 2nd Field, a jemadar named Asanandan Singh. Singh was up for the Indian Order of Merit, Wright said, after they had taken his leave, but deserved even better.

The company's other lieutenants seemed bemused at being so far from Blighty for so long. They worried constantly about their onward deployment and when it would point them back toward Europe – which Britain hadn't touched since 1940 – and home.

But Bobby was burning to hear about what he had missed, about the war the sappers had left behind in Africa. On occasional evenings, he and Wright avoided the officers' mess tent, and introduced themselves quietly to the circle in the jemadars' area, where the Indian VCOs gathered to smoke hashish at sundown.

They carried a tin or two of warm beer for themselves, and first, as a gesture of official purpose, Wright would share the news that came down from brigade, about developments in the desert theatre and the rest of the world. The crack of the tab and the hiss of carbonation announced the end of the briefing. The Indians began to talk, slowly at first with a mind to the officers' presence, and then in frank but mellow voices which slipped inconsiderately into Punjabi and then resumed Urdu again, and their stories came out, beginning with the story of Asanandan Singh.

10

The Jemadars' Story
Eritrea and Libya, 1940–41

It was August of 1940, and away at the base of the Himalayas, Asanandan Singh led the recruits' anti-gas training. It was still hot in the day so they drilled at night, wearing gas masks as they dug trenches, looking like boars rooting up the soil by moonlight. Under the circumstances, Singh welcomed the news that the 2nd Field Company had orders to mobilise, to fight Mussolini.

Italy had taken the plunge, declaring war on the British Empire, and right away in Africa, its colonial armies invaded neighbouring British possessions. From Libya, they moved east into Egypt. From Abyssinia, they marched north into British Somaliland, and began nosing south into Kenya and north-west into Sudan. This open country was defended only by small garrisons, and the cry went up all over, to call in the Indian Army. Within a week, the company was on board the HT *Akbar*, preparing to cross the Arabian Sea. On the day of their departure, a German radio broadcast aimed at India recited the exact shipping schedule from Bombay, and concluded: 'None of them will arrive at their destination of Port Sudan.' On the tenth day of the voyage, Italian planes smashed up the sea to either side of the *Akbar*. But on the thirteenth day they did reach Port Sudan, and it was as they had been warned: the advantage in the air was entirely the enemy's.

The platoons came down in good order; they had drilled, on board, to disembark quickly. Still, it was hard on the men to be greeted at a foreign front by the full wail of air-raid sirens.

Singh was more worried about the trucks, as they'd never had trucks before.[1] Their engines had to be primed after two weeks sitting in the hold. For an enemy bomber this would look like three birds in one shot – docks, trucks, men. The vehicles came down in a great sling, one by one, and as soon as each had bumped down onto the dock, he was beside it, bellowing over the siren: '*Clear sling; quick inspect; connect battery terminal. Fill up! Cranked to fill the carburettor? Drive off, drive off!*'

So the 2nd Field Company entered Sudan, and the African war. At Khartoum, they painted their lorries and staff cars with the sign of their new division, the 5th Indian Infantry Division: a simple red circle on a black field, hastily contrived by the chief of staff, and called 'the Ball of Fire'.[2] They patrolled the banks of the river Atbara while the infantry arrived, and their formation grew to full strength, and was joined by the 4th Indian Division from Egypt. By the time the two divisions could go on the offensive it was the new year of 1941, and the Italians had pulled back across the border, to fight in the highlands of Eritrea. They were concentrating in Asmara, the capital and the key to safe shipping in the Red Sea. The key to Asmara was Keren, high in the mountains, and the sole approach to Keren was the Dongolaas Gorge.

At the gates of the gorge, Italian sappers had blown down half a hillside. Basalt rocks, the size of three-ton lorries, lolled in the road. The company spent five days cutting, blasting and clearing under fire from the Italian rearguard, and lost seven men. When they entered the gorge, the mountains rose around them like iron plough teeth, sharp and crusted, digging at the sky. Singh's platoon were Hindus from the hills of Garhwal, not far from Roorkee, a place where the wind came through green valleys carrying the electric smell of snow, to shock their skins and dismay their cattle and bounce the crops in the high terraced beds. But these hills were barren, or covered in camel-thorn bushes that tore skin like barbed wire. Singh stripped down a solid bough to use as a walking stick while they marched.

Ahead, a more dreadful obstacle awaited: the fortress of Dologorodoc. It was a concrete eyrie commanding the gorge, surrounded by other, higher peaks, all horned with Italian gun positions. The fort was defended by the strongest of the Italian regiments, the Savoy Grenadiers, and it fell to Singh's brigade[3] to capture Dologorodoc itself. The opening attack, 15 March, went badly: a Highland battalion went straight into concealed machine guns, which pinned them down in a streambed for the rest of the day, game for Italian snipers. At nightfall the Marathas went around to the steeper face, and climbed the dizzying incline foot above knee, shouting *'Shivaji Maharaj ki Jai!'* Singh's sapper detail was right behind them. Small red grenades poured down on the Marathas, and thrice they were pushed back, but each time they fought on, till they took the first rise toward the summit. The Sikhs passed through them to capture the next rise, and at night men from Yorkshire stormed the low walls of Dologorodoc.

Then began the greater ordeal, of holding the fort. Across the gorge, the 4th Division had failed to capture the peaks of Sanchil and Brigs Peak, from where the Italian guns hammered steadily on Dologorodoc. The noise alone was an assault. Explosions reverberated in the stone bowl of hills and returned as concussive shockwaves. Before long, sound was joined by smell, of rotting corpses and human waste, which rose from the ravines into which they'd been thrown. On the acre of bald rock at the summit, Singh's platoon tried to raise sandbag barricades in between the waves of Italian counterattack, pushed back with rifle fire and rifle butts. Officers struggled to keep their men from going berserk. Singh saw one Maratha machine-gunner clinging to his weapon on the fort wall, emptying belt after belt into strewn corpses, until his colonel physically dragged him off it.

For ten days the counterattacks continued, but while the bodies mounted around the concrete perimeter, Singh was called away to a new task. The Army Commander had decided that progress must be made down the gorge road, to give the 4th Division new routes of attack on Sanchil, and thus to finally relieve Dologorodoc. But the Italian sappers had blocked the way again, with a hundred yards of fallen boulders alternating with craters in the road.

On 25 March, Singh and his platoon crept down the gorge. It was not yet dawn, and explosions lit the profiles of the peaks above them. This was their third attempt to clear the rockfall. The sappers carried gelignite and ammonal, detonators, primers and fuse, sandbags, picks, shovels, pliers, wire cutters, rifles and two days' dry rations. What weighed most on Asanandan Singh, however, were the after-images – not yet reduced to memories – of their earlier attempts. Both times they had been spotted from the Sanchil slope, and machine guns chiselled up the rocks around them. The second attempt had cost their infantry escort sixteen lives.

A familiar, jagged black screen rose up between the jemadar and the paling sky. He was back at the roadblock, but this time with an idea. Before the enemy could find them, the sappers pulled the grilles off a culvert beneath the road, scuttled inside and walled themselves in with sandbags. Once the shelling began, it rattled the culvert and sent grit down the sappers' collars, but the men stayed focused on preparing explosive charges. Singh counted in his head. The guns, he knew, were old-fashioned artillery pieces: they broke off firing for fifty seconds to reload. That was the sappers' window to place the charges.

Each time a charge was blown the dawn light blacked out, then came streaming back through clouds of cordite and powdered stone. Between detonations, the sappers attacked the rock with crowbars. At this rate, the boulders would be cleared by afternoon, but the danger remained that enemy tanks would come through the breach first, and massacre the company. Someone had to cover the far side. Singh volunteered. He assembled twenty sappers at the head of the culvert, where Lieutenant Selkirk crouched, eyes on his wristwatch. The jemadar flexed his fingers around his walking stick. As the second hand clicked into 0900 hours the lieutenant said go. He went. He ran out past the demo parties and scrambled over the final boulders.

Nobody was visible on the far side, and they were not receiving fire. The sappers spread out at once, giving cover and laying anti-tank mines and concertina wire. Singh jogged from point to point, supervising. The work was quick and uninterrupted. It was almost too easy. The enemy's silence made him uncomfortable. He stepped away to the edge of the road, where the ground sloped away and the dark mouth of another culvert was visible. Without any noise, he slipped down to the level of the culvert, squeezed his eyes shut for a second, and swung himself around to stand before it.

His eyes opened and he could see down the tunnel. Two rows of men stared back from within. His figure blocked their exit, visible only as a dark silhouette with the light behind it, holding what looked like a sub-machine gun at the level of his chest. He was screaming in a language they did not know, *Drop your weapons! Drop your weapons!* His voice flooded the tunnel, so none could make out their superior's orders. They dropped their rifles. Other sappers were down by the jemadar's side now, sighting down their rifles as a score of men, Abyssinians and Italian officers, filed out with hands above their heads. They blinked and stared at the morning light and at the realisation that all the jemadar held in his hands was a walking stick.

By the next morning, the road was clear through that last block in the Dongolaas Gorge. The tanks went through, then the armoured troop carriers, trucks and jeeps. White flags rose over Brigs Peak and Sanchil. A day later, the 5th Division marched into Keren unopposed. At the capital, Asmara, the garrison surrendered. The bishop and the heads of government and police received the commander of 10th Brigade at the gates.

As the division trundled on astride the main highway, a grey python of Italian prisoners crawled away in the opposite direction. Eritrean villagers gathered on bluffs and rises above them, ululating and cheering at their masters' defeat. The Italians faced some risk of reprisals from their own, now disbanded native troops, but the prisoners overall seemed in good cheer. They were on their way to the railhead at Agordat, from there to be transported to camps in the Deccan, to idle away the next four years. They would be in India long before the jemadar or any of his men.

In the lull that followed Asanandan Singh's story, only the dry wind slapped at the canvas walls. What he had left unsaid was that the prisoners had one thing over their victors: they knew they would survive the war. Keren was one of Britain's first victories, most welcome at a time when the Empire fought its enemies alone. When the divisional commander, Lewis Heath, was promoted in April he paid a departing tribute to 'the Sapper and Miner Companies' almost superhuman energy, quite undaunted by shot or shell ...'. But the only reward for bravery was to fight even harder. Beyond Asmara were more granite landslides and burning lorries; more battles, at Massawa by the sea, and then at the deadly mountain redoubt of Amba Alagi, and eventually at Gazala.

The pipe was packed again, and Wright and Bobby crushed their empty cans and smoked. The only one not smoking now was Gurbachan Singh, jemadar of the Sikh 'B' Platoon, who sat further back from the light and the corruption. It was his turn to speak, however, as he had been at Gazala and had gone into the Cauldron – and he was one of the few who returned.

Why talk about Gazala? The sahibs knew enough already. The brigade John Wright was meant to join was the first to be destroyed there, and their own brigade, the 10th Indian, was destroyed before the end. It came a year after Keren, and they spent the intervening winter in Cyprus, fortifying airfields against attack by German paratroopers. Four months on an island of fruit and shade, watching the sun suck jewel colours out of the sea, and forgetting the war being fought just past its horizon.

There, on the huge, flat field of the Libyan desert, Auchinleck's Eighth Army faced the Panzerarmee Afrika in a deadly game. This time it was an even match. Twice each, they had pushed into the other's half; twice each, they'd faltered and fallen all the way back. Armadas of tanks, trucks and wheeled artillery sailed back and forth across the desert, making movements vast in compass, without a thought for roads or bridges. At first, like most Germans, their commander Erwin Rommel had been insulted to find brown men set against his Aryan heroes. The 4th Indian Division taught him to feel otherwise. They had led the advance on Benghazi, and when the tide turned again, they fought a savage rearguard action, all the way to the coastal town of Gazala. This was meant to be Britain's forward bastion, a massive triangle of minefields and fortified brigades anchored in the open desert, just before the fortress of Tobruk.

By the early summer of 1942, when they were relieved by the 5th Division at Gazala, the men of the 4th were thanking their stars. At last they were escaping the black magician Rommel. Gurbachan Singh learned all about his powers: about his command vehicle, a captured British truck he called 'Mammut', the Elephant, which was enchanted and could float over minefields. About the death ray, a weapon he wielded personally, that lanced out of the sky to wipe out full battalions. And Gurbachan Singh would experience for himself the necromancy of desert war: its boundless expanse, on which enemy Panzers rose up out of nothing; the unstable hex of landmines, which turned bare ground deadly; the occult rituals of desert combat and the dread dimensions of a desert retreat.

The 5th arrived there just as Rommel struck again – if not with magic, then with supernatural daring. He whisked his tanks deep into the desert and punched through the weak apex of the Gazala triangle. By the first day's end, his forces had rolled into its centre, backed up against the barrier of minefields, facing out to the bristling Allies. Their position was defensible, but hazardous in the extreme. Petrol, water and reinforcements could not reach them, and General Ritchie let Rommel's strike force stew in 'the Cauldron', their throats and fuel tanks drying up. When the 5th Division's recon group climbed a low ridge, they panned their binoculars over a hundred Panzers dead in the water. The sappers prepared to infiltrate and wreck the stranded tanks with explosives. But they were ordered to hold back, awaiting Ritchie's *jhatka*, his death blow.

More days passed, still but stirred by the delirium of June heat. Allied forces massed around the Cauldron, but still no orders came. Only the *khamseen*, a running cliff of sand that raised the level of the desert to the sky, and buried the company a thousand feet deep in stinging sand. When it passed, and they cleaned the grit out of their eyes and their field glasses, they took in an awful sight: as if by magic, the Panzers had sprung back to life.

Under cover of the sandstorm, Rommel's reserve troops had breached the minefield and carried supplies and fuel across. His force no longer looked like exhausted quarry in a trap – more like an angry steer swinging its horns at the belly of the Eighth Army. Ritchie ordered the attack, a week too late.

At half past two in the morning of 5 June, Gurbachan Singh roused his men into the icy air. Each sapper platoon would provide a detachment to one battalion of 10th Brigade, which would be the first into the fray.[4] At three, as Singh's group climbed into their transport with the 4/10th Baluch, the blowing night silence was split by the roar of a hundred field guns firing together. The barrage lasted twenty minutes, and their column rolled forward. In half an hour they had their objective: a ridge of naked, stony ground called the Dahar el Aslagh, marked only by two wooden barrels. As Singh dismounted, he heard cheers from the forward companies of the Baluchis. 'They are obviously mopping up,' their colonel reported. The earth turned briefly vivid green from the flare signalling the battalion's success.

With the pallid, heating dawn came the enemy shells, landing with great accuracy. By noon, the forward companies reported seventeen Panzers advancing, but they were engaged by the Highland Light Infantry, with whom were the sappers of 'A' Platoon, badly exposed. Their own tank cavalry stayed flea-sized in the distance, outclassed and demoralised. From what Garbachan later heard, the Highlanders left 180 of their men dead on the ridge before they were withdrawn. Well, they were the lucky ones. The Baluchis and the Gurkhas were told to hold their ground at all costs – the attack would be renewed the next day, with fresh troops. The 'C' Platoon sapper-officer went back to bring up extra tools and mines, and even bulldozers to improve the defences, but he never returned.[5]

When the new dawn revealed the horizon, Gurbachan Singh could see the Panzers himself, and now there were sixty of them. Every undulation seemed crested by a turret. They halted just outside of range, hulls down, and knocked out the British anti-tank weapons one by one.[6] Still their own tanks did not come. By nine thirty, the Panzers were crawling up the ridge and through the forward positions. They crossed trench after shallow trench, blasting the men out of the bottom, with nothing but small-arms fire to oppose them. As they expanded into terrifying detail, Gurbachan Singh felt a hand on his shoulder, and an officer shouted in his ear, pointing at a field gun stranded in the distance. Then he was sprinting toward the gun and lighting a bag of ammonal underneath it, and when he turned he saw a Panzer squatting over his position, and the enemy infantry pouring in, rifles levelled at survivors. So he turned again and kept running.

Bobby had to ask: didn't they signal to headquarters for help?

The Sikh jemadar nodded at Asanandan Singh – ask him. They signalled again and again for help. They did not know that the brigade HQ was gone, that their brigadier was a prisoner; that divisional headquarters too was gone, and the radios lay in pieces. They did not know that their fight was long over, so they fought on. The sun closed its eye to the sight.

Asanandan Singh exhaled a feather of smoke and took a moment before he spoke. He did not like to tell the story of a retreat. That day and the days that followed had shamed their commanders, and he did not like to talk of that. It was true that he was at the brigade base, watching as a traffic jam formed in the middle of the desert. It was a mess of the withdrawn and the wounded, and soon more vehicles came stampeding through the company area: lorries and carriers, in no order, simply running east. Something was badly wrong, and that became clearer when USAAF Tomahawks flew over and strafed the sapper camp, taking it for a camp on the enemy side. Major Scott ordered the company back two miles, onto higher ground. From there they had a fine view of the enemy sweeping over their brigade HQ, while the staff smashed their wireless sets and leapt into their jeeps. The last to leave was their colonel, Arthur Napier, whose group of five jeeps was tailed by white streaks of tracer.

'On trucks!' the major shouted, and the sappers joined the rout. They ran east through the dusk. Asanandan Singh looked up and saw yellow squares forming in the blue sky, as bombers opened their hatches above him. When they reached the temporary safety of the El Adem escarpment, the vehicle carrying the jemadar and the major pulled over, and they climbed out.

The stars were out, and below them the ground too was dotted with light, where flames gulped at burning trucks. New fires were lighting up along the main track, and the major marvelled at the precision of the German guns in the dark.

'It's our minefield, sahib,' Singh pointed out.

Their own panicked army was running onto mines that 2nd Field had laid the month before.

'And there is Potts-sahib,' said the jemadar, pinning down with his field glasses some smaller points of light that danced to and fro.

Captain Potts and his group of sappers, with men from the 3/12th Frontier Rifles, ran along the edge, trying to wave off the drivers, who were paying them no attention. Seeing the surrounding trucks explode, the drivers assumed the Germans were closing in, and redoubled their charge onto the minefield. Three hundred British vehicles ran onto the field that night – 'a striking tribute', the major said drily, 'to the quality of the company's work'.

Back in the Cauldron, hundreds were left to die of their wounds and be buried with the secret rites of the desert. The survivors regrouped at El Adem, where 2nd Field counted its losses: of the entire 'B' Platoon detail, only Gurbachan Singh had escaped. Of the 'C' Platoon detail, there was no sign of anybody. All told, two British officers and fifty-nine Indians of the company were killed or captured.

It was Rommel's greatest victory. The Eighth Army had lost its *izzat* (and nearly all its tanks), yet its disgrace was still far from over. The Panzers chased on. Two weeks later, Tobruk was lost, surrendered with a garrison of 35,000 men: a bewildering capitulation on the scale of Singapore. The sappers raced back to Egypt, running day and night, as their army collapsed around them. By July they were at El Alamein, the coastal town that marked the last line of defence before the Nile. Here the Army held its ground at last, and the running war became a static one. The broad battlefront had tapered down to forty miles – a thin band between the sea and the Qattara Depression, where the earth dropped away to a vast pit of salt marsh and sand bog. The long retreat had levelled the two armies' strengths: it shortened the Allied supply lines, but stretched the Axis thin across the desert.

Auchinleck turned immediately to re-equipping and reinforcements. Second Field's brigade had been wiped out at Gazala, and they were attached to a new one, the 161st Indian Motor Brigade.[7] They joined them on Ruweisat Ridge, a stony belt across the waist of the defensive line. For a few weeks the melee continued, testing the essential stalemate. The opposing armies met in lurching, tired collisions, and then both sank into their trenches, and stayed there. Before them, the no-man's-land filled

with debris: black shells of ambulances, severed braids of telephone wire, petrol tins and dud shells, and more than a million
landmines. Into that lulled purgatory arrived this sahib, John
Walker Wright.

11

The Lieutenant's Story
El Alamein, July–November 1942

Late that night, two lieutenants, escaping the fug of the VCOs' circle, prowled the tented rows of Latifiya Camp and found a pipeline on which to sit, or perhaps lie down. They lay down. The stars hung chandelier-like, so infinitely various and bright that some seemed pinned up, high in the tent of night, and others dangled low, heavy with radiance. Bobby's head spun slowly, and he could not shut his eyes, and the stars poured into them.

In the desert, Wright said, this was the only sight he had not tired of ten times over. On his first night at Ruweisat Ridge, he thought God had taken down the old night-roof and put in a new one. The sky had three dimensions here, which was a mercy, because the desert was so damned flat.

They were engineers, trained to work with inclines, gradients, cambers, but in the Western Desert, just about the only place where vertical relief mattered was up there. The stars suggested it, and men elaborated on the imaginary contours. The launch and drop of artillery shells traced thousands of hills in the sky; the long flight of Spitfires and Stukas drew an aerial steppe. Paratroopers jogged down gentle bluffs, swinging sideways from slope to opposing slope. Bursting anti-aircraft shells made pale vegetation, and even shots from rifles, fired in error or in desperation, added the thinnest pencil strokes to the mad conjured landscape. In night battle it was visible: Verey flares etched the luminous outlines, which glowed in his eyelids when he blinked.

Mainly there was no battle. Only the desert, so woefully flat. Wright arrived in Cairo to the news that his formation, the 3rd Indian Motor Brigade, had been destroyed at Gazala.[1] He was instead to join 2nd Field Company, barely half a mile from the front line. On Ruweisat Ridge rain had parted the curtains of desert haze, and a long blue scratch of Mediterranean water had appeared to the north, beyond the pebbled flatness. The infantry roasted in their trenches, endlessly cleaning the sand out of their weapons and flies out of their ears. In the daytime, an inattentive nomad might walk right through the forward area, veined and scabbed as it was by trenches and sandbags, and barely notice. Brown heads and helmets only rose out of the earth like moles, travelled low along the ground and vanished again. Only the engineers worked all day, fixing desert tracks or blasting rock, or planting and clearing, planting and clearing, planting and clearing mines.

At dusk, as the sky's fever abated and cool winds crossed the camp, life rose out of the blistered ground. Bright points of cigarettes glowed against the indigo sky and the grey earth, and the Muslim sappers bent in prayer, their bottoms to the foe. Cut-off petrol tins mouthed cowbell noises as tea was boiled. Infantry patrols slipped up to the wire, and rifles barked as snipers took aim at silhouettes, in the minutes before they were swallowed by darkness.

It was not until September that the dreary peace lifted, and a battle began that dazzled the eye. Replaying Gazala, the Panzers punched into the southern El Alamein front, then swerved back in behind the British lines, cutting an arc below Ruweisat Ridge. From up on top, Wright watched the fireworks.

If it had been scored by Wagner instead of the machines, it would have seemed a war of angels. To the south, above the main enemy thrust, Fairey Albacores dropped phosphorus flares that lit up the desert with electric brilliance, illuminating targets for Wellington bombers. Above their own sector, the Luftwaffe slit the full-moon sky with tracer fire. Planes dropped cases of butterfly bombs: delicate contraptions with hinged casings that sprang open, releasing a pair of wings that spun in the airflow, and drove a spindle into the bomblet to arm it. Landing, they flashed complex patterns on distant ground. Pulsing scarlet flares arced above the Allied lines, and searchlights swung across the spectacle, long flailing spider legs of light that grabbed at the descending figures. The stars burned on above it all.

'An exhilarating performance,' the major wrote in the unit diary.

The following morning they had orders to move east at once, and lay a minefield to stop the Panzer force from getting any further north. The company's lorries stretched out into the desert, each a hundred yards behind the other, raising a great cliffside of dust and grit.

Wright, in charge of picking up stragglers, drove a jeep all the way at the rear. His windscreen wipers worked non-stop to scrape open a view of the road. Turning to look over his elbow, Wright noticed a stationary staff car just south of their line of march. It didn't seem to belong to the company, but he pulled off the track toward it. He stopped a regulation distance away and hailed the men beside the vehicle, and hearing English voices, walked over.

The Humber had its bonnet up, and a helpless-looking sergeant underneath it, prodding at an engine that was belching steam. By the doors were two older officers, one carrying a fly-whisk and wearing the beret of the 11th Hussars, and the other wearing a flinty expression and a peaked cap with a red band.

'Anything wrong, sir?' Wright called out.

'Of course there is,' the first officer snapped. 'You don't think I want to stop here?'

Wright brought his jeep up to where the staff car was still sizzling. The fan belt was gone.

'I'll have to tow you, sir. Where do you need to go?'

'Army HQ, of course,' said the impatient Hussar. 'At Burg el Arab.'

Wright nodded, and went to unspool the towing hook from his jeep. Perhaps he should ask who they were. Of course he should ask who they were: it was protocol for desert encounters, where anyone might be an enemy infiltrator. He turned and snapped out a salute. 'Mind if I ask for your identity card, sir?'

The older officer's hand drifted to his pocket, but the Hussar exploded. 'Don't be a fool, man! Don't you know the Army Commander?'

Wright made sure his face stayed flat and solicitous. The Eighth Army Commander was General Auchinleck, but this didn't look like him. Someone had neglected to tell him that 'the Auk' had been relieved of his command. The news would be disappointing to any Indian soldier, but especially for the 161st Brigade, which included the regiment the Auk had once personally commanded, the 1/1st Punjab.

'Oh!' said Wright, and saluted again.

He hooked up the Army Commander's car and off they went. Wright's eye drifted to his rear-view mirror for a glimpse of the pinched face of the man who would dictate the fate of the Eighth Army. He was General Bernard Montgomery, the second appointee to replace the Auk, after a German Stuka put a bullet in the chest of General Gott as he flew to Cairo. Montgomery had some antipathy for the Indian Army: perhaps because he hadn't passed out from Sandhurst high enough to join it himself.

Wright was thinking that it would require snappy navigation to get the general to the Army HQ and still locate his convoy before dark. He decided to head straight across on the compass bearing, which meant getting off the main Army track. He quickly found a strategic track, less visible and used by L of C transport to evade aerial observation, and steered onto it. It was rough and covered in fine sand, but the coupled vehicles made good progress. Wright's eye went to his mirror again. The tow-chain disappeared into a cloud of dust. He sighed. Eventually he deposited a beige-masked, sand-blasted Army Commander at Burg el Arab, and waited for thanks, 'which were not forthcoming'.

Hours later, when he found the company, he also found a furious captain waiting, who refused to believe a word of it.

When Bobby's duties had him in the HQ tent, he read through the onion-paper pages of the unit diary, as quick as he could. The story of the September battle was completed here. By the time the sappers' work on the new minefield had begun, Rommel's last thrust was already exhausted. Short of petrol again, his Panzers ground to a halt amidst the fighting. They were forced to withdraw, and the offensive chance now lay with the Eighth Army, which was flush with new troops, new American tanks, raised morale and plenty of fuel.

The 4th and 5th Indian Divisions traded places one final time. The weary 5th piled into lorries to join the enormous reserve lying up in Iraq; only the 161st Brigade, its battalions still fresh, stayed put on Ruweisat Ridge. In the unit diary Bobby found the letters that had come down to the company in October, announcing 'D-Day' at last. 'Together we will hit the enemy for a "six", right out of North Africa,' Montgomery wrote. 'Let every officer and man enter the battle with the determination to do his duty so long as he has breath in his body. AND LET NO MAN SURRENDER AS LONG AS HE IS UNWOUNDED AND CAN FIGHT.' The 4th Division commander had added his own message: they were to fight to 'the last man, the last round, the last bomb, *the last bayonet*'.

It never came to that – Wright resumed his story, while they checked a register of tools maintenance with the stores *naik* that evening – once the attack began, Rommel's ranks were quickly broken. There was one terrible day when a Stuka bomber dropped a stick of bombs over their lines, nearly killing the officers in the mess truck, but saving its rage for the cook staff. They found the water carrier, Maqbool, screaming at a stump of flesh that had been his left hand. Mohammed Sharif the *masalchi*, only seventeen years old, was blown to pieces, 'shattered from head to toe'; Budhu Masi, the cook, was disembowelled. He was twenty years old and healthy. He took three hours to die.[2]

Still the battle moved west of them, and its blanket of noise was lifted, then blown off by the open roar of the wind. Wright's platoon found themselves in a quiet sector by the Qattara track, clearing S-mines. Those were anti-personnel devices that popped into the air and exploded at chest level. It was while clearing a minefield that the sappers looked like the farm boys many of them had been. A serried line of men jabbed their bayonets into the ground and felt for the edge of metal on metal. If they felt nothing, they struck again and again, clearing crescents before them, and advanced this way, scything slowly under the sand. The strange agriculture of the desert. One side planted steel seeds, and the other side harvested them. Only some lived out their natural design, to rise suddenly as a plumed palm of shocked air and sand.

Wright sat on a rock, watching his men till the sand. One NCO, Naik Taj Mohammed, was moving fast – he had cleared about thirty already. But then: the sharp noise, the bomblet hanging in the air. Wright felt the blast, the instant of utter surrender, everything tilting over, followed by long, gaping seconds of realisation. He saw the *naik* sit upright, his belly hanging in his lap like a tongue. It was bad but he would survive; the Germans built the mines that way, since a wounded man was a heavier burden than a corpse. When the ambulance left, work resumed.

Afterward, a jeep rolled up to where Wright stood, and he was hailed by Colonel John Blundell, the divisional Chief of Royal Engineers. The lieutenant explained how things were going. 'Right, well, hop in,' said the colonel. 'They can look after themselves.' They drove west into a minor depression of soft sand, interrupted by great limestone boulders, outrageously sculpted by the grainy wind. Wright was chuffed to be so friendly with the colonel, the CRE, and they spoke idly about the news of the fighting. The Desert Fox was losing, for lack of the one thing he valued even over water: petrol. This time the Eighth Army could exploit its advantage all the way. Both men were offended that the 4th Indian Division, one of three Allied divisions in Egypt since the desert war began, was being held back on salvage duty. Wright was wondering aloud whether that had anything to do with him giving Montgomery a mouthful of sand, when he heard a snap and a whistle past his ear.

It took a moment to register that they were being shot at. His instinct was to duck behind the dashboard, but the colonel floored the accelerator, and the jeep lurched forward at one of the boulders. Sure enough, an Italian soldier emerged from behind it with his hands behind his head. 'Know Italian?' the colonel shouted, above the engine's whine. Wright didn't.

The jeep slammed to a halt in front of the Italian, and the colonel leapt out and bounded right at him. In a flash, he picked up the man's rifle and tossed it as far as he could. Then he gripped the straggler by his shoulders, and in lieu of arresting him as a prisoner of war, the colonel turned him to face due east, stepped three paces back and gave him a running kick in the bottom. The Italian went sprawling in the sand. The colonel dragged him back to his feet, turned him east again and gave him a shove. The Italian took off running toward the Eighth Army reserve.

John Wright watched as the soldier pitched through the sand. His figure grew smaller and lost detail, but on the clear, flat ground he stayed visible for a long while, running east and east while his army ran west. Very soon, Wright suspected, he would be doing the same.

12

Kings of Persia
Baghdad, April 1943

As much as Bobby collected Wright's sapper tales to fill the deficit of his war experience, they seemed counterfeit when held in his account. At Latifiya Camp there was nothing to compare. Each morning he woke for reveille, already sweating, to look out through the close mesh of his sand-fly net at a scene that would have resembled Roorkee, if God had ground Roorkee lightly under his heel. Dusty white tents covered endless acres, in orderly rows marred by jeep tracks. The air was filmed with oily smoke from the jerry-rigged stoves the men fired through the night, and it stayed that way even after dawn gave way to broiling mid-morning.

The overall white and buff was only flecked with dull green where roadside shrubs and palms sagged in dust; a heavy slog for eyes accustomed to Malabar's tropical profusion. Beyond the camp was the first stage of Lawrence's desert, which manifested unfortunately as a knobbly gravel plain. The sappers reported that you couldn't kick a football two hundred yards out without chasing it three hundred back and forth. A brief, spring grass had risen and then died back into the stones, leaving the horizon speckled with thousands of white roses, shivering in the wind: crumpled loo-paper gusted out of the British latrines.

Every day had a timetable of continuation training – rowing, knotting and lashing, demolitions revision, Roman Urdu and geometry – mostly classroom lectures, alternating with parade. Brigade exercises came and went, strenuous but not dangerous, and returned Bobby each time to inspections of bedrolls and next-of-kin rolls, and barracks that reeked of sweat and scum. He inspected his men and was inspected in return.

Bobby regarded his life as an anti-suspense novel: *How will our hero escape his monotonous safety, and find his way to danger?* Manek, as always, was far ahead of him. He wrote: he was flying to Imphal. He could say no more – even to Kosh – because it was a secret operation. *A secret operation!* That was hardly necessary. Bobby even felt envious of his old roommate Mukundan, who was in the Indian Electrical and Mechanical Engineers, test-driving American battle tanks after their reassembly in India. They had just begun to receive Shermans, Mukundan wrote, tanks built for big, beef-fed American boys. The bantam-sized Mukundan had to stand on tiptoe to steer, and slammed his lip on the hatch every time he changed gears. He still liked his job, he said: the Shermans had turned the Allies' luck at El Alamein, and they would turn their army's luck in Burma. Only Bobby's efforts, out in Baghdad, seemed completely irrelevant to anyone's luck anywhere.

The problem was that the company, and the Fighting Fifth, and the whole of the combat army, were no more than house-guests in Iraq. It had been different in 1942, when all of Paiforce stood bracing for the war to burst upon it through the Caucasus or the Sinai. By the spring of 1943, however, the Panzerarmee Afrika was falling back, and weeks before Bobby's landing at Basra, General Paulus's army was destroyed outside the city it had spent six months battering and starving. The siege of Stalingrad lifted, and with it the shadow it had cast over Asia.

Paiforce turned back to porterage, the timeless duty of Indians in the world.

The Army did its best to show them their place in the scheme of things. Wireless stations in Baghdad and Tehran made broadcasts in eight Indian languages, and two newspapers – the weekly *Fauji Akhbar* and the biweekly *Jang-i-Khabarein* – appeared in several languages as well. When an open-air cinema came down from Quetta Camp, a propaganda film played before the main Hindustani feature. The stirring theme of the Ministry of Information struck up, and the screen lit with flickering scenes of the sort Bobby had witnessed at Margil: diverse goods of war moving from ship to shore, shore to barge, barge to train, scuttling at low frame-rate across Iraq.[1]

In the film, the train stops beside long rows of lorries parked abreast, each cab deep in the shadow arch of its carriage, forming trompe l'oeil aqueducts. Here waits young 'Apputy'. Too dark and too slender for the infantry, he was given to the Army Transport Corps, who taught him to drive. He is part of an immense transformation in the Indian Army – its mechanisation – another change bemoaned by its old establishment but forced by Auchinleck and the demands of war. In Bangalore, Apputy learned to take a motorbus, squealing and stalling, around in a circle on a repurposed polo ground. In Khanaqin, he swings into the cab of a three-ton Studebaker.

For a few hours his convoy drives east, following an ancient caravan route that now bears more tonnage each day than it would have done before the war in a year. Before him rises the heat-smudged outline of a mountain escarpment, the edge of the temperate and aromatic Iranian plateau; beyond it, quail hop through mulberry bushes and good red wine is a shilling a bottle; but that is not his destination. From the foot of the Zagros Mountains, the lorries begin to haul themselves up 7,000 feet.

The air grows cool, scented by pines, and then freezing. Apputy sleeps in his lorry, and each morning wakes frozen so stiff that he cannot bend his fingers. He drives with open palms pressed against the wheel and gearstick, until the sun rises high enough to oil his rusty joints.

White flecks his windshield, and the slopes accumulate white stubble. Before joining the Army, Apputy had never heard of snow. Now he and the other drivers pull on their extra winter issue: sheepskin greatcoats over oilskin jackets, fur-lined gloves and snow goggles. Even here, in the passes, there are more Indians: sappers scraping aside rockfall or signalmen guiding precious cables through the sleet, so that GHQ Middle East in Cairo might lift a telephone and hear the voice of GHQ India in Delhi. They drive higher, until even the road is glazed with ice and pebbles spring from under his wheels to come to a rest hundreds of feet below him. He has seen trucks go the same way.

Beyond the Shah Pass, they roll down toward Tehran and the Caspian sea ports, or to Tabriz on the Soviet land border. At the border, he tarries while the cargo is transferred and his officers compare forms with their Russian counterparts. Then they turn around and drive back, through Kermanshah, through Behistun, where the mountainside is carved with the symbol of Farohar and giant figures of the Magi. The words of Darius are inscribed there, singing his own praises – 'By the Grace of Ahura Mazda do I hold this empire' – and listing everyone he killed to keep it.

B obby's own expeditions never took him as far afield, though they did bring him face to face with the relics of the Persian kings. Some days the sappers went sightseeing, bussing north to the spiral minaret of Samarra or south to the ziggurat of Ur. The best of the ruins, the Arch of Ctesiphon, lay only ten miles east of Latifiya Camp, a practical distance for a route march. They could see it rise from afar, walls curving high and unsupported till they pressed together at the top, fingertips of buried hands. Once they reached it, the *langar* – canteen – was pulled off a truck, and the men sat on their haunches chewing dates, squinting up at the vacant clay.

For the regiment, the arch itself was less significant than the ground around it. The names of Ctesiphon and Kut-al-Amara resounded as battle honours of the Bengal Sappers. Asanandan Singh told what he had heard from the *subedar*-major, who had been there himself, when he was a new recruit. That was 1916. The 6th Poona Division landed at Basra and marched up the country, till it met the Ottoman machine guns at Ctesiphon. It left this courtyard full of the dying: men and mules entwined in barbed wire, limbs smashed, weeping for water. It's a terrible thing for a dying man to have a dry mouth – many knew that from Gazala. Five thousand mouths were left open, dry and fly-filled as the arch behind them.

The defeated force fell back to a walled town, and a siege began. That was Kut. For five months the division survived there, out of reach of rescue or provision. The Indians ransacked Arab houses for grain, and slaughtered the mules for meat. Twenty jawans died of starvation each day before Kut was surrendered.

To Bobby, who had never been hungry, that was a picture of cruelty utterly remote from the war of the present. The thought of Ottoman vengeance was as exotic as the imperial adventures of a thousand years earlier, when the men who ruled from Ctesiphon were fire-worshiping kings – Bobby's ancestors. Back then, the wings of Farohar enclosed the world from the Nile to the Indus. Before this very arch, the Muslims defeated the Sassanid Empire, sealing the fate of the Zoroastrians, whose children would become the refugees called the Parsis. Through a millennium in Hindustan, they preserved their flame, their blood and their noble names from extinction. Now a Parsi had returned to reclaim his ancient title. Hadn't his army conquered Greater Persia? Bobby strutted through the hall, listening for echoes of his empire. But the arch was silent, emptied of all prayer, left to do nothing but sunbathe its blank planes through eternity. The Zoroastrians were a race of subjects now, and the terrible names of Persia – Cyrus, Darius, Ardeshir – had become a knot of boys being called in from the yard for dinner.

B y April, the noon sky hissed, a frying pan left on the flame with nothing in it. Even the flies, stunned by the tempera-ture, ceased their singing from the arsenic traps around the camp's perimeter. Men sloshed water on their mattresses and hid in their tents, which filled with tangerine glare. At midday not a soul went outside.[2]

Death did not cease his usual rounds. A machine gun left in the sun with a round in the breech, heated up until it spat a bullet and killed a sapper. At Latifiya, a coolie lit his *beedi* and flicked the match into a dugout full of petrol cans. The conflagra-tion would have made the Luftwaffe proud, and it erased every trace of the coolie.

John Wright's injuries had healed, but he was still smarting from the insult that followed the accident on the bund road. Before long, he and Bobby had a chance for revenge against quick-fingered Arabs. The desert around Latifiya was veined with ancient, decrepit aqueducts, raised some feet above the ground. Near the camp they were draped with drying clothes, and further out they stretched into the desert like distended camel bones. One of these barged right through the company area, running under the wire fence at the camp perimeter.

Inevitably, a rifle disappeared from the company's arsenal and the major, who viewed the canal with a tactician's hostility, asked his two young officers to deal with it. It was a textbook booby-trap: they laid a tripwire inside, linked it to an igniter two feet back, and buried a slab of guncotton under the grit and trash on the floor of the duct.

A week later, at the end of another pattern-copied day in Latifiya, the officers met in their mess tent to empty a bottle. It was near midnight and the radio was off, and the silence hummed in their ears until replaced all of a sudden by a hard blast, the patter of debris, mixed yelling, and the snap of small-arms rounds – the forgotten sounds of battle. For Bobby, it was the first time hearing such noises outside a battle inoculation ground. He rose in a fright, not grasping that it was his own handiwork that had caused the excitement.

The officers ran out through the tent flaps, grabbing revolvers and torches and calling on the guards to cease fire. The cones of torchlight parted the swirling dust, found the concertina wire still intact and bobbing, and then located the very tiny, motionless body in the trench. For a moment Bobby thought he had killed a child. Under added beams of light, the figure resolved into the torso of a grown man, voiding black blood in the direction of his legs, which lay separate, a metre back. He had pushed the trip-wire with his head, setting off the charge right beneath him and blowing himself in two: half inside, half out.

A delegation led by the local sheikh arrived the next morning to take the body away. The sheikh, undoubtedly the very person who had ordered the thief in, affected great cheer and congratulated them for their brave action. The irony cut Bobby deeper than any reproach.

The ordeal of the desert summer was partly alleviated when a common suspicion crystallised as credible news. The Indian

Army was being prepared to invade Italy, to strike at what Churchill called 'the soft underbelly' of the fascist crocodile, while the Soviets forced back its jaws. This lifted everybody's mood. The division had been in a general sulk about being dumped in reserve while the Eighth Army regained Libya. After five months in Iraq, their minds sprang ahead to the round hills and pointed peaks of Italy, deliriously transmuted into a vista of buttocks and brassieres. For the first time since Madras, Bobby heard *La Traviata* strike up in his head: *De' miei bollenti spiriti, Il giovanile ardore, ella temprò col placido ... soriso, dell'amore, dell'amore?*

Divisional staff shared stories from Eritrea where, a signals officer remembered, 'You could always tell we were following the Italians ... Wherever they had stopped for breath, there was an absolute trail of Chianti bottles and French letters.'[3] In Libya, the captured Italian forts had yielded huge swags of Pellegrino, champagne and cured meats stocked for officers. At Giarabub, the Gurkhas found rooms full of Milanese prostitutes, rumoured to have techniques of fellatio as diverse as (and named after) shapes of pasta.

The sappers were equally cheered by the prospect, particularly the Hindu sappers from the hills. In the summer heat it only took an irrigation canal, slimy with larvae and bilharzia, to bring them close to breaking ranks and jumping in. Italy would mean thymy mountains and fast and freezing streams. The boot-shaped country was laced with rivers, falling east and west from the central spine of the Apennine Range. In place of the nervous drudgery of handling mines, they would build bridges, a real sapper's job.

Late April found 2nd Field at Habbaniya,[4] practising bridging on the lazy yellow waters of the Euphrates. They were to build a pontoon bridge for a simulated infantry clash between the

Sherwood Foresters and Assyrian Levies. It was less taxing than a timber bridge, and after three hours of road work, beachhead defence, hollering and hauling, the pontoons were in place and bound up, flossing the current through their rubber hides.

Bobby, exultant, pushed away the pile of schematic paperwork and regarded his company. The NCOs were gathered on the bank, shivering in their soaked-black uniforms, laughing over something Bobby couldn't catch. It was about their first camp in the Sudan, on the bank of the Atbara. Its lazy flow was filled with nubs of water-polished rock, innocent until they shot a plume of spray five feet into the air. Then black hulks emerged – mean pontoons of blubber and ivory, surfacing to breathe. At night the hippopotami climbed the banks and roamed about the camp, issuing loud rubbery challenges.

The infantry demonstration began. About ninety senior officers from GHQ Paiforce had assembled to watch it, milling around their parked jeeps on a raised embankment. The Sherwood Foresters swarmed up to the bridgehead, and Vickers Valencia biplanes droned in over the far bank, dropping 'enemy' paratroopers to assault the bridge. The pale silk bulbs popped open in the sky. As Bobby watched, a solitary pilot flying over the water dipped down toward the crowd on the embankment. He was about to 'buzz' the assembled brass for fun. The officers tensed, crouched, and then leapt off the edge. The pilot had misjudged his height. His wheels smashed into the hood of a jeep. As the officers rolled and slid down to the level ground, the plane bounced off the jeep top, yanking its hood up behind it like a banner. The Valencia strained, revolved and crumped hideously, nose first, into the earth.

It was the most awful spectacle Bobby had ever seen. He turned, aghast, to find the NCOs on their knees with laughter. When they could speak again, they assured him that they'd seen far worse. Even at the very beginning, from their camp by the Atbara, they'd had a grandstand view when Italian bombers obliterated the entire RAF fleet at the Gedaref aerodrome. At Mersa Matruh, during the scrambled retreat from Gazala,[5] a two-engined bomber actually crashed into the sappers' camp.

That was war, sahib. All this was still nothing.

PART THREE

East

13

Enter the Hurricane
Imphal, May 1943

The Hurricane bounced in the air and Manek's gut lurched, though he knew in the same instant what it was. Earlier that month he had felt, for the first time, the leaping black rage of anti-aircraft fire aimed at his machine and at blowing him into gravity's clutches. This wasn't it. He looked over just in time to make eye contact with his wingman, who had nudged Manek's wing tip with his own and was still sliding out. Flying Officer Sarna passed his hand over the 'O' of his mouth in mock apology, then gave Manek a winking salute. Manek tapped his forehead in return, once with index and middle fingers together, and a second time with just the middle.

Manek deserved the nudge, anyway. He had been caught napping, and on missions over northern Burma that could end your life. Sarna's job on these operations was to 'weave' around Manek, covering blind spots and scanning the sky for Japanese bandits. Manek's was to watch the ground like a hawk. Only on a good day, a flare might leap through the treetops and pinpoint their quarry. Other days, the risk of detection was too great for signals, and the pilots spent hours combing the canopy of teak, magnolia and ironwood, waiting for a glimpse of a camp in a clearing.

Nobody at Eastern Command knew the exact locations of the camps, so nobody knew the exact location of Manek and his weaver, apart from themselves – and that barely. They were over the thickly wooded region between Mandalay and Myitkyina, east of the Chindwin and far behind enemy lines. They were even further from their airfield at Imphal, and much further from the rest of their squadron in southern India. They were also barely yards above the blurring treetops.

Manek's journey out here began in September of 1942, when the Winged Arrows, still in Arakkonam, received the welcome news that they were to switch to Hawker Hurricanes, modern warplanes at last. Hurricanes had been the avenging angels in the dark nights of the Battle of Britain, when Spitfires could not fly because their exhausts glowed too visibly. These were the machines flown by 'the Few' to whom, in Churchill's stirring phrase, so much was owed by so many.

Manek was part of a small detachment sent to train in the new aircraft. The planes were a surprise gift, and he arrived in Bhopal intrigued about the occasion. There on the tarmac were the Hurricanes, noses in the air, sleek and sufficiently glamorous to make the squadron's old Audaxes seem like coconut contraptions of an island castaway. The fuselage of the Hurricane was built on a frame of steel tubes, and once in the air it drew its under-carriage into the body to jet through the sky at nearly 300 miles an hour. Its silhouette from below was as modern as anyone could imagine, and if you looked for it, there it was (omitting the length of tail): a convincing outline of Farohar.

This new pair of wings came with a closed cockpit and pipes streaming oxygen, but for reasons yet unknown, they engaged exclusively in risky, low-level exercises. There was no official word, but Manek gleaned that this was training for Burma, where Japanese Zeros patrolled the air, faster than the

Hurricane, but unable to manoeuvre so close to the ground. So he passed the winter trimming treetops, while two of the others, Gajinder Singh and Keki Motishaw, crashed into them and died of injuries. At the end of March, the rest flew their seven Hurricanes east to Imphal in the North-Eastern Frontier. On a map in his mind, Manek traced the path of his service, from the North-West Frontier down into the peninsula and then back up to the north-east: a giant V for Victory, the size and shape of his country – and concluding on the brink of the Japanese empire.

It had been a year since the Japanese army had swept over Burma. That year had brought victories in Africa and relief in the Middle East and established the British as the winners of the Desert War. In paddy and jungle, however, Britons and Indians had done nothing but lose. More was at stake than troop morale or even strategic advantage. The USA were in every theatre of the war now, but above all they led the fight in Asia: propping up China, leading the air operations over Burma, and driving the Japanese back up the Pacific Rim, island by bloody island. Implicitly, President Roosevelt was setting terms for the post-war world, one of which was freedom for the colonies. America was not going to snuff out Japan's young empire simply to revive Europe's decrepit ones.

Churchill was equally adamant that he 'had not become the King's first minister in order to oversee the end of the British Empire'. He knew that Britain's right to reclaim its Asian col-onies must be proved, at least by regaining Burma, if not Malaya as well. Yet its troops on that border were a dismal sight, even a year after their rout from Burma. They lived in a hell of neglect, beneath dripping tarpaulin, eating mean and erratic rations and burning with malaria. For every single casualty from enemy action, 120 men were hospitalised with preventable disease. The Japanese leaflets continued to fall, instigating the Gurkha and Indian troops:

> Lion-hearted Indian warriors! The British Government exploited you to the core. They first made you enslave your motherland; then they took you out of India like hired mules to fight other Asiatic nations. They used you to rob other nations of their independence. The British deceived you into becoming traitors; they made the whole world hate you.
>
> Are you not ashamed of your plight? Would you be Britain's tools of slavery? Or, would you be India's warriors of freedom?
>
> FIGHT FOR INDIA, YOUR OWN MOTHERLAND! INQUILAB ZINDABAD![1]

Morale sank and the Army reports were a litany of Hindus deserting, of Sikhs defecting to the other side, and of Muslims harassing the indigenous Burmese in revenge for what had been done to Muslim refugees escaping Burma the year before.

Since the nineteenth century, when it was tamed, the North-East Frontier had been India's overgrown and neglected back-yard. Beyond Assam, the tea gardens ran wild into forested hills where local levies controlled the tribes, some of whom still fought with spear and shield and collected each other's severed heads. Suddenly those silent hills had become the front line of an industrial war. Two armies were pressed together there, though still back to back: the Japanese faced east, to where the American marines crawled into Guadalcanal, and India west, to the war in North Africa and the impending invasion of Italy.

It was sappers who worked hardest there, clearing the hill tracks of their litter of refugee bones and laying real roads up to

Imphal and down to the Chindwin. In the spring of 1943, Britain's attempted offensive along the coast south-east of Bengal was defeated again. Amid the cliffs and streams of the Arakan peninsula, the Japanese proved immovable defenders and nimble assailants. British commanders had looked up at the tree-tangled ridges of the Mayu Range and judged them impassable, but Japanese soldiers proved otherwise, clambering over to ambush and rout the British and Indians.

In an attempt to raise morale about jungle warfare, Allied command turned to Orde Wingate, a brigadier with a messianic vision of Japanese forces in Burma being torn apart from the inside by guerrilla infiltrators. Wingate proposed to split up the 77th Indian Infantry Brigade into Long Range Penetration Groups, which would be called the 'Chindits', after the Burmese guardian spirits – half-lion, half-dragon – the men would wear on their badge.

Wingate's flamboyant plan appealed to Churchill far more than the costly, fastidious arrangements to strengthen and nourish regular Indian formations. In February 1943, the first Chindits slipped across the Chindwin river. Taking supplies on mule and elephant back, they infiltrated deep into northern Burma where they set about ambushing enemy patrols and severing railway lines. Their real target, however, was the myth of the Imperial Japanese Army's invincibility. Intrepid jungle attacks made for spectacular propaganda. The needle of British and Indian morale swayed forward just as the Japanese reared up and brought their full weight down on the guerrillas.

By April, when Manek arrived in Imphal, the brigade had been reduced to scattered and hunted bands. Many units were famished, begging or bartering for rice with Chin tribals, and cooking it along with the tips of edible ferns. The wounded were left behind in friendly villages, and the rest attempted only to survive and make it back across the Chindwin to India. They could be helped, to the extent that they could be located. British and American squadrons tackled the enemy air presence, and made air drops of food and medical aid to the brigade's survivors. It fell to No. 2 Squadron, Indian Air Force, to find them.

Like two deranged eyeballs, Manek and his weaver pilot rolled out over the Burmese forest, glaring round at the earth, the sky, the sun, the towering cumulonimbus, at each other, and their own instruments. Equipped with long-range fuel tanks, their Hurricanes could fly two hundred miles beyond the front line, searching for Chindits who had broken north for China. By the Chinese border enemy guns spat black flak. More terrifying were the weird convectional currents exhaled by the forest itself, which made the aircraft bob and bounce, as if it hung by its wingtips from two elastic clothes lines; they were known to get strong enough to tip a plane straight into the grabbing branches. The flying was ruinous on pilots' nerves, and halfway through each sortie, Manek's uniform was sodden with sweat.

Once they had located their object – the haggard faces in their hasty camps – Manek could turn back, and spy on the secret tableaux of life behind enemy lines as he went. Curls of blue smoke rose from cooling fires; bamboo fish traps threshed hidden creeks; Japanese soldiers sat cross-legged under oak trees, re-reading letters from home. There were traces of their own work in the canopy, where it was streaked with parachute silk, or sheared by the aluminium blade of a fallen wing. When they spotted 'targets of opportunity', such as a camouflaged sampan on the Irrawaddy, or a line of elephants under burlap burdens, they were authorised to wheel around and strafe to their heart's delight.

Coming to a halt on the mushy airfield was the best part of Manek's routine, because the camp itself was rough living. As the day cooled into dusk, rain came chopping down on the cadjan huts. It usually caught Manek bent over an empty kerosene tin, washing his own clothes. The officers' mess was an enclosure with walls of mud and bamboo and a roof of elephant grass. Inside it, though, was a warm knot of real chairs and tables and a small dynamo that powered a single electric bulb and a radio set.[2] After a day of searching with his eyes, Manek closed them and scoured the ether with his ears for songs to remind him of home and Kosh.

The real toll here was not the discomfort, but the unvoiced apprehension of death. Manek had seen too many go already: Gajinder and Keki downed in Bhopal, their squadron leader 'Bulbul' Khan killed at the end of their first fortnight of operations; others disappeared − presumed, at best, captives of the Japanese. Every morning, before Manek returned to the water-pearled sky, he slipped the picture of Kosh − lovely, haughty − into his tunic pocket. He tried to make sure to carry it every time he flew, so that if he failed to return they might tell her something consoling: that he had carried her photo to the end.

Still, Manek did not dwell on doubts about his purpose there, particularly not after what happened on the riverbank. At the end of one day's reconnaissance, he and his wingman were flying homeward, longing for the sight of Chindwin's broad trunk and glittering bark. The forest cover opened out onto the flat bank, suddenly revealing a pitched battle beneath them. A band of Gurkhas raced across the long, silted plain, pursued by at least thirty Japanese soldiers. Drained and desperate, the guerrillas had broken up and some had fallen. One man lay on his side, holding off ten cautious Japanese with the storied tenacity that never deserted Gurkha fighters. He fired his Tommy gun, dropped it to drag his legs by inches toward the water, then raised it and fired again.

As the Hurricanes sped past above him, Manek saw the small upturned face, and felt his throat catch. The brave, brown fellow was going to die at Japanese hands. A long second passed as the planes shot over the water, and then the weaver pilot signalled Manek and tore off into a steep banking turn. Manek was right behind him, practically pirouetting on the water, until the scene opened up before them again. The Gurkha was still pushing himself back, and now flailing his arms for help, and the Japanese were crouched to spring. They fell flat as the first Hurricane roared over blasting its cannons, then bolted while Manek opened his throttle, tearing down the same path and raising a wall of noise and lead in front of the wounded man. Like parent birds of prey, the Hurricanes swung around again and again, until the Gurkha platoon recovered the lame man and the attackers disappeared into deep cover. Then their fuel gauges gave warning, and they swung out over the river and back to Imphal.

That was that, it seemed, until an evening weeks later, when they dropped from their planes to the earth and the groundcrew nodded toward a couple of figures by the airfield's edge. The two pilots crossed the tarmac, pulling off their helmets and masks, their eyes slowly widening at the sight of a tall White lieutenant colonel waiting beside a short Nepali man on crutches. The Gurkha stood expressionless while the officer did the talking, but once the formal thanks had been made he swung forward on his good leg. Reaching into his coat, he took out a ceremonial kukri, the sort that passed as heirlooms in Gurkha families, and placed it in the hands of Manek's colleague. Then the four men saluted each other, with nothing more to be said.[3]

The wounded man was evacuated down to Assam, and they would never meet him again. The kukri would fly into battle in the cockpit of an IAF Hurricane, until the last of the men who could make it home to India had done so.

14

No Heroes

Madras, May–June 1943

After the deserts of Libya and Iraq, and lately a week on the Arabian Sea, the men of 2nd Field Company had seen enough mirages to doubt the bright, blocky crust accreting on the horizon. In hours, though, the channel grew busy with ships, and then there was no doubting the stench of fish and civilisation. Men crowded the bows of the *Nevasa* as she slipped past the Elysium of Bombay, the Gateway of India and the Hotel Taj Mahal, and returned to the dock from which the company had departed nearly a thousand days before.

As the ship berthed a brass band struck up behind the crimson carousel of coolies' dhotis. Its tooting and bumping were drowned out by the clamour of the troops as they rushed up from below and frothed on the deck. For more than an hour they lay tied up without orders to disembark. Hindi in the dialects of Rajputana and Urdu in the brogue of Wales mingled over softer conferences in Tamil and Garhwali. In content, however, the talk was all the same: the cause of the hold-up before their summer furlough.

At last four jeeps drove onto the quayside, and a hush descended as some very heavy gold braid stepped out. Then the ship erupted in whoops and whistles, not for the Major-General Commandant of Bombay, or the commander of the 5th Division, but for the third man to emerge: the handsome slab of chin and the trim blond moustache that were unmistakably General Claude Auchinleck.

The Auk looked a little diminished from his photographs of 1941, when he had commanded the entire Middle Eastern thea tre. After being relieved in Cairo he had spent a year unassigned, the punishment for his many contretemps with Churchill. His chest had sunk, and he clasped his hands behind his back. His great chin rested nearly on his sternum, but a smile played above it, sending wrinkles to his small enquiring eyes. Perhaps he knew that he would soon be re-appointed Commander-in-Chief of the Army in India, the force to which he had always been most devoted. But his present news was even greater. It was exchanged on the quayside with the brigade staff, and ran like a sparking fuse up the gangway to explode on the deck where Bobby stood. Tunis had fallen, the Afrika Korps was defeated. The 4th Indian Division had accepted the surrender of General von Arnim, Rommel's successor and the supreme commander of Axis forces in Africa.[1] The news was bittersweet, for both Auchinleck and the 5th Division. Neither had seen the campaign through to its end: the general had been fired from his command just before the final turn, and the division had been sent east after paying for the victory with the lives of thousands.

A few days later, there were more pipes and drums at the platform of Roorkee station, as 2nd Field was paraded through the town, representing all the Bengal Sappers still overseas. Europeans, loyalists, cantonment staff and children came out to cheer for them, the victors of North Africa; pi-dogs yapped and scampered. At Roorkee parade ground the commandant announced decorations and promotions. Asanandan Singh went up to be promoted *subedar* and receive the Indian Order of Merit for his 'continuous courage and disregard of personal danger' at Keren and the Falaja Pass.[2] He, with seventy-five other Indians and one British officer, Major Scott, had been in the field from 6 September 1940 to that day, 21 May 1943. They could now go home.

As his train jerked into motion, Bobby sensed a country in motion as well. The atmosphere in India had changed completely from the summer before. The mayhem of 'Do or Die' and the suppression of the Congress had helped India forget how close the Japanese still prowled to its back gate. Relieved of naval invaders[3] and nationalist crusaders, and all that existential bother, the country had settled in to win a war.

In 1943, India's 'phoney war' was at its peak, and all were doing well from it. The vision held by Leo Amery, Secretary of State for India, of a colony 'humming from end to end with activity in munitions and supply production ... the bustle of men training for active service', had become real. Everything was in demand, and India could supply: jute from the east for sandbags, wool from the north for blankets, coir from the south for rope; timber, tea, leather, coal; beans, bullets, ghee, glass, chemicals and compass parts. The industries of the Bombay Presidency, long fettered by the Raj, manufactured steel, ball-bearings and motor tools. The government purchased materiel with loans from India, and India turned from its master's debtor into its creditor. The mints worked overtime, issuing rupees to finance India's spending. Prices spiralled, but the wealthy lived better than ever before, flush with new profit.[4]

In Calicut, the saw mills ran day and night, cutting sleepers for railroads in Egypt and Persia, while in Delhi's Connaught Circus, lavish cabarets kept the same hours, fed by the salaries of US airmen.[5] In Madras, the port would be busier than it had ever been, receiving American ships whose draft did not permit them to sail up the Hooghly to Calcutta. The city would be turning as a happy cog in the newly oiled mechanism of India's war.

As he crossed India's midriff, Bobby passed through a belt of new and wildly disordered complexion. In Bombay, solitary girls from Ukraine sold sex to survive outside the Reich's new reach, and Polish orphans played in Bandra gardens, innocent of the fate of the families they'd left behind. To the east, in the hinterlands of Nagpur, West African soldiers toiled and trained, and in Delawari, Italian POWs built churches and joined the locals in praying for rain. Pale Cockneys of the Queen's Regiment turned Mowglies in the Seoni Forest. Further east, in Ramgarh, bare-chested Kentishmen marched between bare-breasted Santal women breaking rocks by the roadside. Chinese sappers flattened termite hills to expand training camps for 30,000 Chinese soldiers. Further east again was Calcutta, where US airmen, white-skinned boy-kings, swallowed inhuman quantities of ice cream; and then Assam, where Black engineers from Dixie built a new road to China, directing black labour from Travancore. At last, at India's furthest extent, Japanese patrols moved in stealth along the border, awaiting their own entrance to the play.[6]

In the middle of them all, and not the least strange, was Bobby himself. By officers' privilege, he travelled first class. The singed air billowed into his face, and sent him into a reverie of how much had changed and how fast. In the very same season, two years before, he and Mukundan would have been going home on hols. They only ever travelled third class back then. They wore sleeveless vests and lungis in the Maplah fashion, a week's scruff on their necks and the pungent reek of summer in their hair. As the engine hauled its heavy tail over the Ghats, Bobby chafed on the bare wooden berths yet felt like the king of train and track.

Once, when they hissed into a minor station, Bobby had peered into the stationary bogey on the next track. The berths there were upholstered in leather, and a fan whirred: second class.

Bobby looked on until a face appeared at the window. It was a second-class face, too, covered in even softer padding than the berths.

'*Edoh* ... Psst,' Bobby said. '*Edoh!*'

The middle-aged gentleman glanced over, then firmly away.

'*Edoh!*' Bobby insisted. 'Hey. Look here, *da* ...'

The man looked.

'I can tell that you haven't bought a ticket either, right?' Bobby said, in gutter Malayalam, and winked. 'Don't worry, don't worry. Just watch out for the ticket collector at Gudalur, and you'll be okay.'

The stranger's mouth slackened, but whatever he snapped back was lost in Bobby and Mukundan's hooting at the thrill of their reverse snobbery.

Well, the old Seth could get back at Bobby now. Here he was, travelling in first class – not even second. What did that make him? An army officer, of course. A sahib? Parsis were already semi-sahibs. No surprise they made good lieutenants; that was their shelf. Bobby, the Parsi-Madrassi *lootnant-sahib* of George's Own Bengalis, back from Iraq! Whatever he was, from the next track over, it must look pretty funny.

Maybe he wasn't anything at all. Not native or White, not Hindu or Muslim, pledged neither to his King nor his countrymen. He was no-land's man, a narrow strip of ground between all those clear-drawn lines. Maybe the whole country was like that: split between loyalty and liberty, subordination and treason. By being neither one thing nor the other, Bobby might be the most Indian of all.

He was still waiting to reach the fight, to see on which side he'd actually fall. Because he wasn't yet a real soldier, either. He had his first-class ticket, but he hadn't paid its true price. The only foes he had faced were flies and thieves. The 2nd Field Company had earned its victor's parade, many times over: at Barentu, at Keren, on the torn Massawa Road, up in Amba Alagi, down in the hell of Gazala, at Alam el Halfa and on the Ruweisat Ridge. When all that was over, Bobby marched with them, but mentally he demurred. *Ungli katvaake shaheedon mein shaamil ho guyu*, he thought – just a cut on the finger but in the ranks of the martyrs. What Bobby had to prove would be proved after this summer. Until then, the honours belonged to John Wright and Asanandan Singh. And Ganny, rest his soul. And Manek, who even now must be snapping on his flight goggles, taxiing out through curtains of rain toward Burma, where Bobby was in haste to join him.

The telegram arrived at the Mugaseth house the day before Bobby did, informing them of the crash. Manek had been returning to base through extreme low visibility due to monsoon cloud and had flown into a hill inside Indian lines. He'd been carrying Kosh's photograph in his pocket, where they had found it, folded into his maps. He was pronounced dead and buried in Imphal. The telegram thanked them for their sacrifice.

That was it. It was no enemy's doing, and no one's responsibility. Manek had just slipped from God's palm, and gone.

In those weeks, in that house, nothing could be clearly seen from the outside – nor could anyone, decades later, presume to describe it. There were just bare facts. Two boys had departed, Khodadad and Tehmina were back. And there was one more: Nugs and Ganny's baby daughter, not yet six months old. New death becoming known with new life. Wails of the newborn and the newly bereft. Also tears, breastmilk, urine, and of course – it was Madras and summer – ripe sweat.

Kosh was inconsolable, her pretty features twisted into ugly shapes. Nugs helped Khodadad and Tehmina receive their murmuring visitors, including the old Parsis who hadn't visited when her own husband died, and now met her with their excuses. There was little else to do. They did not have Manek's body to wash, or to soothe with the smoke of frankincense, or to follow in pairs down to the Tower of Silence.

All summer, the air stayed swollen and tender. Bobby's family had fallen apart once again – and once again it was rebuilt, but with its original members, as it had been in Calicut. Quietly they knitted back together, and in still moments, when the baby had her breast, Nugs told Bobby about her own journey home.

In December, in Thal, after the warmth left Ganny's body, and the cinders cooled in his petrol-smelling pyre, she had to execute the long, solitary return from the frosted plane of the Frontier, back to Madras and the world of the living. Six nights on a train, empty as Orpheus, with only her full belly and a full urn of ashes, before she stepped onto the sun-blasted platform and into the arms of her sisters.

They tried to keep her calm through the last two weeks of her pregnancy. She went into labour on New Year's Eve, and they hurried to the Women and Children's Hospital where she worked. Ganny's sister worked there as well, and was on duty that night, but refused to come to Nugs's bedside. Instead the nurses cared for her as if she was family. On the morning of the new year, her daughter was born.

New child and new mother went to Subur's, where early the next day Khodadad and Tehmina arrived at the door. 'You didn't bless our wedding,' Nugs screamed when she saw them, and then she fell into her mother's arms, and later they talked. Though unable to forgive Nugs and her husband, Khodadad and Tehmina were unable to forsake Nugs on her own. Once they saw the baby they were reconciled to her trail of mistakes. They would move to Madras to rejoin their daughters, eventually selling the house in Calicut, and recovering what they could of their family.

Nugs had to function, even as she groped for her sanity, so she managed both. The exertions of maternity had her on her feet from dawn. Then dusk returned, and on the beat of patting the baby to sleep, she counted the toll of consequences on her young life – become a wife, become an orphan; become a widow, become a mother – when all she'd ever felt ready to become was a doctor.

Tehmina ran the household, and though nobody could find an appetite, the table was covered as well as ever. Meat, fish, fruits and butter, and blessedly, eggs, were exempt from India's wartime controls. There were dhansaks of eight dals and eight vegetables for dinner. In all this only Khodadad was visibly improved. At the slightest opportunity he bundled the family into the car and dragged them out to the Cosmopolitan Club. His daughters' double losses had given him what his own doubling profits never had: a role, unavoidable, in the world of his children.

Outside, the blistering city (why was it always summer?) mopped its brow and hurried on, missing nobody. Shopkeepers broke from reading aloud from *Japan Varuvaana*[7] to fan themselves with its pages. Weeks became months. Already Manek had begun to fade. His plane had entered a cloud and flown into an invisible hillside. From that invisibility he never re-emerged, not even as a dead man. The pages of the squadron diary which documented the Imphal mission would be lost, and with them the record of Manek's last flight; in time, his name would disappear from the surviving rolls of the squadron's dead. Around the house too, Bobby noticed the gradual disappearance of Manek and Ganny's effects – a tin of hair cream, a stack of visiting cards – as noiseless hands packed them away. Already they were diminishing, their lives shrinking from the run of a subcontinent to the handspan of a photo frame.

Bobby was left alone to contemplate what lay ahead. Grief was grief, with its own authority. But grief was also a pretext to stay silent as the passing days pulled Bobby away from the family and into the company awaiting, which were still embodied for him by the two dead men. The war meant much less to him now, but he was indentured to it, and his real labour was just beginning. It was going to be a sappers' war. The Army planned a full offensive at last, rather than more glamorous folly of Wingate's sort, the sort that had cost Manek his life. A full offensive meant tanks and artillery, and full divisions of infantry well equipped. Out on the slopes of tropical mountains, through knotty forests of bamboo and orchids, their greatest military asset would be a decent road, and Bobby would have to build it.

15

Fascines and Gabions
Calcutta, October 1943

Slow, great and a year too late, like an elephant loosed from its chains, the Indian Army turned from the enemy it fought on orders to the enemy it had to fight for survival. In 1942 the country had faced Japan's carrier groups with fake guns made of tarred coconut stems. By 1944, it would have to beat the Japanese hand-to-hand. In the pivotal year of 1943, however, the Indian Army had new champions, bent on delivering better training, better weapons, provisions and a better chance.

One of these was Admiral Lord Louis Mountbatten, the new Supreme Allied Commander for SEAC (South-East Asia Command). He applied his enormous charisma to managing the Allied high command, delaying the promised campaign until the Army in India was prepared on three critical fronts: 'malaria, monsoon and morale'. A second stalwart was General Sir William Slim, the commander of the Fourteenth Army, the largest army ever raised by the British Empire, now poised on the Burmese border. Slim had led a brigade under 5th Indian Division in Eritrea. He was badly injured there, shot up by Italian fighter aircraft, but recovered in time to lead troops into Syria and Iran later that year.

In early 1942, Slim had stood on a muddy rampart at the border of Burma and India, watching his soldiers struggle across, and vowed to avenge them. Their condition was so pitiful that eight per cent would not survive. Back in Bengal, however, he was dismayed to find that they 'were short of everything': rifles, field guns, wireless kits, ambulances, and medical stores. 'Something vigorous would have to be done to avoid disaster,' he reflected later. 'Luckily, General Auchinleck was the man to do it.'[1]

Even in his previous position, leading the armies of six nations in the Western Desert, Auchinleck had kept an eye out for India's security against the Japanese onslaught. 'Two hundred thousand Indian soldiers in the Middle East is very nice for us, but hardly in keeping with her own apparently very urgent need,' he wrote to Alan Brooke, the Chief of the Imperial General Staff. 'I believe that we can still hold India without the Middle East, but we cannot for long hold the Middle East without India.'[2] His solicitous regard for India's safety left Churchill apoplectic. But the attitude behind it, the value placed on Indian lives, had a steadying effect on Indian officers through the dismal summer of 1942.

Like Slim, Auchinleck realised that the hopes of the Burma campaign hinged on transforming the army in India. Returning as Commander-in-Chief in 1943, he had lost his command of the fighting army to Mountbatten, but he remained responsible for ensuring its arsenal, supplies and training regime. India's self-defence had always been a contradiction in terms: its native soldiers had not been allowed to shoulder modern arms, and only received them in order to fight elsewhere in the Empire. Even in the 1930s, Nehru watched cadets parading at the new Indian Military Academy and secretly worried about 'what purpose this training serves ... Infantry and cavalry are about as much use today as the Roman phalanx, and the rifle is little better than the bow and arrow.'

Rarely had any army been entrusted with so much, while being distrusted so much. Old hands continued to believe that native battalions should remain with their relic equipment, dumb troops with basic weapons, no armour and no field guns. Chief among them was Churchill, who warned India's commanders that they were 'creating a Frankenstein by putting modern weapons in the hands of sepoys'.[3] The new commanders were not deterred. On the anvil of the Chhota Nagpur plateau, the Indian Army was being hammered into new steel.

Jungle warfare was not too bad, if judged by the picture of the 2nd Field Company in September. Reunited in Bihar, the company trained at bridging and amphibious landings on the Ganga. There was plashing in the green acre of the tank in Monghyr Fort, where new recruits learned to swim. Those from the Punjab, land of five rivers and five thousand irrigation ditches, usually arrived knowing how, but for those who didn't, Bobby employed the old Malabar technique, roping together hollow coconuts to make floats. All 'were like ducks in water by the end', the unit diary noted. In October the well-bathed company left Monghyr for Tori on the Chhota Nagpur plateau, to rejoin the 5th Division.

To learn the tactics of jungle war was, above all, to learn from the Japanese. The British had started out with only contempt for the little yellow Oriental. Very quickly that attitude swung, as Slim admitted, into dread of 'the superman of the jungle', from whom the British Empire had failed to wrest a single strategic victory. The jungle was the bane of the British: they regarded it as a depressing obstacle to mobility and visibility, while the Japanese relished the possibilities for deadly stealth.

Yet the rout in Asia had created a cadre of officers who had personally, and bitterly, accepted the lessons of Malaya and

Burma. On their evidence, Slim and the Auk realised that an army long aimed at the arid North-West Frontier must be reoriented for the humid north-east – down to every last man. By 1943, a doctrine of skills and tactics had finally been designed for troops in the Burmese theatre, published as *Military Training Pamphlet No. 9 (India)*. It focused on the Japanese soldier's tactical superiority and his character in combat, which they would mimic: it emphasised camouflage, infiltration, encirclement and ambush. The manual was nicknamed 'The Jungle Book', and its intention was to make them feral, jungle-wise, and oblivious to the conventions of Western war.

It was on board the *Nevasa* that Bobby had his first glimpse of what was to come. It was obvious by now that it would not include Sicilian olive groves or the Neapolitan opera. A day outside Bombay, the ship's captain got on the tannoy to congratulate them on crossing the 70th Meridian, the line chosen by the Axis powers to separate the future spheres of interest of Germany and Japan. The same day, divisional staff handed out envelopes full of photographs. The men passed them around without overreacting. The VCOs, who knew what was expected, muttered oaths. Some stared right through the pictures, absorbing the first official signal about the kind of war for which they were bound.

There was little in the photographs that hadn't already reached them in words, through the rumour mills of the jawans. Prisoners had been found crucified against tree trunks, their legs gnawed off by jackals. Sikhs were trussed up with their own turbans, forced to kneel in rows and used for bayonet practice. All that was known. The Japanese officers drove their own men like slaves. *Afsar sipahiyon ko bhains jaise maarte hain*, the sappers heard – They thrashed their troops like bullocks. Plausible tales mixed with snatches of nightmare. Jap soldiers carried loads like ants ... They were unbeatable in the jungle because they leapt through treetops: yellow-skinned monkey-sized men – apes with aircraft carriers.

Whatever they were, the 5th Division's training made it clear that it would not do to try and take them prisoner. 'The JAP is a fanatic,' one pamphlet explained, who should be regarded as 'a menace until he is dead'. In victory they gave no quarter, and facing defeat, they never surrendered. Their deranged dedication to the Emperor drove wounded Japanese to conceal hand-grenades until they were carried into Allied field hospitals, and then to pull the pin. Two years into the war, the total number of Japanese soldiers taken into Allied captivity alive was still in two digits.

The sappers were assembled in '*josh* groups', informal sessions where Bobby and the other officers could stoke hostility against the invaders. The Hun could be admired as a machine; the Jap was an animal. In order to dent Japanese morale, the training instructions said, 'It will be our fanatical aim to KILL JAPS; hunt him and kill him like any other wild beast.' The officers conveyed the five commandments handed down to all the units of 5th Division. The first: 'Be determined to kill every Jap you meet, and then some.' The last: 'Be determined – even fanatical.'[4] The aim overall, Bobby concluded, was twofold: to make the men hate the Japs as much as possible, and to make them as much like the Japs as possible.

On an evening when they returned from jungle drills in Tori, their colonel, 'Uncle' Arthur Napier, had attempted some encour-agement. 'Yes, yes,' he said to Bobby and Wright at the mess, 'You've got the idea. We're no longer in the realm of modern warfare. It's back to the concept of fascines and gabions – and shako hats, and that sort of thing ...'[5] Bobby wasn't so sure. The days of parade were gone, the days of march past, chin over one shoulder, rifle stock on the other. In Roorkee, the morning glare blurred the marching ranks into stripes of pale and dark – pale turbans, dark faces, pale tunics, dark belts, pale shorts, dark shins – and braided their rows into patterns as tight as a weaver's. That bright, liveried army which had marched for Victoria and Edward now seemed to Bobby like a dissolving dream.

Here the men drilled shirtless, or slogged through bush and brush to charge bare hillocks through clouds of mosquitoes. At dusk they tucked their pant legs into their boots, rolled helmet nets into their collars, and sloped around camp in a fog of Flit. Every soldier headed east was threatened with court martial if he neglected anti-malarial drill, and before he left, each man was fed the bitter course of mepacrine,[6] a new drug that turned skin a dull fluorescent yellow. Bobby watched in grim amusement as a jaundiced glow entered the pale skins of his fellow officers, and their transformation into yellow men seemed complete.

A t October's end, they shouldered packs to head toward Calcutta and the war. The train rattled down the Chhota Nagpur plateau into Bengal, and Bobby looked out the window onto a countryside that was well worked, patched with dark green fishponds and heavy with vines of areca nut. But everything was still; no women, or water buffaloes, moved in the fields.

He expected to see more proof of wartime profits: tea stalls, motor buses, silver on the women's arms. Instead, the sides of the railway track grew increasingly cobwebbed with tents and sacking and dark bodies with thread-thin limbs. Outside Calcutta, a serried line of children at least a mile long held tin bowls above their heads. As the engine slowed to a considered huffing, and the company rose to shoulder packs, they began to run alongside, as children do, but repeating one phrase: '*payter jala*' – stomach burning.

That there was famine in Bengal had been kept out of the papers even till late August, by which time the company was preoccupied in Monghyr. They were warned, but never prepared for the sight of it. At the Alipore station, the platform was thick with imploded bodies. The squeal of the train brakes pulled the jointed skin and bone onto its feet, and dragged it alongside till the train was at a halt. Then the arms and huge eyes were at the bars, scanning the sappers' own eyes for wayward hints of charity. The VCOs went carriage to carriage, slamming down shutters, shouting orders that the men were not to hand out rations.

At the gates of the freight yard, while they waited for transport and Bobby checked inventories, he watched figures diving onto the road behind each departing lorry to search the ruts for fallen rice. The company were driven to their transit camp, at the old infantry battalion lines, away from town but still surrounded by canyons of thin-walled brothels. During the day, they rifle-tested new recruits. In the evenings Bobby escaped, shouldered past the pimps hustling new girls, virgins ('her fee is the last thread of hope for her family'), and went to see Calcutta.

In Calcutta, civilisation stood before a fun-house mirror. Part of it bulged out past recognition and the other part collapsed inwards. There was high life and piteous death, both gross and gaudy, two worlds not colliding but sliding past each other like trams on parallel tracks. Calcutta was the principal R&R centre for the China–Burma theatre, and it was flush with cash. Everyone – generals, GIs, *babus* and *baniyas* – was keen that the soldiers have a good time, and not carry too much of their pay back with them to the Arakan front or the deadly air route to China.

Chowringhee Street was cinemas, chummeries and cabarets, hairdressers and ice-cream parlours; a khaki beau monde. The windows of the Grand Hotel advertised seven-course meals, and when its doors swung open, lobby lights skating on the glass, out burst tangled gangs of young officers and chee-chee girlfriends, billows of air scented with Old Spice and gin and buttery Chicken Kiev, and passages of hectic jazz. Inside, Teddy Weatherford was playing with Roy 'The Reverend' Butler and the gang of Burmese jazzmen they had intercepted as they fled the Japanese the year before. Indians sat primly, while Yankee fly-boys hung off each other's collars, giggling into their gimlets, rifling through their pockets to pull out blood chits printed in multiple languages, including Bengali – 'I am an American airman. If you will assist me, my government will sufficiently reward you when the Japanese are driven away ...' – to thrust at the waiters who brought the bill.

Senior officers took their wives to shows, and sang along to Andy Gemmel's hit song *Adolf* ..., with lyrics that served as well for the Americans in the audience as the Brits:

> A-a-a-dolf – You've bitten off
> Much more than you can chew ...
> Now you may get something to remi-ind you
> Of the old Red, White and Blue![7]

The non-coms preferred Firpo's, where a thirteen-course buffet opened with three kinds of chips, and built up to full trays of steak and spare ribs. With their plates piled, they found tables on the balcony, and avoided looking down to where the gas-blue and pink marquee lights picked out sunken faces and ribs, and lent coloured flames to the invisible pyre of famine.

Bobby too learned to walk like an actor hamming a pretty day, his face turned up, not wanting to know if a dusty shape was a fallen bough of tamarind leaves or a fallen girl. But the famine had a smell – a sour reek that leaked from stretched skin – and it had a sound, the clack of the *ghotis*, the tin bowls, on the hard pavement after the starving lost their voices.

Two thousand were dying every month in Calcutta alone. The earlier they were into starvation, the more difficult it was to look, because they were still trying – searching for susceptible soldiers, for rancid army scraps, for water that had been used to boil rice. The families were still families, and were still able to share. Despite their leathery skin and boar hair, they recognised themselves. The shade of prettiness still lay over women's features. Later they only repelled you. Then the municipal trucks came around to pick up their corpses, and carried them out of the city for mass burial.

The transit camp was not much relief, dripping with gonorrhoea and ghoulish talk. Men returning from the countryside described ghost villages, infants trying to feed at the breasts of dead mothers, children with limbs mangled by packs of dogs which no longer waited for people to die. After four days of this, 2nd Field Company fairly fled to the docks at Garden Reach, onto the rusty tub *Islami* and away. But sailing to Chittagong would only move them deeper into the shadow. The famine was born in the easternmost districts, to a conspiracy of nature, war and human prejudice. It began in 1942 with the loss of Burma, and with it, the Burmese rice surplus on which Bengal's population had long relied. In the border districts, the Army enforced a 'policy of denial', confiscating bicycles, motor buses and river boats, slaughtering elephants, denying the Japanese anything they could use to advance into the country. Families were left marooned, unable to reach their own plots or markets. Once transport was dealt with, authorities turned to 'rice denial', and emptied the granaries of tens of thousands of tons, some of which they set on fire.

After the scorching came the flood. A cyclone hit in October, inundating the region up to forty miles in from the sea. In Chittagong, to pass the time, RAF airmen filled their pockets with incendiary rounds and walked out onto the dykes above the river. They settled down, wearing gas masks against the stench, and took turns shooting at the bloated corpses rolling in the flood. When they hit one, escaping gases popped with flame.

. The cyclone ruined harvests, and farmers ate their seed stores. By the spring of 1943, church and civil groups were warning officials about starvation deaths. Bengal's government, embittered by the Quit India havoc, refused to listen. Following their prime minister, they took the view that Britain had endured shortages since 1940, with unity and resolve; Indians could do the same, or else pay the cost of their own venality. At a meeting of his War Cabinet, Churchill declared his view that only those Indians directly contributing to the war effort needed to be fed.

Some army commanders disagreed, knowing the effect of the spectacle on the morale of Indian troops. They wrote to Whitehall demanding food shipments, but were denied: the ships in the Indian Ocean were being drafted to the Atlantic to service Britain's own food imports. Meanwhile the Civil Supplies Department started to build its private stockpiles, and advised others – Army Service Corps, factory and plantation managers – to do the same. Rice piled up in hoards and stockpiles, jealous provisions against war outcomes and price futures, and continued to be sucked out of the countryside until the very end. The famine would consume 3 million lives before it was over. The newly generous Indian Army rations only made the situation look worse. The mercenaries feasted among the starving slaves.

In Chittagong, the famine was compounded by the seedy chaos of a low-priority war front. After three days pitching about on the Bay of Bengal, 2nd Field Company stumbled down to the docks, anxious to get some rest on dry and stable ground. A Movement Control officer assigned them a guide and shooed them off to barracks that were six miles away, and just as far again from the station from which they had to leave the next morning. There were rest camps right by the station, he admitted, filled with troops going nowhere for days. But orders were orders.

The company marched into the slummy city. Boys drifted up astride the column, murmuring the price to bed their sisters. The dying had been rousted from the main road, but they lay half-visible in the alleys. Some were naked, genitals shrunken, men and women barely distinguishable. It was a vision straight out of the lurid cartoons that the Japanese had dropped onto the retreating 17th Indian Division in Burma – Black Indians lying starving and skeletal, while pink-cheeked John Bulls marched the dumb jawans over their bodies – only this was real and it kept coming.

After four and a half miles, the OC asked the guide how much further remained. The guide nodded. On being pressed, he admitted he didn't know where he was taking them. Eventually they located the lines, but their vehicles, which were to follow with bedding and food, only reached them long past midnight. 'Although this war has been raging now for 4½ years,' the OC wrote in the unit diary, 'and though this campaign has been planned for months, arrangements fantastically bad.' As the exhausted cooks set up the *langar*, Bobby reread the disintegrating Movement Control order. 'Personal baggage and cooking pots will be loaded onto train by 10:00 hours.' The order gave no hint of how that baggage would get to the station. They could not ask the sappers to wake and march six miles back encumbered. That night he barely slept, troubled by the choking cries of children, and he rose before daybreak with Wright and the OC to scour the town for a truck.

Bobby's faith in British order was recoiling in his face. In Bengal, the oldest dominion of British India, the devastation seemed no different from what they heard of the territories now ruled by the Japanese. Bobby felt himself being pulled by a chilly undertow away from the West-facing war and its modern means, its plain purposes and moral clarity, its flat and sunlit field, into a deadly murk in the East in which very little was clear.

The confusion was telling on the men, as well. They were garrulous with fatigue, and were agitating each other with dismal thoughts. The new recruits included men from the United Provinces and Bihar, who were distraught at the idea of the famine reaching their villages. As it was, food was costly. Then they were called up just before the planting. Softer talk concerned Subhas Chandra Bose. On 15 August, over Radio Syonon, he had offered 100,000 tons of rice to save Bengal. The British *sarkar* had declined to even acknowledge it. Bose was a traitor, but at least it could be said of him that he thought Indians were good for more than dying.

In the spring of that year, in Königsbrück, Bose had bid farewell to his two battalions of Legion Freies Indien, both now regular formations in the Wehrmacht. He departed Germany and reappeared in Japanese-held Singapore, still waving the banner of a Free Indian Army.[8] 'To lean on the Japanese to get rid of British power,' Gandhi had written the previous year, was 'a remedy worse than the disease'.[9] But Bose was ready to take steps that the lily-livered Congress would not contemplate. After Stalingrad and El Alamein, he realised that no liberating army would ever reach India from the West. Instead he saw his chance, and his country's, on the jungled frontier with Burma.

In Singapore, he took command of the idle Indian renegades who called themselves the 'Indian National Army'. To Bobby and the other officers, they were the 'Indian Traitor Army', but by official order they were referred to as 'JIFs' – Japanese-Inspired Fifth Columnists. Though it had not yet been in battle, the INA was putting on a good show. It was the force Bose needed and he was the leader, the Netaji, it had been waiting for. For recruits, it drew from the deep pools of Indians languishing since the flight of the British – first the prisoners of war, then the Tamil plantation workers, who feared being press-ganged into work on the Thai-Burmese Railroad. Some troops joined from a captured garrison on the Andaman Islands. Eventually Bose would have 40,000 troops, among them a brigade of women called the Rani Lakshmibai Brigade, to honour a heroine of the uprising of 1857. It was led by another Lakshmi: Lakshmi Swaminathan from Madras, who had been made a captain. If Bobby met her now, he might be expected to salute her – were it not for the fact that he would have to shoot her.

Unlike his predecessor, a captain self-promoted to general, Bose took no rank. Yet he was plainly the most esteemed Indian officer anywhere in the world. He began to make appearances only in uniform, and he crisscrossed the Japanese imperium, leaving a trail of adulation among the Indians, the most vulnerable of the population in every place. On the radio he was hypnotic, but his live rallies drew tens of thousands, crowds that surged forward to fling jewellery at his feet to fund his crusade.

On 21 October, Bose announced the formation of the Arzi-Hukumat-e-Azad Hind, the Provisional Government of Free India.[10] The Japanese ceded the Andaman and Nicobar Islands to its symbolic rule, and Bose visited the islands briefly to raise the tricolour flag of the INA, not noticing the terror in which the real administration held the islands' population. If Azad Hind could be taken seriously, then Kobad's Maplah convicts – exiled here since the '20s – had the fruit of their rebellion, slow-ripening and probably bitter. They had become the first free Indians.

Azad Hind declared war on Britain, and Bose explained, 'When I say war I mean WAR – war to the finish, a war that can only end in the freedom of India.' He had led his crowds in shouting '*Dilli Chalo!*' – Onward to Delhi!, and now they were coming, marching with the enemy. In November their first units moved west to the front, and 2nd Field Company moved east to meet them.

16

The Jungle Book
Arakan,
December 1943–March 1944

At last Bobby was building his road. It was not, in its design or location, anything he might have foreseen; not a concrete highway cut through shoulders of sheer rock, or a track of diamond-mesh netting pegged over desert sand. Instead it was a light sheet of bitumen sprayed onto gravel, providing a casual passage across a bright green pastoral that was almost the Malabar.

The broad tar cambered to the grassy edge of the bund, then dropped into paddy pits, which were clay-cracked or held warm, shallow pools in this dry season. Bamboo thickets grew in narrow footholds, and plantain leaves twitched like elephants' ears in the breeze. On the far side of the paddy, scrubby forest massed and scattered. Burmese villagers crossed the fields wearing longyis, knotting and tucking in abstracted motions, just as the men did at home.

This picturesque plain was only a narrow belt, four miles wide, between the Bay of Bengal and the sudden, sheer rise of the Mayu hills. With the equally narrow plain on the far side of the hills, it formed the Arakan peninsula, the last fingernail of coastal Burma over which the British still asserted control. Smaller hills herring-boned off the central range, and tidal creeks, or *chaungs*, whiskered the coastal strip. Bobby's road skipped and darted around them, connecting the base at Chittagong to the forward operations of the Allied Fourteenth Army, which now included the 5th Indian Division.

The 5th had been reorganised as a 'Combined Animal and Motorised Transport' division, and they were accompanied by new comrades: tough and ill-tempered, champing like betel-chewers. Mules would be integral to their mobility in Burma. They were becoming so essential at the front line that the army had experimented with dropping mules by self-deployed parachute (alas for the mules involved). Any slope that an armed soldier could climb, a laden mule could too, leaving trucks and jeeps to catch up as they could. On operations, a jawan carried his rifle, his grenade and provisions for a day, but he watched anxiously over his shoulder for the mule that brought his blanket, bandages and sugar, stove and tea. The men of the division became devoted to them at once. They had been trained in their handling, loading and care, and when the time came, they kneeled on the mules' anaesthetised heads while doctors did bloody surgery to take out the animals' vocal chords. Debrayed and unable to speak their protest, the mules were ready for battle.

Day and night, a pastoral theatre played out on the Arakan Road. Motor vehicles hurried by, blaring horns, and exited. An occasional elephant ambled through, then returned the stage to its main actors, the mules. They came in trains of plodding hooves and nodding muzzles, flanks buried under heaped stores or pieces of broken-down artillery. It was the dry season and their feet raised the dust on the road, and villagers had to be hired to keep it tamped down. Fine-built men and women in bright longyis spread out beneath the bund, using cigarette tins to fling water out of the paddy puddles onto the tarmac. Each sapper platoon worked about twelve miles of road, and for much of the day, Bobby had his orderly drive him back and forth, watching the leaping walls of spritz as they caught rainbows and distressed the clouds of yellow butterflies in the air. After dark, clouds of fireflies took their place, and the sappers rolled tar by the light of blazing petrol-tin lamps.[1]

Up the road, John Wright found his villagers less than motivated, and on a morning when his jeep refused to start, he fancied he could already see the rising dust cloud, an invitation to an aerial strafing. He puzzled over how to find some transport, and it struck him that the 2nd Derajat Mountain Battery still kept horses, and stabled their remounts somewhere nearby. It was his lucky day after all. The gunner commander was obliging, and they led out a superb charger bearing full army kit: a rolled-up blanket behind the saddle, spare shoes jangling at the cantle, and a real cavalry sabre hanging in its sheath. Trotting down the road, Wright looked forward to busting the Burmese labour corps from this high position on his new mount.

It occurred to him, though, that if they saw him coming his truant wards might hop up and pretend to have been working all along. Suddenly inspired, he turned his steed off the road, across the dry fields, and into the trees on the far side. Crossing over the forested hillock, he could cut a shorter route to his road section. Shortly he could observe, from behind a screen of foliage, the row of villagers seated on their haunches and chatting in the bund's shade.

Wright sank his heels into the horse and burst, triumphant, from the foliage. The Burmese had not noticed. His spirit rose, and he spurred the horse again till they were cantering over the clay. The Burmese paid no attention. Now man and mount were galloping at their victims, and Wright reached for the hilt of the sabre and drew it in a motion, and then he was swirling it above his head, hollering like a Hussar, and at last the Burmese were rising nervously to their feet.

His cry tapered off quite suddenly, and his sword hand froze as he noticed the pennanted jeep that had come around the corner while he charged over the field. Wright paused by the side of the road to squirm the sabre into its sheath, then trotted over to the jeep.

Beside an impassive driver was Brigadier Mansergh, chief of regimental artillery. 'Good morning, lieutenant,' the brigadier said. 'And is this the accepted practice in the Royal Corps of Engineers for road labour inspection?'

The driver smiled behind his glove, but the brigadier kept a straight face until his jeep was back in motion. By the time John Wright dismounted and turned, arcs of spray were rising all down the Arakan Road.

The company tended their road till the end of the year, when they reached Zenganbyin and a military policeman's sign with a crude sketch beneath it. 'STOP,' said the sign. 'If you drive your vehicle past this point, you probably won't come back.' They camped there while the brigade assembled, on the first of a spur of hillocks where their good road ended and the war began.

The retreat of 1942, over a thousand miles, had already turned Burma into Britain's largest land campaign in the world war. It was on its way to becoming the longest lasting. After the failure of the first Arakan campaign, in early 1943, and the passing of the monsoon that year, the pressure had resumed on the Fourteenth Army to provide a visible victory for the Empire, or at least to draw off more enemy divisions from the fighting in China and the Pacific Islands. Slim had planned an amphibious assault down the coast, but the mysterious recall of all landing craft to Europe had scuttled that proposal, and left his options unchanged.

In the new year, then, his army would reprise the strategy of 1943: an offensive down the Arakan peninsula, aided by a Chinese advance in northern Burma and a second Chindit infiltration in the centre. For 161st Indian Infantry Brigade the specified objective was a series of railway tunnels that traversed the Mayu Range, connecting the port town of Maungdaw to the inland river town of Buthidaung. The larger aim was as quixotic as ever: Tokyo was never going to fall to an offensive that began in Chittagong. Slim's modest campaign had only the modest hope, he wrote, of being 'the first step to building a tradition of success'[2] against the Japanese.

At Zenganbyin, from their mild elevation, Bobby could see a fallen pillar of floating dust, his road leading back north to Cox's Bazaar and Chittagong. In the west, the winter sun lit up a filament of the Naf estuary where it met the sea at Maungdaw. To the south, it glimmered on the winding Hathipauk Chaung, beyond which the ground rose into crisscrossing chains of hillocks. What mattered was what lay there: on each hump, concealed by the coarse undergrowth, were Japanese trenches, wire and machine guns. The highest hilltop was Razabil, an earthen fortress fenced in with spiked bamboo, and in its shadow, the tunnels crossing the mountain.

More than a year after his commission, Bobby had found the war. It hadn't reached him by surprise, but seeped into his life as rainwater fills a trench, inch by inch, less exhilarating and more chilling with each drop. Now he had to wade out into it. The first offensive was set for the night of 30 December, according to the three clocks of moon, tide and paperwork. Earlier in the day, the 4th Battalion, Queen's Own Royal West Kents and the 1/1st Punjab had marched off in opposite directions, each with a 'bunker-busting' sapper detachment. They would circle behind the first chain of hillocks to cut off Japanese retreat or reinforcement. At dawn, the 4/7th Rajputs would put in a frontal charge and sweep through, destroying the enemy from the Hathipauk Chaung to the cut-off positions in the rear. Their hundred mules would follow at noon.

The operation was codenamed 'Jericho', after the biblical city vanquished by the Israelites, whose voices and trumpets were enough to flatten its walls. The divisional commander seemed confident of an equally deft victory: 'There will be little resistance to a surprise attack on my objective, except possibly by isolated posts,' he wrote to the brigade. It would be over in a single day.

The moon set. The tide fell. Down below, the sappers had raised a timber bridge over the *chaung*, and the Rajputs streamed over it and disappeared in the dark. Their war cry was audible at first light, answered by a red flare from the nearest hilltop, and then the chatter of machine guns like an insect swarm rising with the sun.

By nine o'clock the battle was fully joined. Bobby retired from the banks of the *chaung* to a vehicle park further back and up, where the cooks were doling out a morning langar. There was a partial view of the facing ridge, and everyone looked south, watching for the yellow triangular pennant that would signal the first objective being taken. The miniature figures of the Rajputs were periodically visible as they moved through the cover of Frate's rhododendron, or mustered a charge through black puffs of grenade smoke. If they were Hindus, Bobby knew, they would be crying out, *'Jai Bajrang Bali!'*, or if Muslims, *'Nara-i-Haidri Ya Ali!'* But under the hellish din of machine guns and mortars, which rolled directly over him here, he heard only a high, thin note like children singing. It seemed the Rajputs' battle cries had not the power of the Israelites'. The attack was not going as planned. Only once he saw a few of them reach the top trench, where other small figures rose to meet them with bayonets.

It was his first glimpse of the enemy, dug into burrows on an anonymous knoll in the Arakan. Their war was a crusade, Bobby thought ruefully; a duty to an emperor who was no less than a deity, and to an imperial destiny they held equally sacred. They fought under these orders from their army commander, General Mutaguchi: 'If your hands are broken, fight with your feet. If your hands and feet are broken, fight with your teeth. If there is not breath left in your body, fight with your ghost.' Bobby wished his own army fought for more than wage and pension – or that he had any conviction about why he was there himself.

By afternoon the chance was lost, the leading platoon virtually destroyed. But each day a new Rajput attack was thrown at some innocent-looking rise. Each time, the defenders shot a flare and vanished deep in their trenches, while surrounding positions brought down maximum fire on their own men and the exposed Rajputs. Every evening the dead and the wounded came back dangling in their mule saddles, and a gridlock of shouting stretcher-bearers built up at the *chaung* crossing.

The new year came, bringing rain, which washed the bloodied hillface in sleets of chilly water. The creek banks were churned to froth by hooves and tyres, and Bobby and the sappers laboured to ramp down the sand, lay new matting, and keep in place the guide ropes and pickets that kept the grisly traffic going. Snipers perched in trees drove them from the banks, but they returned to work under fire. On the sixth day, the Rajputs and the West Kents stormed a final feature, and found it had been abandoned during the previous night's rain. A pencilled note in the Rajputs' diary shares the secret of their eventual victory: 'Strangulation, starving, attrition.'

The brigade pushed on south over the hills toward Razabil, now with tanks alongside, firing solid steel shot over the heads of the infantry. Howitzers were dragged up the slopes and sent shells arcing from hill to hill, lifting geysers of shredded vegetation, soil and life. Vultee Vengeance bombers fell like spear thrusts from the sky, making eighty-degree dives and only twisting out instants before their payloads scalped the hills. Further north, one of these bombers was being flown by Manek's little brother Edul, a pilot with No. 7 Squadron IAF, wreaking vengeance in more than name. Sometimes the Allied echelons bombed their own side. By the end of the month, the Rajputs alone had 247 dead and wounded, and still they struggled to prise the deep-lodged enemy out of the soft ground.

As the Razabil assault ground on, the war broke the dykes of the front line and poured in all around them. The 5th Division, descending the western coastal strip, was mirrored across the Mayu by the 7th Indian Division, which advanced on the eastern end of the tunnels – and into a trap. In February, an enemy division made a cunning sweep around them, encircling the 7th, and cutting them off from the steep passes through which they were supplied.

Its infantry, dispersed in readiness for an attack, dug into their positions and refused to fall back. They inadvertently left the forward headquarters at Sinzweya – the divisional stores, signals centre, medical stations, all gathered in a natural amphitheatre in the eastern foothills – barely defended. Shells began crashing into the 'Admin Box', spreading fire in the vehicle park and letting loose a chain explosion in the ammunition dump. Cooks, clerks and signalmen, muleteers and quartermasters were handed rifles, and charged with helping to hold off thousands of Japanese.

The fight for Sinzweya was bestial, even by the standards of an animal war. On 7 February, the main medical dressing station was overrun by a force of Japanese supported by JIFs. The doctors and orderlies were stopped mid-surgery and led away, roped to one another by the neck. Bayonets dug in where their scalpels had been working. Thirty-six hours of fighting later, as British and Indian troops pressed back, it was the doctors' turn to be executed, one by one. The Indian orderlies were forced to carry out the Japanese wounded, and then they were shot as well. One doctor, Lieutenant Basu, had a revolver fired twice at his temple. Both times the bullet exploded in the chamber. When he realised he was still alive, Basu slipped his hands into the wounds of his friends, borrowing blood to cover his own head and neck.[3] Then he lay there in the gore, playing dead until he could be rescued.

After word reached Bobby's brigade about the atrocity in the field hospital, a change came over the men. They began to fight with relish. The jawans had been ambivalent about their country-men who marched with the enemy, but that was now swept aside by simple loathing. Wright had no compassion left either, he said. In view of the Japs' fondness for easy targets, his idea was to build a dummy hospital to lure them in − and booby-trap it to blow them to pieces.

The enemy offensive to the east of the Mayu swept over the passes, and knifed into the rear area of the 5th Division. All the way down Bobby's road, enemy patrols stalked each other and the bamboo groves flashed with fire. On his own patrols, Bobby learned to spot the spoor of Japanese snipers, fresh pockmarks in banks of earth. Sometimes he caught a glimpse of the men on the other side: a soldier washing his tunic in a stream in the rain-chased sunlight, indifferent to the demands of war, until shots rang out and he slipped into the water; a row of thin conscripts knee deep in a creek, bowed at the waist with bamboo yokes on their shoulders, forming a human bridge for their officers to cross.

In the evenings the jumbled silhouettes of the woods stirred to life. The wind raced over the hills, and the trees on the horizon were like dark creatures bounding. Any shape might be coming to kill you. Behind the screen of jungle noise the Japanese signalled to each other, mimicking woodpeckers and scops owls. They prowled around the camp, blasting grenades at random. These were 'jitter parties', intended to scare the men into returning fire: wasting ammunition and revealing their positions. The sappers were forewarned. In Tori, trigger-happy recruits had been forced to wear saris, making the point that real men controlled themselves and did not shoot prematurely.[4] Now they lay silent, even as the enemy passed near enough to toss rocks into their camp.

One night a jitter party strayed inadvertently through a gap in the wire. Shots rang out, and the Japanese went to ground in the middle of the brigade encampment, with no idea how to get out. The alert about an infiltration came down to the sappers from a Hyderabad machine-gun company dug in on a rise behind them. Nothing was visible in the silvered darkness, and the platoon hunched in their foxholes, bleary but breathing hard.

There was a shout from above: '*Khabardar, risala aa gaya!*'

It rang in their ears, and was repeated.

'Look out! Stand by to repel cavalry!'

An astonishing sound – a trampling of hooves – built up around the lone voice, and Bobby half rose in his trench, mystified, imagining a squadron of spirit lancers materialising up the hill. What appeared instead was a seething dark cataract, sounding, above the hooves, of indignant snorts and bits of bouncing harness. Then the brigade's entire mule pack cantered by, concealing in its midst the infiltrators who had found the mule lines, cut the tethers, and bolted out clutching at the animals' manes. The stampede passed right over the sappers, and bursts of gunfire lit up in it.

By morning light, they found no enemy felled – only twitching animals, their coats bloodied black. 'Well, we're able to say that we've withstood a cavalry charge,' Wright said, in consolation. 'And one from behind.' But there was little humour in his voice, because the men had grown protective of their mules, who were so stout and unfaltering. Nobody felt a deeper camaraderie with the mule than the sapper. Engineering in the forward areas often meant building mule tracks, and Bobby learned a careful appreciation of the gradient, breadth and zigzag turning radius a loaded mule needed to stay on its feet. Like the sappers, mules were half-warriors, half-carriers; together they opened rough paths to take troops to the front and sustain them there.

Other creatures joined the fray. Kites and vultures speckled the sky above the battlefield. Mosquitoes hit against Bobby's face and arms each time he moved, and leeches hung off his ankles and thighs like shining mulberries. Both armies lost thousands of casualties to the common adversary of ticks, scorpions and kraits.

Herds of wild elephant crashed through the woods. On one occasion, a patrol of 1/1st Punjab near the Rehkat Chaung was saved by a wild elephant who 'moved in close support', drawing fire and revealing an enemy strongpoint. 'The first recorded use of elephants in close support since the days of Hannibal,' their unit diary bragged. Chained tuskers were a more frequent sight, used to haul lumber to bridging sites. A bull elephant could drive his tusks under a log and lift it ten feet, and push it gently into place on the joists – making a few minutes' work of what would have taken the company hours. 'To watch an elephant building a bridge,' Slim would write, 'was to realise that the elephant was no mere transport animal, but indeed a skilled sapper.'[5] Bobby had joined the army with dreams of a fantastical, mechanised war, but they had left that behind in the desert. This war was fought off steaming backs and raw flanks, of men as well as beasts.

The Japanese had their own elephants, commandeered from the teak plantations to build roads and causeways and bring up supplies for their own side. Just like the elephants, serving masters on one side and then the other, were the men of the Indian National Army. In physical appearance they were identical to the men of the Indian Army, but the one extra word turned them deadly enemies. The company's rear base at Ngangyaung was attacked with flame-throwers, and as they pumped fire onto the supply dumps, voices shouted out in Punjabi calling the men to fight for their own. Two sentries vanished that night, in defection or in flames.

The meaning of the JIFs' presence at the front was not lost either on the ranks or up the chain of command. As the offensive against 7th Division began, 'Tokyo Rose', on the Japanese propaganda broadcast, had sung:

> The March on Delhi has begun.
> Tanahashi, the victor of Arakan,
> will be in Chittagong within a week.
> New British Fourteenth Army destroyed.

> ... Why not go home? It's all over in Burma.

The offensive had aimed to deal quickly with the Arakan, and to reach Chittagong where the perfidious Bengalis would be roused by their countryman Bose, casting eastern India into havoc. The Japanese columns had moved fast, not weighed down by rations. As with captured British supplies, Slim saw: 'None of our transport was to be destroyed. It was all wanted intact for the March on Delhi.' This grand strategy was held up by the resistance of the embattled 7th Indian Division. The largest air battles yet seen in South-East Asia took place above the eastern Arakan, giving cover to a great effort to air-drop supplies into the Admin Box. So, reversing the logic of centuries, the men in the siege received food and ammunition, while the besieging soldiers went hungry. The diary of a captured Japanese officer described their perspective: 'Their planes are bringing whisky, beer, butter, cheese, jam, corned beef, and eggs in great quantity,' he said. 'I am starving.'

The retraining of the Indian Army had had its effect, on ability as well as morale. Within weeks, the enemy division was scattered and its famished soldiers hunted down across the Mayu slopes. Razabil was taken, and the railway tunnels. It seemed certain that the tide had turned, that from here the Fourteenth Army could march into Burma – until new orders reached 2nd Field Company: mobilise immediately to Dohazari Airfield. They were being airlifted back to Assam, where the true offensive and the real wrath of war were impending.

17

Fight with Your Ghost
Kohima and Jotsoma, April 1944

The steel jaw fell open, banged hard on the tarmac, and the mouth of the plane lay agape, waiting for men to enter. It looked to Bobby like a great sacrifice, the feeding of the whole 5th Division to the bird gods, the Dakota and Commando transports. They never stopped coming – materialising in the heavens and descending to the airstrip, where they moaned until they were fed.

Their mouths dropped open and hundreds of loaves of bread, stacked like bricks into long parapets, snaked in. Jeeps drove up the long tongues to be swallowed, with the help of some manual hauling, deep into their bellies. It was, to be sure, a matter of ritual precision and the shamans presiding were surly pilots of the USAAF. They pawed at their red eyes and barked orders for the exact loading of the very inexact paraphernalia of an army division – folded acres of canvas tentage; small, shining stupas of cooking pots, one for each caste; typewriters, water *pakhals*, camouflage netting, crated mustard, bootlaces, blood plasma and a thousand other things. The planes swallowed it all.

Bobby looked down the loading table, which detailed exactly which men of 2nd Field Company, by rank and trade, would board each aircraft, along with which equipment. The idea was to avoid concentrating any class of personnel or gear in one plane, in case that plane did not reach its destination. The emplaning orders changed constantly, so Bobby had told the men to drop their packs in a patch of forest shade at the edge of the airstrip, where they sucked on their *beedis* and mulled over the prospect of lorrying through the sky. The British platoon nearby regaled them with some newly composed verse:

> Japs on the hilltop
> Japs in the Chaung
> Japs on the Ngakyedauk
> Japs in the Taung
> Japs with their L-of-C far too long –
> As they revel in the joys of in-fil-tration![1]

Bobby's attention was on the mules, the only element of the brigade that was resisting the Dakota's maw. The airmen had devised a mechanism to encourage them, a rope run through the steel handles on either side of the bay door and looped behind an animal's rump. When they yanked on the ends, the mules were flung into the dark fuselage. Inside, they were tethered at the fore with a wooden spar behind them to keep them still. The pilots scowled at all of this, and warned that any animal that got out of hand would be shot mid-flight or pushed off the plane. The idea of the dear grey bodies dropping through the blue was enough to persuade one volunteer in each plane to sit leaning against the spar, and risk a reproachful kick in the ribs.

For the first and only time in the war, an entire division – 15,000 men, with guns, jeeps, mules – was being pulled out of action on one battlefront to be airlifted to another. The urgency was plain to the men on the ground. Thirty of Curtis's

Commandos had been diverted by Mountbatten from their routine flights over 'the Hump', without even waiting for sanction by US air command. He had taken a liberty with that, but there simply wasn't enough time.

The 161st Brigade would be the last to fly, and the sappers of 2nd Field spent three days waiting at Dohazari – three days of hot dinners and haircuts, and motion pictures flickering through the night – before their turn came. By then, the pilots of that air-group had already made more than 700 sorties ferrying the division to Imphal.[2] Bobby had barely ducked under the vibrating palate of the aircraft and found a seat among the piles of stores before the bay door slammed shut, and they were off.

This was Bobby's first time in flight. Five years ago he had sat in the Loyola College canteen, picking the skin off his filter coffee, listening to Manek explain that it was aeroplanes that would win the war for Britain, or lose it. Nearly a year ago one of those planes had met the rushing rock and blown Manek's soul out of his body, sending it into flight eternal. Somewhere in these hills below him.

He wiped the window where it was fogged from his breath. The coastal plain had boiled up, first into low hills like scoops of chutney, then into vast green furrows, the Lushai Hills, which merged in the east with the Chin Hills, and in the north-east, along their path of flight, with the isolated ranges of the Naga tribes. Together they formed the awesome barrier that ran unbroken from Tibet to the Burmese coast, and had sealed eastern India against invasion for so long – though no longer. The enemy was lunging across it, racing Bobby to his destination.

Deep within the sea of hills was a single stepping-stone: the flat, oval valley of Imphal, speckled with villages and the ancient capital of Manipur. Barely a cart track had linked Imphal to the Assam plains two years earlier, when the piteous refugees and the 17th Indian Division dragged themselves through there from Burma. By 1944, it was the site of a corps HQ and humming Allied airfields, the keystone of the frail bridge between eastern India and the central Burmese front.

Japan's offensive in the Arakan had been a diversion. An army thrice as large was deploying against Imphal, and the Allied brass were stunned by its size and speed. Three full Japanese divisions had crossed the Chindwin by stealth, leading 12,000 horses, 30,000 oxen and more than a thousand elephants. They had formed an arc three hundred miles across, then closed in a circle around Imphal, cutting it off from the plains of Assam. With them was a brigade of Bose's soldiers, despatched with his promise: 'We shall carve our way through the enemy's ranks, or if God wills, we shall die a martyr's death, and in our last sleep we shall kiss the road which will bring our Army to Delhi.'

The spearheads of the Japanese Empire had pierced India at last, and they seemed to be driving at its very heart. If the invading horde captured Imphal, Japan could raise its head over Assam, Bengal and the country beyond. The retreating British government would scorch the earth, and the eastern provinces would starve afresh. Bose would ride the juggernaut through a country put to flames in his welcome. Indian troops would fall in with him to march on Calcutta, even Delhi, and Britain, overwhelmed by mutiny and massacre, would sue for peace. Gandhi and Nehru would be pulled out of jail to meet their new masters and learn that the days of empire were anything but over.

For two hours the Commandos' engines strained, spooling in the horizon. The planes carrying Bobby's brigade did not turn east to unload them in Imphal, as they had done with the rest of the division. They droned on, north and slightly west, and descended in the late morning over the slushy airfield of Dimapur.

When the aircraft banked to land, Bobby looked down on the grey clutter of the town. Dimapur looked from above like the underside of a truck, obscured by grime but holding all the springs and sprockets that could move this campaign to its end. It was a depot town, formed by the static build-up of things that wanted to be moving, things which had piled up into a city before a front line that had not shifted in two years. Dimapur held sufficient supplies to provision an army for an entire year. Trains entered and went no further. It was the final railhead at the end of Assam, beyond which a single road wound east and up to a hill post called Kohima, then turned south to Imphal.

On the ground, Dimapur was in a state of high alert and consternation, with no coherent end. Bobby felt at once the déjà vu of a defenceless city awaiting invasion. That same day, the Japanese had captured the road beyond Kohima, and dug in with a northern vantage over the Imphal Plain. Imphal was surrounded: still, half an army was garrisoned there for its defence. More appalling was the discovery of another enemy column coming over the hills, directly at Dimapur itself. The town's cornucopia of stores, vital for besieged Imphal, was just as vital for the Japanese, whose dwindling supply line was stretched over the jagged wilderness.

British commanders had anticipated a light enemy force, a battalion at most. But what was emerging over the hills was the whole of the Japanese 31st Division. At Sangshak and Jessami, two border villages, bloody resistance had slowed it down by a few days. But Kohima remained poorly defended, and Dimapur not at all. The officer-in-charge had told Slim that, of the 45,000 mouths he had to feed at Dimapur, he 'might get 500 who know how to fire a rifle'. They could do little more than wait while 15,000 Japanese soldiers crossed the ranges and rivers to destroy them.

The 161st Brigade was spat out of its aircraft straight into lorries. At first they sped between pasture and terrace plots of mineral-tinted water, but then they slowed to climb, and the earth beyond the shoulders of the road went wildly aslant. One side went right up and the other right down, falling to the floor of sea-deep valleys. They crawled between peak and precipice, and by sundown, a final lunge brought into view the Kohima Ridge.

It was a mile-long green saddle, slung from the heights of Mount Pulebadze in the south and a Naga-settled peak in the north. In between, in expanding detail, Bobby could make out red tin roofs of a colonial settlement, a hospital, bakery and stores; a sight that reminded him of Coonoor, the hill station north of Malabar. On one rise was the bungalow of the Deputy Commissioner, skirted with flower gardens and a clay tennis court, and surrounded by pines. Beyond it, the colonial postcard gave way to the rough woodcut of the tribal village: clustered dank thatch shivering on its height, exhaling wood smoke, snatching up and casting off wet blankets of cloud. The Nagas had emerged to watch their arrival, shining like beads strung across the hillside in their shawls of martial red and black. Behind them, the colossal herd of blue hills raised their heads and humps and filled the world to the horizon.

The sappers spread their bedrolls in the rooms of an evacuated hospital and shuttered the windows against the creeping mist. While they settled down, the OC called in Bobby and the others for a situation briefing. The garrison in Kohima was desperately unready to face the coming attack. Prior to their arrival, the town held only a single battalion of proper infantry, the Assam Regiment, which was itself the remains of a crumpled rearguard that had slowed the Japanese advance from the border. The other troops were a mess of hill levies, men pulled out of convalescent wards and stray recruits clubbed into new units under unfamiliar officers – what the local commander called his 'odds and sods'.

Even with the 161st Brigade they were far too few, and their brigadier 'Daddy' Warren confessed he was on tenterhooks. Orders from above kept changing. At his headquarters in Comilla, General Slim was locked in argument with both subordinates and superiors about how best to deploy the lone brigade between two towns forty-three miles apart. Dimapur was the real prize the Japanese wanted, but it was already on the plains, too deep into India. A stand at Kohima might halt the onslaught, but if Kohima fell it would doom Dimapur and the country behind it.

Already the 1/1st Punjabis had been shunted east and back, south and back, like a piece in the hands of a nervous chess player. At Kohima, the sappers needed every precious hour remaining to dig trenches, improve local tracks and sandbag their water points. At dawn, the men swung into confident action. The mountain wind pushed between them as they worked, flipping tarps and exciting the pennants on the tents and jeeps, and it was a glad sight for the local troops, at least till dusk closed in, and with it the Japanese.

On the second morning the order arrived: return to Dimapur.[3] Cursing and spitting, the men pushed their gear back onto the lorries and started the dismal drive down, leaving Kohima to its original, now-panicking, garrison. It was raining, and Bobby knew that their trenches, left half dug and without revetments, must be crumbling and flooding. Kohima would go the same way, with as little resistance. The brigade convoy spread out and the sappers bivouacked on the rain-frothed road, only straggling into Dimapur the next day, the first of April.

Forty-eight hours later, they were ordered back.

Second Field's 'A' Platoon, led by John Wright, left Dimapur at daybreak with the West Kents and a battery of gunners. Blaring vehicles hurtled past them on the narrow road, carrying away the sick and non-combatants. Outside Kohima, Wright watched the last of the opposing traffic, a regiment of Nepali state forces, rattle past him and down to Dimapur; they were wide-eyed with fright, officers as well as men. As Wright rounded the final bend, their debussing point came into view a half-mile ahead, crowded with the lorries of the West Kents – one of them in flames. Shells were landing amidst the vehicles: men leapt out, some already hurt and screaming as their feet hit the dirt. The Indian drivers were shouting and reversing to get out of range. The West Kents piled up in a roadside gutter, lying flat on their bellies and then rising, platoon by platoon, to sprint off in the direction of the DC's bungalow. An inauspicious way to get into town, Wright thought. He ordered his sappers to dismount, and carrying what they could on their backs, they jogged quietly into Kohima.

A few miles back, with the 1/1st Punjab and the 4/7th Rajputs, Bobby rode in the cab of a truck, alternately fiddling with his Webley, packing and emptying its chambers, and leaning out the window to peer ahead. The road was shrouded in the exhaust of the descending traffic. They were barely creeping forward. To Bobby's right, the hill-cut extruded the pale roots of the forest; to his left was the windy abyss. Directly in front of him, sappers took turns vomiting over the tailgate of their lorry – sickened by the fumes, the fatigue, the fear and the swerving ascent. Bobby swayed in his seat, urging the convoy to move faster, less for the sake of Kohima than to catch up with Wright. Whatever reckoning lay before them, he had to meet it and not be too late, as he had always been before. The road would not cooperate: already a captain of the Rajput battalion had caught his drivers sabotaging their vehicles, stuffing cigarette papers into the fuel pipes so they could drop out of the column.

After a point, Bobby was distracted from his silent urging by the numbers of men shuffling past on foot toward Dimapur; anxious groups who only met his gaze sidelong, some of them armed and seeming healthy. As they passed, some of the stragglers began to toss their rifles and ammunition belts into the brigade transport, shedding the signs that they belonged to the army. They were deserting, for reasons that became clear once a few were arrested.

They were terrified. They moaned and pleaded utter confusion. All was disarray in Kohima, they said: the night after 161st Brigade had abandoned them, enemy soldiers snuck into the Naga village in the north and slaughtered the Gurkhas on guard there. The next day they came from the south, and began to shell the town. Already the Japanese had captured the general hospital and the only water springs, and had forced back the defensive perimeter. Men in the garrison had been put under command of officers they had never seen before – officers who then ordered them to face an enemy at suicidal odds. Voices rose in the night to counter them, calling out in Urdu and Punjabi, 'Brother! Kill your officers before they get you killed!' The troops answered with random fire, contagious spasms aimed at ghosts.

Other soldiers had defected, the men said – gone over to the INA. They themselves had only fled.

The deserters were released, to be picked up in Dimapur. The convoy pulled off the road for the night and pressed on in the morning, a silent accordion of vehicles and men on foot, rifle-ready. The low drumming of distant guns and their echoes broke suddenly into the close, shrill whistle of falling shells. The first ones hit the tree canopy. Trunks cracked and branches burst loose over the brigade. Somewhere, a gunner adjusted his range. Then a screaming came down at Bobby where he stood.

Earth bucked. The blast rushed over him. It tumbled him, bodily, into a dark and quiet place he hadn't seen in a long time – not since the first time he had thought he would die, when he was a spindle-limbed boy swimming off the Calicut pier, and a big wave knocked him under with its hard rubber palm. He'd thought he was drowning before the sunlight pulled him back – as it did now. Bobby rose choking, with a throat full of leaf litter instead of salt. He clung to the earth as he had once clung to the furred leg of the pier. He had never known anything could be so loud. When his ears started working again, he heard someone nearby screaming at the top of their lungs.

Bobby got to his feet, and seizing the boy's shirt, pulled him over onto his side. He wasn't injured, and his scream subsided into a sobbing. Bobby looked up and staggered out across the carpet of dust and shattered bark. There was another body – down, and not moving – a sapper named Jagannath, a new recruit, concussed from the blast. He would survive. A platoon havildar, Keshwa Nand, had wounds from shrapnel but refused to be evacuated until they persuaded him that Jagannath must have an escort. Both were thrown into the last trucks heading downhill.

At the front of the convoy, the Rajputs had been approaching the forty-two milestone when the Japanese guns found them. Fires now burned greedily down their column, and ignited the mule trucks. While the men recovered, the animals burned, voiceless and unattended in the confusion. After the flames were extinguished, half the mules had to be dragged out of the charred carriage, demented from burns. They were shot through the forehead by ashen-faced jawans, then pushed over the edge of the ravine.

The Japanese division had seized the Dimapur road behind Wright's platoon and the West Kents, and it was still advancing. The enemy was a flood and Kohima was an island, five hills and sinking; now the water rose around the brigade in turn. Once Brigadier Warren's phoneline to Dimapur went dead, they knew they were encircled too. They must get off the road. The brigade struggled up through the dark, moss-dressed forest, towards a Naga hamlet called Jotsoma. It occupied a high spur of Pulebadze, with a clear and parallel view across the two-mile distance to Kohima. Here they held fast, a second island in the storm.

The five hills of the Kohima Ridge hung like a stage curtain across their western prospect. The slopes of Pulebadze at one end and the Naga village at the other were already crowded with Japanese, and for the next two weeks, Bobby watched the forests of Kohima explode and the line of ash and fire converge on the centre of the picture. They had only two goals in Jotsoma: to endure until relieved from Dimapur, and to protect their artillery, the 24th Mountain Regiment, as it helped Kohima endure. The two guns that had entered Kohima were now at too close quarters to be any use. Instead, with rising desperation, the eight guns at Jotsoma slung their fire into that narrowing gap of pulverised earth. All in the Jotsoma 'box' felt the same rage and urgency as they watched. It was hard to imagine anyone surviving in there.

Though a very long way from Roorkee, the company OC thought the situation also called for some cantonment drill. 'Raise-strike, break-rake,' the *naiks* sang out. 'Swing, handle low, throw.' Digging by numbers, three cubic yards per man per day, even though the soil was mostly rock. The familiar drill kept the sappers focused and calm, even though they were deemed 'fighting infantry' now, under command of the Rajputs. With the West Kents inside Kohima, the brigade was a battalion short; one

Rajput company soon disappeared into the trees, aiming to slip through the siege and add a last few rifles to the Kohima defence.[4] Each day the sappers fanned out further along the perimeter, as the infantry sent new patrols to the intervening slopes, or onto the road itself, trading ambush for ambush. Sometimes sappers went with them, bunker-busting details, to run through smoke toward an enemy momentarily subdued, push a pole-charge into a sodden dugout and blow it into smoking timber.

Every time they advanced, counterattacks dragged them back to defend Jotsoma. At the wire, Bobby shared a dugout with his orderly, and kept a close eye on the platoon that had lost their havildar. They were especially on edge. The first night in the box, a nervous bout produced an endless fusillade, riddling the vacant dark. In the morning the Rajput CO coolly informed Bobby that he had counted 250 wasted rounds – each of which betrayed the lay of their defence to the jitter party presumably watching to learn just that.

Days passed under breeze-blown heat. Even with the crush of men in the box, and the enemy swirling around it, what Bobby felt constantly was not fear but loneliness. The scale of the valleys demolished any sense of a lone human's significance. That was apart from all the lethal metal streaking through them. Out here on the green baize of the Naga Hills, the gods were rolling dice for men's lives and limbs. Each day the brigade brought in its dead – Jat Sikhs, Hazarawals, Punjabi Mussalmans – to be burned or buried in the wilderness. At any moment, Bobby could fall to the snap of a bullet or the sighing arrival of a mortar shell.

In the evenings, the wind towed clouds over the ridges, which scraped their bottoms of rain. When the clouds reached Jotsoma, a grey mist charged in like a ghost battalion, leaping overhead and closing up in front of them, and opening fire with needle-sharp drops, flying sideways. Through one such blindfold of rain,

Bobby first heard, and then saw, the white bursts spouting from the blue shadow beyond the wire. His mind emptied clean of the thoughts it had been working on the instant before, of the words on his lips. As the roar of voices and gunshots rose around him, his life behind him went dark and only the present showed in flashing fear-vision.

Bobby sat down hard, and for a minute, or how long he didn't know, he only sat. Bullets cast the sound of pure and lethal speed wide overhead, and he twisted around to watch the stabbing flames multiply before him. He watched the battle, and then he could see himself watching the battle, and then for a moment he saw someone else, far away and in the future, watching him watch himself, at this moment.

And then he was back, his will at work again and his eyes swivelling over the scene around him. Mortars fell on both sides, flashing among the darkened trees over there, silhouetting thin men and thin packs. A sapper's face lit up as a child's, round-eyed and square-mouthed, exhaling panic. Asanandan Singh was crawling up the trench, bellowing into sappers' ears, and Bobby rose on legs like tubes of water to do the same.

He had grasped the words and could say them. But the Bren guns roared to life, hosing the woods with returned fire and turning Bobby into a soundless mime, manhandling boys up against the parapet. The *naiks* got their Tommy guns going. A few gallants were up behind their rifles, sighting over the edge for a target in the spasming light. Taking courage from them, Bobby fell to his knees with the Webley that had tugged at his hip since Baghdad. Now it was out and seeking its shot, but no new flash issued from the grey tree shadows. The raiders disappeared, leaving Bobby with the blood banging in his ears, acid in his mouth, and a lead-heavy sidearm wavering in his hands.

18

The Cremation Ground
Kohima, April 1944

The wireless set at Jotsoma was rarely let go by the gunners, who needed to stay in constant touch with their observers inside Kohima. It wasn't until 13 April, a week after their separation, that the OC of 2nd Field had a moment to check in with John Wright. He returned with an uplifting report, noting in the unit diary: '"A" Section in good heart and mainly engaged in blowing up houses containing Japs ...'

As Wright scampered zigzag back to his trench in Kohima, he considered all the details he'd omitted. He hadn't mentioned, for instance, that he was a hero. He wasn't dwelling on it, under the circumstances. It had happened on the one good day that anyone in Kohima had had since the siege began.

After sneaking into the Kohima perimeter without casualties, Wright's platoon had 'dug trenches like billyo', only about a foot deep to start with – enough for them to lie nuzzling the earth. Forty-eight hours later they were dug in on the central feature, Garrison Hill. The Japanese battered in on all points, but their main offensive press was from the south, where the defenders had been driven off two more hillocks. A third, the Detail Hill, was under heavy assault. At sunrise on 7 April, a company of West Kents found a large population of Japanese in their midst

– hunkered down in a set of vacant trenches and buildings on Detail Hill. They turned a mortar onto the thatched huts, which burst into flame and drove some Japanese into the open, where the Kentish gunners cut them down. But nearly a hundred infiltrators still sheltered in one large building, a bakery, and were shooting out of its slit windows, tearing up the ground against a counterattack. Japanese snipers on Jail Hill, a hundred yards back, covered the approach as well. The West Kent captain Donald Easten thought it looked like a job for the sappers.

The captain laid out the situation to Wright and Lance-Naik Abdul Majid: the bakery had a tin roof, one brick wall and three walls of bamboo. In Kohima, this amounted to rock-solid defences. The men inside were also taking cover in the bread ovens, which gave protection against grenade blasts. Could the sappers make a breach in the wall?

Wright exchanged a few words with Majid, who sprinted away and returned with the platoon's Bren gunners. Above his head Majid carried a light wooden door frame panelled with hessian, scrounged from the debris of the general hospital. Kneeling together, Wright and Majid pasted slabs of guncotton onto the frame, and plugged them with a detonator and a tail of black safety fuse.

At a sign, the Bren began to flash and crackle, and the lieutenant and the lance-naik sprang up the slope, carrying the door between them like a battering ram. They reached the bakery wall and slammed the frame up against it, fumbled a light to the fuse and fled back downhill to shelter.

Once the ammonal blew and the gauzy smoke lifted, it revealed a neat, door-shaped hole in the brick, and bodies sprawled in the shadow within. The West Kents pitched grenades through the doorway, and the Japanese came staggering into the sunlight, some of them on fire, falling to roll on the earth, others running for the safety of Jail Hill. Very few made it. The Bren gun and the infantry rifles knocked them down – like a pheasant shoot, thought Wright. Everyone got a kill, and some West Kent NCOs claimed more than ten. The figure for enemy killed that morning was put at 120, forty-four of them left strewn around the bakery itself. The sappers had saved the hill.

To avoid further trouble, Captain Easten asked Wright to raze the other building still intact on Detail Hill, a grain godown not far away. Three sappers got to work while Wright stepped away to examine his handiwork at the bakery. They had taken only two prisoners; one a dying lieutenant, with a backpack full of maps. Bodies gouted blood onto the ground. A British private nudged a corpse's cheek with his rifle, bent over and then laughed. The dead men's mouths were smeared with a pale, sticky fluid: they had spent the night licking clean tins of condensed milk.

At the godown, Wright's demolition party ran a daisy chain of explosive charges around the sacks of flour. After clearing the vicinity, Wright shoved the detonator home. There was silence. 'God,' he remembered thinking, 'the circuit's broken, I'm going to have to go and —': a cyclonic roar sucked his mind bare. An enraged fireball billowed up into the sky. Wright was horrified: he hadn't counted on the flour combusting as it dispersed. The secondary detonation whirled the air above the hillside as the flour fed the flame. The pillar of burning wheat rose and rose, a finger of fire addressing every eye on the surrounding hills with a portent of what was still to come.

D etail Hill would not hold. The garrison was too small, surrounded and outnumbered ten to one, and its defence too costly. Japanese artillery pounded the defenders day and night. The men called them the morning and evening 'hates'.

Salvos turned the town buildings to rubble, and shells landing near trenches made the earth lurch with the force of a car crash. When the artillery fell silent, it gave way to the racket of the Japanese assembling to attack. The defenders braced for the moment when the alien chatter turned into a unified scream. Then they came crawling and scrambling up the slope. Bullets stopped hundreds, but hundreds more were massed and waiting. When they reached the perimeter, the fighting was the worst that fighting could be: murder done hand to hand, face to face.

Trench after trench on Detail Hill was overwhelmed by bayonets and body weight, until the West Kents dug in there begged their captain for permission to withdraw. On 10 April, they fell back to 'Field Supply Hill', where Wright's sappers had fifty yards of perimeter to defend. Spread before them was a *shamshaan*, as his orderly Raham Ali called it: a cremation ground, earth belching fire, covered with cold bodies. At night the Japanese crisscrossed the hillside, dousing the corpses with petrol and, indifferent to their race, set them burning.

In the north-east corner, the Assam Regiment held out against the worst of the onslaught. The DC's pretty bungalow was long gone. The defenders hung on, barely, at the tennis court, and the earlier use of that ground was perversely echoed in the arcing of grenades and charges back and forth. It was a microscopic replay of the trench battles of the Great War: the no-man's land diminished to twenty yards, and at times to barely five. A successful charge ended in bestial struggle, with daggers, rifle butts and worn muscle. Death had no ceremony there, as one officer learned when he slipped into a dugout at the tennis court and landed among several jawans, crouched over their rifles to face the enemy: all of them unresponsive to his commands, he found, because all of them were dead.

There was no respite, no reinforcements and no water: the thin pipe that brought them their only steady supply had been found and cut. Since then the defenders had subsisted largely on what the RAF could drop in inner tubes, less than a pint a day for each man. There was no barbed wire, not a single coil,[1] nothing between the defenders and the attackers except the open air and as much lead as they could fill it with. The men who had been at Ruweisat Ridge fantasised about wire, the taut double aprons and the bouncing concertinas, the thorny monoculture that had seemed to cover the desert. They recalled also the desert's huge and utter flatness, so unimaginable from a place where every bluff and gully mattered. On the eastern face of Supply Hill, the Japanese used ladders to try and scale the slope. At the northern end, a fifteen-foot cutting above the Imphal Road was all that denied the enemy's encroachment. In the south, each degree of the hillside gradient could mean the difference between survival and the tip of a bayonet.

There was no sleep. The Japanese charged at sundown and the break of dawn, and in between they tried to sneak in through the dark. At odd hours the voices of the JIFs rose like delirious dreams. Half the time they called out in the wrong language, appealing in Urdu to the West Kents, while the Japanese mocked the bewildered Rajputs on loudhailers, saying: 'Johnny, Johnny! … Come over to us … We'll give you a cup of tea!' As the nights passed, the temptation to go over to the more numerous enemy grew, yet not a single Indian defected.

Night was also when the sappers could move in the open, to assist infantry counterattacks or to lay booby traps at weak points in the perimeter. Wright spent most of those hours staring into the abyss that tipped away before him. If he nodded off, he woke in panic to check that it was still a friend in the next foxhole. By daylight he would be trembling with exhaustion, and if no enemy came, he closed his eyes until they did. NCOs slithered out to shake the sappers' shoulders and wake them, but that was only necessary till the shells came screaming in and punching up the mud.

Inside the perimeter – which meant, at most, a few hundred yards back – the sappers worked exposed on the hillsides, digging, which was barely less dangerous than manning the trenches. They dug latrines: a measure of sanitation, if an increasingly futile one. As the attacks intensified and the perimeter shrank, more men caught dysentery, including Wright himself. Eventually they just squatted on empty coffee tins, then sent them flying toward the enemy trenches. In the worst areas, such as the tennis court, they squirted down their pant legs in despair.

They dug the battalion HQ, the artillery observers' post, graves and surgical dugouts. Some of the sappers were in those dugouts already; one was in a grave. This was Wright's first casualty, a new recruit who had joined 2nd Field just days before they drove up to Kohima, and a picture of innocence. His NCO had told him to stand guard – meaning be alert – but the boy climbed out and stood up on the hillside as if on sentry. He was shot in the gut before anyone noticed. Wright visited him in the aid post, and nearly cried as he watched the boy die.

On Garrison Hill, they dug the ever-extending pits to hold the wounded. There were hundreds, each stretcher-length, and it was a morbid moment when a living man was lowered into one. Those men suffered the worst, gasping in agony day after day. From where they lay, some could watch the Japanese mortar-men dropping rounds into the hot pipe, the charge flashing, and the bomb sailing over toward them. Shells punched into the denuded treetops, and the air bursts plastered the trenches with shrapnel, dealing new wounds to the wounded. On Thursday the 13th, the day Wright spoke to the OC, the enemy guns found the main dressing station and shelled it steadily for an hour, creating a diabolical lab: each man's bits grafting onto another's, hair in gut, gut in bone, bone in brain. It ended the lives of twenty-one wounded men.

The fate of the wounded, if the ridge was overrun, was only too apparent. That image helped the defenders to hang on past blind exhaustion, adding hour after impossible hour to the calendar of endurance. Daily the message flew from Dimapur to Jotsoma, from Jotsoma to Kohima, and was rolled into the foxholes: 'Hold on, and you will have made history.' 'If you let go, India falls.' Relief would come tomorrow, hold on.

Tomorrow came again and again, and so did the attacks. The guns at Jotsoma bucked and spat, sending down to Kohima an invisible giant that stamped out onto the enemy each time they formed up. The guns never rested. In one period of five hours, on one bearing alone, they launched some 3,500 rounds; entire Japanese companies could be obliterated overnight by the barrage. The guns were joined by screaming flights of Hurricanes and Vengeance bombers. The Japanese soldiers' ears bled from the shockwaves. They were running out of time as well, but their sheer numbers, iron discipline and suicidal ecstasies kept them rising and charging.

Wright did his best to keep the sappers sane, though there were signs they were losing that battle as well. One jemadar, Nazir Hussain Shah, had his orderly dig a hole for him – as deep as possible. He went in and refused to emerge until the end. Wright's own orderly, the staunch and weathered Raham Ali, fully thirty-eight years old, was near the brink. He shared Wright's dugout, and during one lull in the shelling, he asked, 'Sa'ab, when we are out of here, can I go back to the depot?' Then he said: '*Bahut ho gaya, sa'ab*' – It's been too much.

Wright felt himself coming apart too: his hands were badly burned from a grenade explosion, and although he had them salved and bandaged at the aid station, they seemed to be going rotten. Blood throbbed in the burns when he had his hands down, so he held them continually above his head. The worst wasn't his hands, though. It wasn't the skin rash or the fatigue or the ribbons into which his stomach had been torn by dysentery. The lack of sleep was physical torture, but even worse was the toll of the ceaseless, mounting fear. Every man there felt it. Only a matter of time.

Time itself seemed to reel from the blasts. Night's bright inferno passed into black dawns streaming with cinders. Overcast afternoons lit up as evening fell and flares rose into the sky, small suns guiding in the supply drops. On the night of 17 April, the Supply Hill was overrun, and the defenders fell back into bunkers on Kuki Picket. Wright felt his heart stop as a body plunged into his dugout. It was the West Kent company clerk, Private Tom Jackson.

'If they come up the hill, we've had our chips,' Jackson shouted.

'We'll use bayonets,' Wright replied.

Their flank gave in before they could attempt it, and they fled back again to the edge of Garrison Hill. Fewer than fifty men were still in any condition to resist on their sector: shreds of the Assam Regiment, West Kents, Rajputs and sapper Mussalmans. Behind them were the desperate commanders, the petrified noncombatants, the 600 wounded men lying in their not-yet graves. In the medical station, officers on stretchers asked to have pistols by their sides. They backed into their burrows like rats facing a terrier's teeth.

Hours passed. As the sky blanched they tensed one last time, waiting for the screams that would announce the final onslaught, and their last stand. There was grinding and firing in the distance, to the west; otherwise nothing. Then Raham Ali touched Wright's arm and pointed back to the hospital spur: eight Lee-Grant tanks were coming up the road, covering a platoon of the 1/1st Punjab and a detail of Bengal Sappers.

Bobby worked his way up the road more slowly, pothole by pothole. Now and then he scooped out gravel and lifted out a Japanese landmine. The enemy guns had been redirected onto the road to halt the relief column, and the tarmac bounced with each explosion up ahead. The sweat rolled hot off his scalp and left tracks on his dusty forearms and the scuffed, tea-plate sized munitions.

On 15 April, the tanks of the 2nd British Division had finally forced open the Japanese vice around Jotsoma. By then, Bobby's brigade had held off attacks that cost the Japanese as many casualties as the attacks on Garrison Hill. The Jotsoma box was now suddenly filled with boys from Dorset, Norfolk and Berkshire, allowing the 1/1st Punjab to turn at once and hurl its full weight in the direction of Kohima. The sappers were needed as well, ducking under tank turrets and the Punjabis' machine guns to 'de-louse' the road for the main force behind them.

At 7a.m. on 18 April, the relief column broke through to Kohima. The battle was anything but finished: the Japanese were still barely yards away on every side, and the rest of the ridge and the peaks looming over it still bristled with bayonets and deep-set bunkers. The Japanese shelling pursued the wounded even as they were carried to the trucks waiting at the Hospital Ridge. It would be two more days before 'A' Platoon could follow them out and Bobby arrived at Garrison Hill to escort them.

It poured all that morning, slowing the evacuation, but at least the rain parted the caul of smoke above the ridge. Nearer Jotsoma, the leaves and air shivered in the gleam of the silver cloud cover, but Garrison Hill was a different, deformed world. Veteran officers, including General Slim, would invariably recall the Somme in 1916: every yard of ground was gored by the shelling, leaving a black and trampled mire of soot, rainwater, debris and faeces. Just the smell that came off it was enough to break a man. Corpses rotted in the noon heat, with only flies to pay them any attention. Pale parachutes hung from the blackened trees, trailing their lines in the mud, ghoulish fungi sucking at the decay.

Bobby retched as he climbed the hill toward 'A' Platoon. They were an amazing sight – filthy as Bombay beggars, looking ready to cough once and dissolve into a heap of rags. Here came Wright, ever the hero that Bobby dreamt of being, to stand by the lorry wobbling slightly, his bandaged hands raised in an ironic pose of surrender. Here was grinning Sirajuddin, who had attempted to flee with the Nepalis on the first day of the siege, but crept back in on the second. In the last war, his commanding officer would have pushed him against a wall and shot him; instead Wright let the fugitive be redeemed through non-stop latrine-digging duty.

Here came Havildar Mohammad Vilayat, who had managed the miracle of cooking the platoon's dal and roti through the siege. 'You know, sa'ab ...' said the havildar, never a man too fastidious about prayer, '*five* times a day from now on.' One by one they clambered into the lorry, and Bobby hoisted Wright in last of all.

The fear fell away as they fell back toward Dimapur, and while Wright shut his eyes to elated oblivion, Bobby felt another ache rise and overwhelm his relief, from knowing that his English friend was a hero – surely slated for a Military Cross – and was alive, while Ganny and Manek were dead, and already taking their leave from Bobby's own mind. They were no heroes. Nobody would know them, not even Ganny's own daughter. And the sharp, exquisite pity Bobby felt extended not only to them, but to himself.

A drum of tea was brewing at the military hospital in Dimapur. The nurses cleaned the dressings on Wright's hands, and took him to a bed with white sheets fresh from the depot. Before he could lie down, he was led out onto the sun-warmed stones of the hospital compound, through a hooting, splashing, sudsy mass of black and pink skin, to where soldiers sat in rows of improvised bathtubs, each one an oil drum sawn lengthwise in half. Wright sank his body into the water, his eyes closed and his arms motionless; and Bobby bathed him like a child.

19

The Elephant
Tiddim Road, June–October 1944

They opened the roads from Kohima like roots open stone, slowly, and with an anguish inaudible to the rest of the world. The Japanese were as rugged in defence as they were reckless in attack. They had soldered themselves into deep bunkers, and they held them to the last man. More Allied soldiers died prising the Japanese from the Kohima Ridge than had died already in halting them there. The gruelling melee was led by tanks – 'tin elephants' to the Nagas – which were led in turn by sappers firming the tracks, to keep the tanks from sliding away down hillsides unlaced by rain. Then there was more killing, with pole-charge and bayonet,[1] and inside the sodden bunkers troops ate K-rations off handkerchiefs spread over the enemy's corpses.[2]

The grisly attrition lasted the summer, and then the monsoon arrived to kneel on the Naga Hills. Second Field Company moved east, scraping open the road and clearing mines ahead of the infantry, pushing the Japanese back the way they had come. On bamboo poles they raised high screens of camouflage net, the only protection from enemy snipers – apart from the funereal light and the torrential rain. Laying a Bailey bridge on the Jessami track on 17 June, the unit diary recorded '24 hours of continuous work in knee-deep mud'. At the end of each day, Bobby returned to his one-man bivouac tent, dragged his uniform off his body, dumped it outside, and slithered under the canvas to towel off and sleep. At dawn he crawled back into the rain to pull the same sodden clothes on again.

They passed through the villages of the Nagas, still staunch but bewildered, as their hermit hills were ground under the millstone of modern war. Every jawan had heard of, or seen first-hand, the Nagas' loyalty: their willingness to scout, to bear the wounded, and even to attack Japanese patrols with cast-off guns and tribal swords. At Jotsoma the Nagas had led the Indians to fresh water, moving bravely ahead onto the stream banks in case they were under enemy observation. Now, with nothing to hunt or harvest, the Nagas were going hungry or being poisoned by scavenged army rations.

Still, they were spared the real famine in the hills, which befell the Japanese as they struggled back toward the Chindwin. They had come unburdened by provisions, as in the Arakan, counting on the capture of *Chachiru kyuyo* – 'Churchill supplies' – in battle and at Dimapur. It was a bad wager, for which the men would pay an unspeakable price. The Japanese 31st Division was already short of food by the time it encircled Garrison Hill. When the siege was broken, its troops were ordered to cling to the ridge, first eating their mules and then their horses. Only when one general broke the chain of command, and pleaded with the Emperor directly, were they allowed to retreat. By then it was too late.

The supermen of the jungle had fallen, further than anyone could have imagined. As the 161st Brigade pursued the Japanese to Jessami, they found the tracks and villages littered with bodies. In the bamboo biers of the forest, the Emperor's men lay in groups of two or three, craving company as they chose between suicide and starvation. The insides of their helmets were dusted grey from when they had ground rice chaff in search of the last grains. There were silent field hospitals where the wounded had been laid out in rows and shot, one by one, through the head. Those gave way to sites of more desperate self-annihilation, where groups had huddled over a single grenade, leaving corpses petalled in rough circles.

Each week, a patrol would net a brace of JIFs with their hands above their heads. The enemy propaganda rained onto Indian troops in Burma was now being repaid, with interest. Amnesty notes offered food and repatriation, and the JIFs, hungry or half dead from malaria, were ready to accept. The regular jawans of the brigade had curdled with contempt, for now the JIFs were losers as well as turncoats. Officers had to intervene to let them surrender, sometimes without success.

On 22 June, troops fighting southward from Kohima met the 5th Indian Division pushing north out of Imphal, and the road into the valley was opened. The town of Imphal was unmolested, and remarkably, had not gone hungry – it was kept supplied through its three-month siege by air drops on a magnificent scale. With relief, the brigade turned off the road of bones and onto the southern route to Imphal. In Imphal, it was reunited with its division, and the sappers spent their first night since Dimapur billeted under a roof. For a week they had dry floors and hot food, and awaited the order suspending operations till the end of the monsoon.

In the week of respite, Bobby had time to brood over what had passed. He had seen India racked by three ersatz wars: in Madras, an invasion that never came; at Roorkee, an eruption from within; in Bengal, a circumstantial holocaust that killed only the most innocent. The war had rippled constantly over India, but the stone never struck it direct.

If Kohima had fallen, though ... That fate was spelled out in a Japanese order, intercepted and passed down as brigade intelligence. 'The prestige of the Empire will spread over the whole world,' the order concluded. 'Our glorious colours will fly bravely over the great plains of India, and 400 million Indians will realise their hopes when we enable them to live under Imperial influence. That day, I am confident, is not far off.'

Instead Bobby's army had defended its own border, and dealt the Japanese land army the greatest defeat in its history. For once, they fought not to preserve a foreign empire, but to preserve India itself. The victory of the Fourteenth Army would belong to soldiers and pilots from five continents and many nations: Britain, Nigeria, Gambia and the Gold Coast, East Africa, the United States, Canada and China. Yet more were Indians than were from all the other Allied nations taken together.

Theirs was more than a victory. It was a baptism. Bobby realised he had seen in the smoking kiln of Kohima the hardening of a new army of Indians. For those few days in April, the jawan stood in a new light – a light that passed through his mercenary colours and made him visible as a hero defending his homeland. But the light had closed like a monsoon beam and passed unnoticed. Back home, news of the siege of Kohima was suppressed in the papers, at least for its actual duration.[3] Churchill made no speeches about it. By the time the news came out the crisis had receded, and its drama was dwarfed by the Allied landings in north-west Europe. Radiant new heroes at Normandy ensured that no one need glance for any length at the Naga Hills.

Bobby saw no more of the Nagas, who were missed, because the plain of Imphal was occupied by Meiteis, a people more settled, less guileless, more political and far less supportive of

Britain's war. Outside Kohima, on top of what would later be called Congress Ridge, the JIFs had raised a fluttering tricolour, green, white and saffron, stamped with Bose's leaping tiger. It was simple, then: an enemy device, a challenger to be overcome.

Now, on the Imphal Plain, they found it was the JIFs who stood in the light. They had evangelised in every village taken by the Japanese: the same villages where Bengal Sappers had destroyed private rice stores as they made their retreat.[4] In the town of Moirang, the renegades had flown another tricolour, and young Meiteis lined up to join Bose's army. The JIFs had lost, and badly, but the future was on their side. Bobby's army had won, but it had fought on the side of the past.

Orders arrived sooner than expected. Abandoning two years' precedent, General Slim decided to fight through the monsoon. He would press his advantage and beat the enemy back south into Burma. The Japanese 33rd Division, astride the southern road, was the last of the three invading forces still retreating in good order. The 5th Indian Division would pursue them across the Manipur river, up the perilous ascents called the Ladder and the Chocolate Staircase, to the town of Tiddim where the last massif of the Chin Hills dropped away to the plain of Mandalay. There the recoiling Japanese would turn and face them, and would have to be defeated before they could all go home.

Through the ruined paddy and the marshes by Loktak Lake, and on the high dewy pastures above Bishenpur, the two divisions grappled and crashed south away from Imphal. In September they crossed into Burma, and into areas that had no map names, only figures. The 161st Brigade moved into the lead now, and 2nd Field Company with it. The hills massed in, wooded and ravined, mounting so far overhead that Bobby could crane his neck and see sun-bright slopes above, a mirage afloat in the sky.

The quality of the Tiddim Road reflected the nature of the war on it: pathetic and physically brutal. Wrecked once in the British retreat in March, the road was newly cratered and collapsed by the Japanese. Each downpour or bomb fumbled from a passing Hurricane could loose tons of waterlogged clay onto it. As a later account had it, 'moving streams of shale and mud, trees and boulders, flowed across the road like lava from some volcano'.

Vehicles bogged down had to be winched out, or towed free by elephants. Early on a convoy of Bailey bridge trucks sank into the mud, and sat immovable for four days until a spell of sunshine hardened the surface. All along, the road was rutted so deep that the lorries churning down it keeled from one violent angle to another. The men inside flew around as if the tent pegs of gravity had come out, and they reached the front bone-weary and nauseous.

The sappers pressed on, splitting through hardwood and hillside, using explosives, earth-movers and teams of pick-and-shovel. At the close of one day, the *subedar* of 2nd Field announced they had moved 'at least half of Assam'. There were smaller, lateral tracks that could collapse into spear pits, concealed in the ground and caked with septic human dung. Also under foot was the ghastly debris of the retreating division, bodies disinterred by the sapper work. The Japanese survivors still fought, with the supreme tenacity for which they were legend. Their officers, out of ammo, drew their sabres and fell under the Rajputs' rifles. An Indian lieutenant of another company of Bengal Sappers described a Japanese officer with part of his arm missing, maggots crawling over him, but fighting still.

It was harder now to hate the enemy than to pity them. At times the only difference Bobby saw between the Indians and the Japs was what grew on them: fungus on the winners, maggots on the losers. Death felt common after Kohima, and unexalted, dealt as easily by a crate of tinned peaches swinging from a snared parachute as by a hostile bullet. There was no fascination any more, no feeling, in seeing the precious red secrets of a human skull ransacked and spilt on the ground. It was left to distant adjutants to write citations describing the victim's valour and high purpose. Here there was only going on, or not.

The noises of the forest seemed to absorb all the blood and grow more bloated. The heat and the nerves and the gulp of water began to make Bobby ill. He shook with fever, and there were longer and longer periods he could not remember, pure blanks in his mind. His OC ordered him back to be treated for malaria at the divisional hospital. Death was even louder there, and packed in. Scrub typhus, septic sores, malaria, dengue fever, jaundice and jungle rot gnawed on men's bodies beneath their stained sheets; that was not counting combat wounds. Bobby stared out the window of his ward, watching taut cables turn slack and bowed by the rain. Every length glistened with water, and dripped in perfect order and time, like men on the march. Each drop, advancing down its narrow black road, grew from an intrepid bulge to a shining half-pearl. Then it reached the bottom of its arc, and cut, and fell – a hundred a minute, from a hundred cables, in identical discipline – to break on earth already so sodden that not a shadow of any one remained.

Bobby was discharged and returned to the brigade to find a pinpoint of cheer on the landscape: their new pet, an elephant adopted by the 1/1st Punjab. Wright had been with the Punjabi patrol when they followed the tinkling of bells up a cloud-shrouded spur. There they discovered three nervous, abandoned elephants – remnants of the fleet the Japanese had used to pull guns into India. Wright made bold and stepped up to one of them. He was only yards away when it flung its trunk up and screamed in his face. It felt as if someone had lifted him off his feet and shaken him. He turned on his heels and ran.

Fortunately, the orderly to Daddy Warren had once worked as a mahout, and he arrived in time to collect the gentlest of the three. Thereafter the orderly spent more time attending to the beast than the brigadier, commandeering enough chapatis to meet its great appetite, as well as a dugout made for a three-ton lorry, to which the animal learned to hurry at the sound of falling artillery. It became a brief mascot of the 161st Brigade, especially beloved of the Punjabis who had an elephant on their regimental badge. For a while, there was no sight as soothing as the creature bearing the piled laundry of brigade headquarters down to the river, where it lay in the water and consented to let the dhobis use its rumpled skin as a scrubbing board, and to smack drenched uniforms on its legs. Then it was led away back to India, to join the stables of the Raja of Cooch Behar, while the brigade turned back to its road.

From five miles away, they heard the Manipur river. 'Its roar,' Slim wrote, 'was like that of a great football crowd.'[5] The river was in monsoon spate, whirlpooling and wild, and would suffer nobody to cross. Brigade and sapper officers conferred on the banks, shouting to be audible. Second Field Company had a new OC who was keen to prove his mettle by making the first crossing. He called up an assault boat – a collapsible canvas tub powered by an outboard motor – and pushed off into the stream. It covered about five yards before the river lifted the boat and flung it in the air, dispersing the sappers like spray. All were saved, thanks to Jemadar Jehan Dad[6] who had sidled off downstream ahead of time, and then plunged into the water to drag out the drowning men.

It was two days before they got a rope across, by clamping it to a dummy mortar round and firing it over the water. Once a heavier cable was pulled through, the sappers hitched up a 'flying ferry', a pontoon raft attached to a traveller on the cable, which would be propelled to the far bank by the river's own force. Worn-out units turned back at the river, and a thinned division began to cross. By now the current had risen from twelve to seventeen feet per second, and the truculent river hurled debris and timber against the sides of the inflated raft. Each day a pontoon burst or a bollard was ripped off. On 5 October alone, five sappers drowned: Bhan Singh, Chanan Singh, Keshar Singh, Sardara Singh, Surjan Singh; sons of faraway Ludhiana, Patiala, Jullundhur. Still the sappers ran the crossing through the days and into the nights, under the shelling of the Japanese 105mm guns. By mid-October they had ferried across the larger part of the division with its supplies and equipment, as well as two hospital units and six Lee-Grant tanks, at the cost of ten sappers' lives.

Ahead was the Chocolate Staircase, a muddy track that climbed thirty-eight bends, writhing and twisting like a snake with a broken spine. From there on, it was impossible to maintain the full route, and they let the road close over behind them. They would rely on air supply, as the Chindits had; they would carry their wounded with them, and not think about the way back.

Men kept dying – blown up by a landmine, killed by gangrene after a foot was chewed up in a bulldozer's tread. The weight of one tank broke the road into the ravine below, and it plunged out of sight, taking a sapper with it. Near Tiddim a rockface leaned heavily over the road, and the ground on the other side fell away in a sheer drop of five hundred feet. Clinging to the rock, Sappers Karam Singh and Santokh Singh bored holes that could take explosive charges and bring the rockface down. It collapsed as they worked, burying them four feet deep. Shale gushed down along the length of the track, spilling off the cliff's edge. Still the other sappers ran in to dig the fallen men out. Karam Singh was dead. Santokh Singh was pulled out with a broken arm and a fractured skull. There was no way he could be evacuated, and Bobby could barely watch as he was dragged along on the juddering bed of a jeep.

The mules suffered too, toiling hock-deep in the mud while their loads chafed their hides and gradually exposed the warm pink dermis of their flanks. The sappers hacked mule paths through the steaming verdure, over forest floors flowing like gutters, to get rifle companies around the enemy flank. Blinking up at the trails, Bobby couldn't always tell if he was looking at men climbing hand and foot, or animals; now they were men, now mules, and now they and their drivers were joined into crawling six-legged creatures with trembling sinews holding one half to the other.

A memo arrived from Daddy Warren, their former brigadier now promoted to command the whole of 5th Division. 'So far the major burden of the advance has fallen on the engineers,' he wrote; 'I fully realise that, with the equipment available, it has been next door to a miracle to pass a Division down this road and across the Manipur river in the time in which you have done it ...' Bobby read down the letter, but the words skimmed like water bugs on the film on his eye. He set it down before reaching the end.

Warren's appreciation would not make the world know the men who died here; even those living called themselves 'the Forgotten Army'. By now the 4th Indian Division had lunged up the boot laces of Italy: heroes in everyone's sight. The Americans had liberated Paris, and the Soviets were in Germany. They believed they would end the war in Europe by Christmas, and those who did not make it back would be remembered for it.

Their combat through the sacred cities of Western civilisation made Bobby's army look like ants disputing anthills. Second Field Company had been ordered all around the weedy edge of the Empire, farm boys toiling from acre to distant acre, until they reached here, the final field but one. Their greatest campaign was this feral fight in a place far from everywhere, a place that turned men into animals to blunder and maul and die on the banks of shit-filled *chaungs*.

When the slaughter of Whites by Whites was over, who among them would remember the Black men they sent running and shooting in the jungle? The Empire was ending and they were too late to find a place in that epic. In India how many would know, as Bobby did, the cost in boys' lives? A new nation was forming, and they were too early to belong in its story. Those who had fallen like Manek and Ganny had fallen in the middle, and Bobby felt himself wanting to fall too.

O ne afternoon Daddy Warren, on his way back from the front, drove over to the company in person. His jeep passed by Wright where he sat atop a bridging vehicle, and he called Wright over.

'We've had dead mules, and dead Japs,' the general said. 'But please, lieutenant – when you see this elephant we're following, do dissuade the tank people from killing it?' Wright now had an ironic reputation for his courage facing elephants. He hadn't realised it had travelled as far as the divisional commander. He returned a stiff salute.

Wright was sent forward the next morning to examine the dead elephant. It had been gunned down but by a Hurricane pilot, who must have taken it for an animal still in Japanese employ. The elephant had bled to death, with a minimum of mess. Wright phoned back to the company to ask for someone to deal with it.

Bobby arrived soon afterwards with a detonation kit and a bag of ammonal. He approached the elephant with a detachment equal to the task of disposing of it. It was very large and very still, and it hadn't yet begun to bloat or to stink. Within two days it would soften into a giant, diseased mushroom dribbling its stench down the cliff road. This was really a situation that required a bulldozer, but the machines were few and constantly occupied with the avalanche of clay and rock. This smaller avalanche of flesh would have to be dealt with using explosives.

Bobby stepped in closer and placed a hand on the elephant's firm hide. He had never blown up an elephant. He edged around the carcass, examining how it lay, taking in its matted tuft of tail, its violent expulsion of dung, the sagging belly stained black from exit wounds and the head streaked black with tears. He put his hand on the bristled brow, and for a moment he felt like he had travelled in the company of this creature for a long time, from Calicut where it was chained and fed holy offerings, through the dumb toil and idleness of Roorkee, turning with it west to east until Burma, and the labours and terrors on the Tiddim Road.

He moved around the elephant again and his hands worked on their own, tucking charges under the folds of the belly skin and the loose flap of lip. Bobby's mind was on the single, long-lashed eye, half-drowned in its pool of black wrinkles. Sorrow welled up in him at the thought of what had raced through that eye in the elephant's last days and hours: turning and turning again, not knowing its master, bewildered and blundering on the Tiddim Road, until shot down at last by who-knows-which side, and blown out of the way by a man as bewildered as itself.

His hand fired the fuse and he stepped away. The ammonal detonated with its deep *whoomp*, but the carcass did not lift or land clear of the road as it was meant to. The elephant exploded. It rose for an instant and then burst, separating into a million strands of wayward gut and muscle, which snagged in the high branches by the roadside and rushed as a pink mist into Bobby's glazed eyes.

20

The Road Ahead
Madras, November 1945

K hodadad observed that he could snap the morning news-paper out of its fold – it wasn't yet humid, it must be November. Then he did it. They smiled around the table, as they seldom had that year. Then he vanished into its private corner, and all that emerged for a while was the rustle of pages passing steadily from right hand to left.

Nugs tried to chart out her day in her mind. She was back on call now at the obstetrics department, but she had today off to manage the house. This house, on Montieth Road, was her own; she had bought it and found ways to fill it: with the remains of her family, and their old retainers from Calicut, and *their* families, with icons of Zarathustra and other prophets on the walls, with two Dalmatians, and on most days, a constant ringing of guests and friends. And all of that together did not fill Nugs's home as much as her daughter, who was nearly three. Already she had turned from a plump puzzle of flesh into a small person. If the Mugaseth family had survived, it was because she had saved them. Nineteen forty-two, '43, '44: every year had hollowed the house, but the growing child filled it, and brought youth to a family that had aged quicker than time.

Nugs was staring down at her scrambled eggs when she sensed it coming. She didn't need warning. She could feel the blow coming, and the memories rising beneath it like a bruise. Khodadad began to read aloud: 'Indian Troops Smash Indonesian Attacks. The fighting at Surabaya has only just reached its full intensity ...' He browsed quietly for a moment. 'The latest reports indicate no slackening of Indonesian resistance ...'

It was news from Bobby's division – or what had been Bobby's division. Three months had passed since The Bomb and Japan's surrender. Down the arc of South-East Asia its soldiers stood in disbelief as their godly empire vanished into thin air. Thanks to Khodadad, she knew that the 5th Indian Division, then in Burma, had sailed out to accept the surrender of Singapore, an honour for its troops. Then it sailed for Java to start to fight again.

The war hadn't ended, even though it had. The winners were now fighting over who got what. None of it mattered to Nugs any longer, though it did to her father. He wouldn't let the war end either, because once the war was over, it was the end of the story. Then they would never learn the truth of what had happened to Bobby.

The family knew little more than what they'd read when the telegram came last November. Official records were mum too – even the diary of 2nd Field Company, on the date of 4 November 1944, merely said: 'Lieut Mugaseth G Kh IE admitted to hosp.' Nugs could only brood over the final photograph he'd sent her, around the time that his company prepared to leave Imphal: a picture she had looked at and failed, at first, to recognise. Bobby was transformed. The shirt he wore was unbuttoned, its collar askew and his lieutenant's pips seemed to droop from his shoulders. His face was drawn and dark, suddenly like an Indian's, but also like a stranger's. The smooth cheeks were carved away, and that teasing, translucent expression was gone. His once sappy eyes were hard under new shadows.

It was not a picture she wanted to look at again, so she hid it in the back of the silver photo frame: behind the younger, truer portrait of Bobby which had joined the other two on the sitting-room table. What Nugs had to do now was forget. She had spent too long lost in the corridors of grief, where each door led on to new halls but the way overall led only from wholeness to emptiness. She couldn't afford to go there any more. The only victory for Nugs in 1945 was the cumulative moments she spent in possession of her own life, not pierced by memories of the dead.

Yet Khodadad was adamant. His dolorous keystrokes produced letter after letter, which were posted to new offices and authorities, seemingly pushed under every door of the Indian Army. He had to have a better accounting for the loss of his son; as if any story would help them endure it. It was futile. There were no longer any replies. A year had passed since the telegram, and everyone else already had their versions, or at least their bare theories, of what had happened to Bobby. Each was brief and hard as a seed, but grew into a kind of memory of what they had never known in the first place.

The gun went off in error, most of them said. It was the merciful consensus, offered to the Mugaseths by every visitor who came with condolences. It happened on the front, where the rain and muck ran constantly into gunpowder, and sidearms were drenched in the wading of streams. At the time it happened, the 161st Brigade wasn't even on the road, but cutting a jungle track south of Tiddim, to hook around enemy positions on Kennedy Peak.

Imagine: it was dawn, and the air was patterned with arabesques of noisy birdsong. Around the clearing, men rose out of warm envelopes of sleep into the chill of the battlefront. Wearing sweaters over their battledress, fumbling with stiff fingers, they moved to strike camp. Bobby must have stood, facing east for the light, scraping his cheeks with a razor while his orderly folded clothes behind him. The sky was quicksilver running to gold behind the outline of Mount Kennedy. It was beautiful. His orderly handed him a stack of clothes and kit, and went to bring tea. Bobby dropped the pile onto the ground. A shot rang out. Bobby fell. It was quick. He did nothing wrong.

That story probably wasn't true at all. The people who believed it didn't know Bobby, not the way the boys in Madras did – Mukundan and Kurien and Sankaran Nair. They knew that fate did not sneak up on Bobby; he pursued it. That's how they would always think of him, through his youthful caprices and his impulse to roll the dice. Well, he couldn't have meant for it to happen, but he must have asked for it.

Deep in the killing fields of Burma, life was cheap, maybe even cheap enough to play with. The war made men crazy. The mepacrine dosage made some men psychotic, giving them strange waking dreams and manic rages, and whispering voices in their ears that caused them to stagger out alone into the jungle. Besides, everyone drank hard, and harder as a campaign ran on, as the monotony of army scale and their physical ordeal wore them down. Air-dropped rations kept them moving, and even when the division had barely enough to eat, the quartermasters in Imphal made sure they had plenty to drink.

The way Sankaran Nair told it, it was dusk, and the air had filled with the screaming of the woods. 'Returning from a jungle patrol, he went for his bath after ordering his batman to empty and clean his revolver,' Nair would say. 'Later he picked up the revolver, and went to the mess.'

John Wright and his platoon were elsewhere, and the other British officers sat together, playing cards around a gas lamp. They had risked their lives too much that month, and the rum ration was their only consolation.

The officers' mess tent was tattered and sewn up again, and it didn't keep out the night wind. Bobby drank until the liquor rocked in his head. 'Then,' Nair said, 'he dared his British brother officers to play a game of Russian roulette. They asked him not to be stupid, and to continue drinking. He ribbed them for being funks and said he would demonstrate the game.' He couldn't remember the words he'd just spoken which brought his hand to his holster. The Webley .455 was heavy, but not as heavy as it would be loaded, it was heavier then. The iron finger tapped hard on his skull. He forced himself to laugh as he pulled the trigger.

'The batman had left one round in the gun ...' Nair said. 'Fate had engraved Bobby's name on this cartridge.'[1]

Nugs closed her eyes and her mind to the horror of that thought, as she had learned to do from constant practice in the last three years. She never believed the ghastly fancies of Bobby's friends, that he had died like a lunatic spinning a revolver's chambers. After all their family had suffered, he would never have sold his life so cheap. She didn't accept either that he died by accident, hit by a dart of chance.

The truth was that she would never know what took away their last boy, her little brother. Nugs didn't know, beyond what she read in the papers, about the lives and deaths on the Tiddim Road. She only knew that the men there called themselves the Forgotten Army, and it must have been intolerable to feel forgotten. They had fought the most savage battles of the Empire's war, but the world looked elsewhere, and already they were closed out of its memory. Maybe Bobby thought he was forgotten, too, out there where death was in bloom and bodies fell by the thousand, dropped from the boughs by the rain. Or maybe, as the thick bamboo crossed out the road behind him, he did the forgetting – lost sight of his far-off life and family, and of Nugs – and surrendered to the loneliness of those awesome, empty valleys.

A grooved, leaden instrument rested in his lap.

Perhaps Bobby looked down the long road, past his own death, to where he was but a memory, a brief exposure on the minds of a few who survived, before that too dimmed and disappeared. Ganny and Manek had gone this way ahead of him, into the field from which no one returned. And even after death there was a field, the farthest field: it was where you went when even the memory of your name was gone, and you were forgotten completely.

A puckered steel mouth was breathing at his temple.

Before him, the rutted track ran toward the mountain. And Bobby saw it darkly, beyond the peak, the farthest field, and he prepared to cross.

When it was too late, but before the end, perhaps he remembered.

In the moment that remained after the revolver's roar, he felt warm liquid coming down his cheek and ears, like the bath of milk his sisters gave him on his birthdays. He looked down at his arms and saw the rose petals landing, one after another, until they covered everything.

Nugs raised her head and blinked her eyes. The family was watching her from around the table. She had wandered off again, and hadn't heard her daughter calling from the top of the stairway. Her chair fell back and Nugs fled up the steps. Her day was just beginning.

Epilogue

The 161st Indian Infantry Brigade was airlifted out of Kalemyo, at the end of the Tiddim Road, on 28 November, 1944: less than three weeks after Bobby's death. They had spent fourteen months at the front. The brigade remained a part of 5th Indian Division through the campaign to reconquer Burma, the formal surrender of Singapore, and the pacification of the Dutch East Indies.

A Dutch colonial administration waited to be restored to power in the East Indies, even though the Netherlands itself had only been liberated six months before. Indonesian partisans had a different view: they had opposed the Dutch before, and then the Japanese, and they did not intend to stand and watch as the Dutch returned, after a three-year absence, to rule them again. The vanquished Japanese Army had accepted the terms of the surrender: including the bitter condition that they would now help restore Asian colonies to their old European masters. But some Japanese commanders were more inclined to surrender their arms to natives than to Allied victors. The partisans were well established on the islands, and now, besides their guerrillas' rifles, swords and bamboo spears, they had armoured cars, machine guns and tanks.

The Ball of Fire, celebrating in the streets in Singapore, was made to arm and sail for Java. Pending the arrival of competent Dutch troops and administration, it was to secure the island against a partisan takeover. In the town of Surabaya, a fragile truce with the nationalists cracked under the strain of Britain's ambiguous intentions; fighting spread across the city, and had to be suppressed street by street. So began the inevitable final act of the 5th Division's five years of war. Indonesians, armed by the Japanese, would fight Indians, commanded by the British, on behalf of the Dutch.

The 161st Indian Infantry Brigade remained in Java well into 1946, aiding in 'the systematic disposal of extremist elements'. Through two operations, named 'Pounce' and 'Purge', the 1/1st Punjab cordoned off towns, turning back residents who attempted to leave, while a vengeful Dutch police force 'swept from south to north on a wide front, and destroyed all extremist elements discovered'. On 31 January, between operations, the battalion were added to a ceremonial parade in Batavia to celebrate the birthday of Princess Beatrix of the Netherlands.

In 1947, the 2nd Field Company, Bengal Sappers, was reorganised as an entirely Mussalman unit. Along with its former brigade-mate, the 1/1st Punjab, it became part of the army of the new state of Pakistan.

Field Marshal Claude Auchinleck retained his appointment as Commander-in-Chief of India until the date of Independence. On 14 August 1947, he issued the final military command of the British Raj: 'This is the last Army Order.' After presiding over the division of the Indian armed forces, he spent most of his retired life in Marrakesh, Morocco.

Aspy Engineer and Arjan Singh, Manek's superior officers in No. 2 Squadron in 1941, would both rise to the rank of air marshal and between them head the Indian Air Force through most of the 1960s. Arjan Singh retained the facial scar from his crash in the rivulet at Asad Khel for the rest of his life.

Asanandan Singh won an Indian Order of Merit and survived the rest of the war as a *subedar*. No further record of his life could be found.

John Walker Wright won the Military Cross for his courage in Kohima, and was promoted captain before the war's end. Afterwards, he returned to Cambridge to finish his degree, and then worked as a civil engineer at postings around the world, including back in India in the 1990s. He retired to the village of Bisley, near Stroud in Gloucestershire, where he died in 2002. A diorama showing him and Lance-Naik Abdul Majid blowing the door off the bakery in Kohima has pride of place at the museum of the Royal Engineers in Gillingham, Kent.

Verghese Kurien, Bobby's classmate at Guindy who was offered an army commission but forbidden from joining by his mother, accepted a government job to run a milk-processing unit in the village of Anand in Gujarat. Eventually he built Amul, a cooperative organisation that revolutionised milk production in India, and still provides dairy goods for half the country. I met him a few months before his death in 2012, when he gave me one account of Bobby's life and death.

Sankaran Nair became the first chief of India's intelligence agency, the Research and Analysis Wing. His memoir, *Inside I.B. and R.A.W.: A Rolling Stone that Gathered Moss*, provides another version of Bobby's death.

P. Mukundan left the Army and became an officer with Indian Telephone Industries and the national telegraph service. Through his retirement, he lived in Palghat, in the hills midway between Madras and Calicut.

After the war, Subur and GP thrived in the service of a newly self-governing country. GP left *The Hindu* to enter Nehru's diplomatic corps, in which he rose swiftly to become India's ambassador to Indonesia, to the People's Republic of China, to Pakistan, and finally to the United Nations. Subur's academic career earned her an appointment as a Member of Parliament in the upper house. She died in New York City in 1966.

Manek's death, on a hillside behind Indian lines on 25 May 1943, occurred on the final day of the squadron's mission in Imphal. He was twenty-four years old. His younger brother, a pilot with No 7. Squadron, died in the Imphal area a year later, while Bobby was on the ground there. On 1 April 1944, Edul Dadabhoy flew into bad weather and ordered his navigator, J. E. Dordi, to bail out. Dordi survived a parachute landing twenty-five miles behind enemy lines and made it back to a British unit with the help of Naga tribesmen. Edul died attempting a forced landing. Both Manek and Edul are commemorated at the Commonwealth War Graves Cemetery in Singapore.

In 1948, Kosh was married again – to Ganny's younger brother, Kodandera Thimayya, thus completing the serial self-exile of the Mugaseth sisters from the Parsi fold. They had two sons, divorced, and she spent the rest of her life with Nugs. Kosh died in 2008.

Ganny's death, in Thal on 10 December 1942, was attributed to asthmatic bronchitis. He was twenty-six years old. He is commemorated at the Commonwealth War Graves Cemetery in New Delhi.

Nugs never remarried. She continued working in the government health service in Madras and raised her daughter – my mother – while never speaking about the war years and what they took from her. She kept a large house full of staff, guests, and dogs: a house from which, people would say, no one was ever asked to leave. She died in Madras in 1998, with her daughter by her side.

Bobby Mugaseth was declared dead on 11 November 1944. He was later buried at the Commonwealth War Graves Cemetery in Imphal, where his epitaph reads:

Lieutenant Godrej Khodadad Mugaseth
King George V's Own Bengal Sappers and Miners

He lived as he died, everybody's friend.
May his beloved soul rest in peace.

Afterword

History is written by the victors, but not by all of them. As a part of the British Empire, India had won its war. Then, ceasing to be a part of the Empire, it won its independence. To a large extent, one was born of the other, yet India's part in the world war is absent from its own history. The lives and deaths of those who fought in it are stories mislaid, and which now, seven decades later, are about to be lost for ever.

In a way, it is amazing. No war has ever been committed more seriously to the conscience of memory. The years 1939–45 might be the most revered, deplored and replayed period in the history of the modern world. Although India was spared the devastation of a war on its soil, it was profoundly and permanently changed; the course of the war accelerated the end of the Raj, and dictated what would follow it.

The fall of the British Empire in South-East Asia, and the disgrace of its White ruling class, deepened the nationalist mood in India in ways that activism may never have achieved on its own. The general military crisis of 1942 – the squander of Indian forces in the East, the defeats in the West, and the dreaded invasion of India's coast – heightened the stakes in the Congress bid for independence, to the point of ultimatum in August of that year. Gandhi never intended for the Quit India Movement to burst into mass violence and reprisals, but it did, and the Congress paid the price of being banned until the end of the war. The more acquiescent Muslim League used those years to deepen its hold on Indian Muslims. By the time Congress leaders emerged from their jails, India's partition was written on its forehead.

Even as the war tilted Indians toward nationalism, it drew many others to the urgent cause of the British Empire. By their good fortune, most Indians who were touched by the war were involved in carrying goods to the fight nearby; not like Gunga Din, but with real dividends for the economy of the country. Millions contributed to the war effort, if only by putting their labour into the burgeoning industries that supplied the empire's mobilisation. The industrialist G. D. Birla, even as he financed the Congress through 1942, simultaneously established Hindustan Motors, and his assets grew sixfold during the war.[1] J. R. D. Tata established Tata Chemicals, as well as the Tata Engineering and Locomotive Company in those years. The war secured a measure of financial health for free India, which saw its entire debt to Britain liquidated against war purchases, and then grown to a £1 billion sterling balance.[2]

Above all, Indians in the armed forces, eventually numbering 2.5 million, formed the largest volunteer force in the war (larger armies relied on conscription). India lent its manpower to practically every theatre of war in which Britain was engaged, from the mule lines in Dunkirk to the garrison of Diego Garcia, from the snowfields of the Apennines to policing pipelines in Persia or suppressing communist partisans in liberated Greece. Around 36,000 Indians were killed or went missing in action, and more than 64,000 were wounded. They fought on three continents, facing every Axis adversary: Italians, Germans, the colonial troops of the Vichy French, the Japanese, and of course, other Indians.

Just as the uprising of 1857 dictated the form of the Army of the Raj, the Second World War dictated the form of the modern Indian Army, which it retains today. For ninety years, a weak colonial army, held back in the past, had been preferable to a volatile one armed for the present. The world war forced the change.

India's Army entered the Second World War as a mildewed 'mercenary' service of 200,000, in a pact with select races of the country's north-west. It emerged as a huge, modernised and vaguely universalised army, marbled with diverse ethnicities.[3] It possessed new weapons and new esprit de corps. After Kohima, Indian battalions fought so well that they were used to stiffen the morale of British troops, reversing a century-old equation. By 1945, Auchinleck wrote to the Viceroy: some high commanders 'actually asked that British units should be replaced by Indian'.[4] The reconquest of Burma was the Japanese land army's most conclusive defeat, and the Indian Army's prize.

In this new army, Indian officers now numbered over 8,000, including scores of battalion commanders and four brigadiers. The first Indian to lead a brigade was 'Timmy' Thimayya, the Kodava officer who had been told by his CO that 'you people just don't have it in you'. Watching his army's transformation, Thimayya likened it to 'the reincarnation of Lord Krishna', the god who drove the chariot of the victorious hero in the final battle of the Mahabharata.

Once stirred in, Indian officers could not be stirred back out. In a letter to Churchill in October 1944, Wavell conveyed that it would no longer be possible to hold India by force after the war. With its racial formulae corrupted in both the ranks and command, the Indian Army of lore was no longer a trustworthy instrument. For imperial hardliners, this was a fell realisation. The Empire would have to depart, and quickly, before the army's loyalty could be weighed in the scales against British lives.

Many young nationalists who joined the British Indian Army had only hoped to live to someday see India's freedom. They didn't guess that before their thirtieth birthdays they'd be serving an independent country – let alone two separate ones. On 14 August 1947, a new state was sawn off from the shoulders of the old one, and India and Pakistan awoke to self-rule and immediate war. The 'brother-officers' of the old army, the army of a few weeks prior, met as enemies in Kashmir – which was the war that would be treated as the first chapter in the authorised saga of India's military.

More terrible still was the work of tens of thousands of demo-bilised soldiers in the Punjab. Auchinleck had protested the rushed schedule for demobilising Indian troops and withdrawing British ones. His concerns were overruled, with grave consequences. Many veterans would shepherd their communities across the new border, as witnessed of the Sikhs of Lyallpur by Ian Morrison in the London *Times*: 'The Sikhs move in blocks of 40,000 to 60,000 and cover about twenty miles a day. It is an unforgettable sight to see one of these columns on the move. The organisation is mainly entrusted to ex-servicemen and soldiers on leave who have been caught by the disturbances. Men on horseback, armed with spears or swords, provide guards in front, behind, and on the flanks. There is a regular system of bugle calls. At night a halt is called ... watch-fires are lit, and pickets are posted.'

Yet others, hardened by encounters with Nazi SS platoons and Japanese suicide squads, turned their skill at arms against inno-cents in their own village lanes. As a Congress Party report on the massacres described: 'These were not riots but deliberately organised military campaigns ... The armed crowd which attacked ... were led by ex-military men on horseback, armed with

Tommy guns, pistols, rifles, hand-grenades, hatchets, petrol tins and some even carried field glasses.'[5]

Every month that an Indian battalion had spent on the front line deepened the extent that minorities were purged from its home district.[6] The intention of Sir Charles Wood, the Victorian Secretary of State for India, that Sikh may fire into Muslim, and Muslim into Hindu, 'without scruple', came into effect at last – just as the Empire it was meant to protect departed.

The surrender of Japan was signed on 15 August 1945, and two years later, to the day, the British Raj was over. It was the intimacy of the two events that ensured that one or the other must be elided. In the decades after the Second World War, as its empire declined, Britain cherished evermore its image as the brave little island that had stood up to global fascism. The war was its redemption. Nazi Germany was such a monstrous regime, and Japan's war-making so phantasmagorical, that they cast a general moral absolution back over the regimes that had held the world under force before them.

It was preferable, almost justifiable, to forget that Germany and Japan had mainly copied and outstripped Britain's own example. Their arguments were Britain's own ancient argument, now wielded by maniacs instead of MPs. Hitler had always admired the British Raj, and the horrors sprung upon Europe, the bombings and concentration camps, were traditions of colonial rule unhinged by the fascist mentality and guided by 'the lights of perverted science'. Even with the war begun, and the Abwehr conniving with rebels in the North-West Frontier, Hitler was loath to undermine something as fine as the Anglo-Saxon dominion over the Black millions. 'The basic reason for English pride is India,' he once said. 'What India was for England, the territories of Russia will be for us.'[7] In the centre and east of Europe, meanwhile, he pictured a racial colony as freely exploitable as the ones Britain founded in the New World. This war was nemesis risen from the hubris of the British world order.

Even as it fought bravely for the freedom of nations, Britain remained the world's colonial hegemon. And the most terrible imprint of colonialism – famine – would, before the end, tarnish all of Britain's enlightened designs. The Bengal famine was, in Nehru's words, 'the final epitaph of British rule and achievement in India'. Its cost in Indian lives was ten times the cost of the whole war in British lives, military and civilian. It was the last epidemic famine in India, and its toll meant that Britain could not step off its 200-year-old throne looking noble.

Avoiding these scenes, we grew accustomed to viewing the war as Western Front, Eastern Front and Pacific. To risk an anachronism, we only take a First World view of the Second World War, as if the Third World had slept. The reality, that the Second World War was a war continuous with the world order before it, was apparent in places that faced colonial suppression before and after. For societies in North and East Africa, in the Middle East and on India's North-West Frontier, the distinction between the two world wars may have been elusive. Many had only known a continuous climate of imperial control and contestation. The reconquest of Burma, after the victory at Imphal, was for General Slim necessary as a moral and military redemption. To Churchill it was a play for the empire's survival. This was widely realised even at the time: in some quarters, what SEAC stood for was not 'South-East Asia Command', but 'Save England's Asian Colonies'.

Afterwards, the Second World War flowed straight back into colonial hostilities, as the winners divided and claimed their shares of territory. The strategy of propping up empire with air power, which had worked so well in the aftermath of the First World War, was attempted again after the Second. Within weeks of their own liberation, the French were bombing rebellious towns in Algeria and Syria.

In the East, Japan's surrender ended the fighting between states, but not between armies: many 'forgotten armies' remained, the seeds of free states that sprouted where the Japanese scythe had passed through colonial Asia. The terms of surrender required the Japanese Army to help restore the territories to the Allied masters. Nowhere was this more absurd than in the Dutch East Indies. In Semarang, Japanese troops were put under British command to suppress Indonesian nationalists[8] – and a Japanese major was even recommended for a Distinguished Service Order. Where the Japanese were less amenable, as in Surabaya, the Indian Army fought on behalf of the Dutch empire.

In the closing weeks of 1945, in Bombay, workers rallied at the DeLisle Road Maidan to demand that Indian troops not be used against Indonesian freedom fighters. At ports from Madras to Sydney, unionised seamen refused to work on ships carrying Dutch troops back to Java. 'I am very eager to go to Java at the earliest opportunity, but so far passport and air travel facilities have not been granted to me,' Nehru said, speaking from Moradabad. 'Meanwhile, I would like to assure Dr Sukarno that the people of India stand by the Indonesian demand for independence and will give all help they can.'[9] But the very day of Nehru's statement, the 5th Indian Infantry Division entered battle in Surabaya.[10] Native partisans were strafed by the RAF and shelled by destroyers off the coast. Fifteen thousand Indonesians were killed, and there were 600 Indian casualties – some of whom had served with the division all the way from Eritrea.

Further off, in Indo-China, the 20th Indian Division was suppressing guerrillas in the outskirts of Saigon, in order that the territory could be returned to the empire of France. On their departure, SEAC left much of their military hardware to the French, including aircraft and artillery, fuelling a war of resistance that would burn for thirty more years.

To the extent that a kind of imperial war goes on today, reverse-engineering political crises to justify new conquests, it goes on in much the same geography. British forces were back in Basra, suppressing local resistance, sixty years after Bobby left from there. The world's current empire is still bombing tracts in Waziristan, trying to drive new fakirs out from under their rocks. Ahmed Khel and Datta Khel, the very villages that Manek's squadron flew out to discipline in 1941, were still being punished by Predator drones in 2013. The empires of the world, old and new, have let these places vanish from the atlas of the Second World War, so we are able to think of those years as a hiatus, rather than a climax, of the West's imperial obsessions.

When it comes to remembering the Indians who served in the Second World War, however, nobody could do less than India itself. Like the subcontinent's many War Graves cemeteries, which lie in stillness behind walls of bougainvillea, the memory of those men and women rests in caches private and unvisited. Within the walls of their cantonments, Army regiments still keep a discreet communion with their exploits for the Raj. In the end they had defended India itself from invasion. But there is no notion, widely held, that that ever occurred. Their own families would eventually not know them, the brown men inexplicably saluting the Union Jack.

We search for our present selves in the mirror we call history. Looking back to the height of the freedom movement, India wants to see itself united in a single struggle. In the autobiography of a new nation state, there was no place for an army that fought for the Empire in the very hour that its countrymen fought to be rid of it. To the extent that Indians are aware of their countrymen in the Second World War, we revere the Indian National Army, which took the ultimate steps to force India's freedom. The INA was never militarily strong; at its peak, it had 40,000 troops, against more than 2 million in the British Indian Army, and many of its volunteers only joined to escape the deadly POW camps and forced labour corps. Its power was on the imagination – mainly of British administrators, who were forced to treat Indian troops with greater care, and after the war, to accept the fact of divided feelings in the breasts of its loyal jawans.

As history, the INA became embodied in the figure of Subhas Chandra Bose, who was either killed in an air crash or spirited into the occult only days after the Japanese surrender. What could India do with his icon, or the image of their liberators marching in step with their dreaded invaders? That was answered a few months later, when the Army decided to court-martial three INA officers: one Hindu, one Muslim and one Sikh. Nehru and his colleagues stepped forward to defend them, and thus the loose strand of the INA was braided back into the Congress epic. Bose's valiant, violent failure would burnish the trophy of the Congress's pacifist path.

This wasn't instantaneous; the rogue ambitions of Bose still rankled with Nehru, and for a generation after the war, still carried 'a nameless aroma of treason'.[11] Seven decades later, though, the INA – nevermore 'the JIFs' – is as well couched in the Indian national regard as the regular Army of the time is exiled from it. The INA is rarely recognised for what it was: a fallen branch of the British Indian Army, grafted onto Japan's ambitions, but of the same genetic constitution as its parent army. The real ideological fissure did not run between the INA and the

Indian Army, but ran through them both together: the dilemma of choosing loyalty or liberty, subordination or treason.

The Second World War in Burma and India's north-east was the British Empire's largest and longest-lasting campaign. Yet in 1944, while the fighting was at its peak, the men there already called themselves 'the Forgotten Army'. The prescient phrase would later be used to title books about the Allied Fourteenth Army, about the INA, and about the wide array of nationalist militias which sprang up in the crescent of Japanese-held Asia. Two books about the RAF in Asia are called *The Forgotten Air Force* and *The Forgotten Ones*. Claude Auchinleck, the champion of the wartime Indian Army, was called 'the forgotten warrior' in his obituaries. Each forgotten force encloses others more forgotten, whether they are the women's regiment of the INA, or the Légions Indiennes; the East Africans or the sappers, or even the mules.

It's obvious that it is the preserve of neither one side nor the other – regular forces nor irregular, rebel nor royal – to be forgotten. Rather, it was a fate that awaited everyone whose service occurred too near the overlap of colonial rule and world war. In the end, the annals of the West would prefer to forget the colonial factors, and the annals of the post-colonial world would forget the war effort: each found their narrative too deeply unsettled by the other. Between the closing chapter of imperial history and the first volume of the national record, we let drop the page that had Indians fighting on both sides.

For their own personal reasons, the bereaved and the survivors of India's Second World War would collude with the state in forgetting those who died. The men who held on to their commissions after 1947 would go on to fight more wars, holding more senior and more admirable commands, against enemies that remain threats today. Their subaltern service to the British

Empire became a quixotic memory, its political valency vague and its heroism diluted. Those who were bereaved would go on, as well, and learn to live their lives unburdened of the memory of the dead.

Today, seventy years after the war's end, they too are making their exit from our lives, and taking their private memories with them. Nugs, my grandmother, died in 1998, before I could ask her about Bobby and the others – before I even knew Bobby had existed. The farthest field is not just a conceit about Bobby's death but one that applies, and at this moment, to all those Indians who were lost to the Second World War. Writing the personal story of these three men was my attempt to draw back the dead, when even their memory had passed into the shadow. The rest of this book is an attempt to keep the common story with us, as the people who lived it take their leave.

Acknowledgements

I feel indebted to everyone who is or was a link to what has passed, especially to those with the generosity of memory to remember Bobby. Indian veterans comprise most of the new friends I've made in the last three years: the late C. M. Beliappa (Dalu Uncle), General Sundara Rao, Wing Commander Hoshang Patel, Brigadier Furdoon 'Duck' Mehta, Brigadier John P. Anthony, Air Vice Marshal Randhir Singh, Subedar Naranjan Singh, Major General Kuldip Singh Bajwa, Brigadier Dhillon, Colonel Jamsher Gill, Subedar Ram Swarup, Brigadier Sant Singh, General S. K. Sinha and Lieutenant General J. F. R. Jacob. Their patient explanations helped me understand the Indian military experience of the war.

I'm most profoundly grateful to Squadron Leader Rana Chhina of the Centre for Armed Forces Historical Research at the United Services Institute, Delhi. Gillian Wright, for introducing me to him. In Chandigarh, the generous and knowledgeable Mandeep Singh Bajwa. Narender Yadav and the staff of the Ministry of Defence History Division in Delhi. Jagan Pilarisetti of the online repository Bharat Rakshak, Mukund Murthy, Somnath Sapru and K. Sree Kumar, for their marvellous work chronicling Indian Air Force history.

In Roorkee, the staff of the Bengal Engineers Group, including Captain Lakshmi and Lieutenant Colonel Bedi. Ajai Shukla for passing his expert eye over a severely inexpert manuscript.

In Palghat, the Mukundan family: Ram, Shailaja and Aunty Padma, and the late P. Mukundan – the resilience of his affection for Bobby made it possible to tell this story. In Indore, Bomi and Shireen Heerjee. In Calicut, the Marshall family, especially Jasmine Marshall. In Anand, Gujarat, Verghese and Nirmala Kurien. In Manipur, Chitra Ahantem, Hemant Singh Katoch, Leisangthem Surjit and Mr Surchand of the Manipur Mountaineering and Trekking Association, Freddy Longleng, Somi Roy, Grace Jajo and the esteemed Yangmasho Shishak.

In Bangalore, Sankaran Nair, Ramachandra Guha, Theodore Baskaran and Bhairav Acharya. In Kodagu, Gowri Monappa and Kushi Cariappa. In Madras, K. T. Ganapathy, S. Muthiah, P. Athiyaman, Kalyan Raman, T. Adhiraj, Mathangi Krishnamurthi, Anna Varki, Siddharth Varadarajan, and the staff at the Alumni Office of the College of Engineering, Guindy. Naresh Fernandes in Bombay and Kai Friese in Delhi, both writers with such erudition about the war years as I could only dream of having.

In the United Kingdom, Gordon Graham for his blessings; Martin Pick, Denzil Fernandes and Michael Dwyer; Nigel de Lee, who interviewed John Walker Wright of the 2nd Field Company; April Philips, the niece of John Walker Wright, and the many residents of Bisley village who came together to help me locate her (among them Derek Hunt, Roger Utley, John Ellis and Bob Brooks). The staffs of the Commonwealth War Graves Commission, the Imperial War Museum, the National Army Museum, the Royal Engineers Museum, the British Library and the National Archives at Kew.

This manuscript was carried through the final lap by the faith and keen criticism of my agents and publishers: David Miller and Melanie Jackson, Arabella Pike, Starling Lawrence and Karthika V. K., Essie Cousins, Kate Johnson, Stephen Guise, Ajitha G. S., Amrita Talwar, Helen Ellis, Elizabeth Riley and Ryan Harrington, besides other friends in publishing, Chiki Sarkar and Nandini Mehta. For personal support: Arshia Sattar, who has encouraged my writing longer than I have been writing; my cohort at Sangam House, Lynne Fernandez and the dancers of Nrityagram, who respectively inspired and humbled me; Maria Aurora Couto and the late Alban Couto (for the use of his library), and Krishna Bisht and the staff at Aldona; Tara Kelton and the T.A.J. Residency, Bangalore; Sarita and Ramneek Bakhshi, Omesh and Anuja Kapila.

Many friends were integral to the long process, and they include Anmol Tikoo, Andrew Stobo Sniderman and the boys of 7/10, Ajay Madiwale, Ajay Krishnan, Sonal Shah, Shruti Ravindran, Anand Vaidya and Veejay Sai. My most insightful reader and loyal friend, Tara Sapru. For all the rest, my family: especially Saraswathy Ganapathy, my mother, constant accomplice, critic and guide.

Notes

Prologue

1. A single exception is the end of the chapter 'No Heroes'. The rescue on the banks of the Chindwin did happen, but the identity of the specific pilots from No. 2 Squadron is unknown, and unclaimed.

PART ONE: HOME
Chapter 1: Everybody's Friend

1. The place was fifty years older, but not very much changed, since the time that Edward Lear visited, seeking landscapes to draw. Lear observed with an artist's eye that it was 'all but impossible to give any idea of these beautiful Malabar lanes, since their chief beauty consists of what cannot be readily imitated: to wit, endless detail of infinitely varied vegetation ... The colour, too, of these scenes, the deep and vivid green, the red soil roads, the brilliant white and scarlet dresses of the people.' He made note of the palmy roads, the plantain leaf – 'Surely no leaf is lovelier!' – and 'the river scenery about Calicut and Mahee more lovely than any I had before imagined ... All more or less qualified by the odour of stinking fish.' From

Edward Lear's Indian journals, online at the Digital Library of India, http://maddy06.blogspot.in/2010/09/edward-lear-at-summer-isle-of-eden.html

2. In the best-known Parsi legend, their first refugees arrived at Nargol in Gujarat, where they were met on the shore by the Raja of Sanjan. There the King held up a full glass of milk, to communicate that his kingdom had no place left for foreigners. In reply, the Parsi leader poured a spoon of sugar into the brimming glass, and it did not overflow; thus answering that the Parsis would sweeten his kingdom without disturbing it.

3. To have 'eaten someone's salt' is a popular idiom in many Indian languages meaning to 'owe someone your loyalty'; in Hindi, a traitor can be called *namak haram*, or a violator of the salt.

4. Not all Parsis were opposed to the nationalist movement. At Navsari, the final stop of the salt *satyagraha* before the coast, Parsi families had paid for the electric lights and dais from which Gandhi addressed a gathering of ten thousand.

Chapter 2: *Hukm Hai*

1. Sankaran Nair, K., *Inside I. B. and R. A. W.: A Rolling Stone that Gathered Moss*, p. 44.

2. The very first pilot licensed in India was J. R. D. Tata in 1929. He was the heir to the largest Parsi industrial fortune.

3. Nirad C. Chaudhuri, *Thy Hand, Great Anarch! India 1921–1952*, p. 592.

4. The Viceroy was, in reality, neither a hawk nor a British bulldog. He was a mild and sympathetic statesman, sent to India to administer the new constitution. When Britain declared war, he had been required by law to automatically

follow suit. So he became a wartime viceroy who, by no will of his own, condemned the chances of a constitutional solution.

5. The castes mingled in the classrooms, but Guindy College did not dare intrude on the sanctum of Indian scruples: food. Separate messes spared the students the worst violations. Messes A–E were vegetarian canteens for Brahmin Tamils, non-Brahmin Tamils, and caste students from Andhra, Kerala and the north. Bobby patronised the others, enjoying whatever they dished out by way of grub and politics. He could breakfast at the Anglo-Indian mess, where toast and omelettes were served with cutlery, porcelain, and learned rumours of the preparation 'at home' for an invasion. At lunchtime, the Andhra non-veg mess had a spicy tamarind fish *pulusu*, and heartburn over the Tamil refusal to cede a Telugu province. The Muslim mess served up mutton curry, pulao, and hot speculation on whether the Aga Khan might come out on Hitler's side. Non-veg D served Chettinad seafood curries to middle-caste Tamils, who argued about whether Rajaji was right to use the same sedition laws against communists that the British had once used against him.

Chapter 3: Savages of the Stone Age

1. It was here that Winston Churchill, as a newly minted subaltern, had joined the punitive expedition that became the subject of his first book. In *The Story of the Malakand Field Force*, young Winston described the Pashtun as a chimera of racial terror: 'To the ferocity of the Zulu are added the craft of the Redskin and the marksmanship of the Boer ... The weapons of the nineteenth century are in the

hands of the savages of the Stone Age.'

2. In 1936, twenty-eight battalions.

3. On 23 July 1941, General Archibald Wavell, the new Commander-in-Chief of India, wrote to Air Marshal Arthur Tedder about a visit to Risalpur in India, where he found a squadron 'training as fighter squadron with Audax machines. Most modern aircraft possessed in India. Does this not make your heart bleed? Could you not now spare some Gladiators, as many as possible, to enable pilots in this squadron to be trained in comparatively modern machines?' Quoted in Michael Carver's *The Warlords*, London, 1976, p. 223.

4. Jasjit Singh, *The Icon: Marshall of the Indian Air Force, Arjan Singh, DFC*, pp. 19–20.

5. Before the war, there had been a massacre in Peshawar. In 1930, the government had arrested Abdul Ghaffar Khan for preaching civil disobedience. He was the leader of the Khudai Khidmatgars, 'Servants of God', a non-violent movement of 50,000 red-shirted Pashtuns. At the news of his arrest, the redshirts swarmed into the walled city and gathered in the Qissa Khawani Bazar, the Storytellers' Market – but the Army would not hear any new stories that day. Being Pashtun, they met a thin-lipped British ferocity which the Congress activists had never had to face. Four hundred were shot and killed: as many as fell at Amritsar ten years before. Only a single regiment, the Royal Garhwal Rifles, had refused to open fire, resisting their officers and the provocation of the crowd. For that insubordination, 67 soldiers were court-martialled, and their NCOs received sentences of life imprisonment.

6. As both Sven Lindqvuist and David Omissi have written, the very existence of the RAF as an independent service is

owed to the policy of colonial 'air control' – the idea that an air force could undertake colonial policing, and relieve the costs of managing the Empire's sprawl.

Victorious in 1919, but gutted by the war, Britain had urgently needed to shed its military load. The security of the colonies had returned as the central objective, and few senior commanders saw any use for a full-fledged air force. The RAF may have been disbanded, but for a daring manoeuvre by Winston Churchill, then a young minister. Along with the first Chief of Air Staff, Hugh Trenchard, he insisted that military aviation could take the lead in securing the empire by conducting 'policing' actions. Churchill argued that an Empire in rebellion needed an air force; in reality, the air force needed the Empire to rebel, and give it a chance to demonstrate air control.

The Empire obliged. Popular eruptions occurred across the British Empire in 1919, and the air force was deployed in Waziristan, Somaliland, Aden, and on one occasion, Punjab. Throughout what Europe called the inter-war years, to be bombed from the air was the privilege of the colonised world. Nowhere was aerial bombing more common than in the 'mandated' territories of the Near East, newly annexed from the Ottoman Empire. Arabs were in mass rebellion, and the RAF seized its chance to practice new techniques of bombing human settlements. Annual campaigns in border areas kept the squadrons busy; in one case, at the end of 1923, the RAF bombed villages in the province of Samawah to enforce a new tax. In Iraq, as in the North-West Frontier, air control was routinised into 'proscription bombing', wherein warning notes were dropped ahead of time, to minimise killing and restore pax Britannica.

Chapter 4: The Centre of the World

1. The first two women enrolled in Guindy Engineering College, A. Lalitha and Leela George, contributed an essay to the college magazine that dwelt in part on the war. An excerpt: 'The present war has brought the fight to our own doors – and when our men are up in the air keeping back the enemy, he comes under cover of darkness and bombs Factories, and does not spare hospitals, churches or schools. It is a war of the machines and the latter have to be produced by the stay-at-homes, viz., women. How can we produce machines if we do not know the science of engineering? Large number of women have been recruited for driving motor vehicles and piloting aero-planes. In peace time, we are only typing automatons, living components in the Telephone Exchange, showcase mannequins or dancing marionettes. But the war has compelled men to give us more urgent and important places in handling machinery. Gifted as we are with equally-sized brains – can we not learn about the principles of machinery and electricity and take our place as engineers-in-charge?' From *Survey School to Tech Temple: A History of College of Engineering, Guindy 1794–1994*, Madras, 1991, p. 162.

2. In 1914 the European war had become a 'world war' only when Japan joined the Allies, relieving the Royal Navy of escort duties in the Indian Ocean and Pacific. It expected in return, but was denied, any share of Germany's colonies in the Far East. A special credit for foresight belongs to Rabindranath Tagore, who wrote in 1915: 'I am almost sure that Japan has her eyes set upon India. She is hungry – she is munching Korea, she has fastened her teeth upon China, and it will be an evil day for India when Japan will

have her opportunity.' Quoted in Pankaj Mishra, *From the Ruins of Empire: The Revolt Against the West and the Remaking of Asia*, p. 233.

3. George Orwell, *Orwell: The Observer Years*, London, 2003, pp. 2–3.

4. Another inter community marriage was making headlines in early 1942. Jawaharlal Nehru's daughter, Indira, was to marry a young Parsi party worker named Feroze Gandhi. Nehru, mid-stride in the national emergency, suddenly found himself tripping over offended Brahmins from his community, the Kashmiri Pandits.

   Nehru was compelled to make a statement to the press, which is quoted in Tariq Ali's *An Indian Dynasty: The story of the Nehru-Gandhi family*. 'I have long held that though parents may and should advice in the matter, the choice and ultimate decision must be with the two parties concerned,' Nehru wrote, and ended with a nimble pass: 'Mahatma Gandhi, whose opinion I value not only in public affairs but in private matters also, gave his blessings to the proposal.'

   It was then Gandhi's (the real Gandhi's) turn to deal with the enraged Pandits. 'His (Feroze's) only crime in their estimation is that he happens to be a Parsi ... Such unions are bound to multiply with benefit to the society,' Gandhi said, and called on 'the writers of such abusive letters to shed your wrath and bless the forthcoming marriage. Their letters betray ... a species of untouchability, dangerous because not so easily identified.' Indira Nehru and Feroze Gandhi were married on 26 March 1942, with Stafford Cripps attending.

5. See Herbert A. Friedman, 'Axis and Allied Propaganda to Indian Troops'.

6. George Orwell, 'Not Counting Niggers', July 1939, *The Collected Essays, Journalism and Letters of George Orwell*, London, 1968.

Chapter 5: Madras Must Not Burn

1. Quoted in Indivar Kamtekar, 'The Shiver of 1942', p. 86.
2. 'Invasion Must Be Resisted', *The Hindu*, 12 April 1942.
3. From a report by the Joint Planning Staff and a Joint Intelligence Committee, titled 'Defence of India':
   'Direction of next Japanese drive cannot yet be established but there is no reason why she should not stage a full scale attack on India. We calculate ten divisions plus what could be spared from Burma ... Air Forces would be limiting factor but calculate Japan might make 600 available for India and Ceylon excluding carrier-borne aircraft. This force possibly insufficient for advance through India from Bengal but in our opinion ample for invasion of India from East Coast or South. In this case enemy's final objective likely to be Bombay area and would have good prospect of success.'

   Under the headers 'Enemy Invasion of Ceylon' and 'Enemy Attack in Madras Area', the report continues: 'If the situation when Ceylon falls is such that its early re-capture is unlikely, Southern INDIA should be given up, our forces withdrawing towards the Central Reserve so as to cover Japanese approaches towards Bombay, ie to, successively, Bangalore, Guntakal, Poona.' India Command Joint Planning Staff Paper No. 15: Defence of India I, 23 April 1942, National Archives, UK, AIR 23/1967.
4. In a conversation with Canadian Air Commodore Leonard Birchall the British Embassy in Washington DC, quoted in Michael Patterson's *Battle for the Skies*, p. 20.

5. 'Keep Calm', *The Times of India*, 10 April 1942.

Chapter 7: Do or Die

1. This situation provided less relief to the hapless civilian administration in India, which spent the monsoon contemplating the prospect of billeting thousands of Europeans, and building refugee camps for millions of Indians from Assam and Bengal.

2. Khanduri, C. B., *Thimayya: An Amazing Life*, Delhi, 2006, p. 57.

3. Because the IMS was staffed by doctors, it had been the first service to commission Indians. The concession led to anxieties about its being flooded with 'native surgeons', and ratios were set for Indians to Europeans, first by the Escher Committee and then the Ogilvy Committee (one-to-two, and two-to-three respectively). To maintain the ratio, the IMS paid British officers an overseas allowance that nearly doubled their total salaries over their Indian colleagues. One consequence was that the pre-war establishment of the IMS was only 364 regular officers, and fifty-five on short-service commission. With the war begun, constraints on recruiting Indian doctors were abolished, but the IMS continued to favour Europeans; in 1942, its civil wing had three times as many Whites as Indians.

4. 'Army Medical Service Deputation to Mr N. R. Sarkar: Racial Discrimination Alleged', *The Hindu*, 16 April 1942.

5. Thal was besieged, and relieved a force led by General Reginald Dyer, only a month after he ordered the firing on unarmed Sikhs in Jallianwala Bagh. Thanks to the victory at Thal, however, he retired a hero.

6. A newly discovered antibacterial compound of sulphonamide, it was used to treat Winston Churchill after

he contracted bacterial pneumonia during the Tehran Conference in 1943. The prime minister later declared: 'This admirable M&B from which I did not suffer any inconvenience, was used at the earliest moment and, after a week's fever, the intruders were repulsed.'

7. Even in 1939, Rajaji had been sorry to lose his government. In the spring he had urged Gandhi to accept Cripps's final offer; now he was fed up with the disruptionists in Congress, and he disdained the August *kranti* as a 'grievous mistake'.

8. In the end, though, there were only 295 sentences of whipping in the Madras Presidency, and only twenty-one occasions when the police had to fire on crowds (compared to 226 in Bombay). One textile strike in Ahmedabad held out until November 1942, and was praised by nationalist leaders as the 'Stalingrad of free India'. See Gyan Pandey (ed.), *The Indian Nation in 1942*.

9. Nirad Chaudhuri, *Thy Hand Great Anarch!*, p. 567.

Chapter 8: The King's Own

1. See Appendix 2: 'The Army of India'.
2. Charles Wood, the Secretary of State for India in 1862, quoted in Madhusree Mukerjee's *Churchill's Secret War*, p. xiii.
3. By coincidence, this was reportedly Hitler's favourite Hollywood movie.
4. The school was formerly St Thomason's College, a rival of Guindy College for the title of the oldest engineering college in India. Later it would become the Indian Institute of Technology, Roorkee.
5. In eighty years, the loyalty of the Indian Army had rarely come into question, but under the strains of war, two

collective insubordinations – technically, mutinies – took place in 1940 alone. The first was by a Sikh squadron of Central Indian Horse, which was persuaded by communists to refuse to embark at Bombay to serve in an imperialist war in the Middle East. In the Middle East itself, Sikhs of the 4th Indian Division's Ammunition Company had refused to carry ammunition boxes on their heads, saying they were not 'coolies'. They were already disgruntled about theatre orders requiring them to carry around steel helmets, which could not go over their turbans. Both incidents led to courts martial and executions.

6. Quoted in Philip Warner, *Auchinleck: The Lonely Soldier*, p194.

7. Quoted in Tarak Barkawi, 'Culture and Combat in the Colonies: The Indian Army in the Second World War'.

8. The doctrine of 'martial races', later euphemised as the 'enlisted classes', drew on an elaborate pseudo-scientific typology of castes. To some extent, the designated races were groups, like the Sikhs and Pathans, that did have martial traditions. Other criteria of a martial race, however, included phrenological measurements and questions of diet. An overarching qualification was that the regiments of that ethnic group had remained in order during the uprising of 1857. The corollary to the list of martial races was an implicit blacklist of castes that led the uprising, such as Awadhi Brahmins. (The Bengal Sappers were the only regiment of the Indian Army that continued to recruit Awadhi Brahmins, in recognition of the role of one sapper who blew up the Kashmere Gate of besieged Delhi, allowing the Army to storm the city and crush the uprising.) Eventually, the military's caste science allowed it to discriminate even between sub-castes, so that Jadhubansi

Ahirs were treated as excellent soldiering material and Nandubansis less satisfactory, while Gwalbansis were unusable except for labour.

9. For the Mahars, an 'Untouchable' community of the Bombay Presidency, the tradition of Army service had been the sole route of social advancement. After the Great War, the right to re-enlist was a perennial issue for their leaders; among them an especially inspiring Congressman, Bhimrao Ambedkar. Ambedkar's father Ramji Sakpal had been a sapper with the 106th Company, Bombay Sappers and Miners. His maternal grandfather, meanwhile, had been a *subedar*-major – the highest rank that could be held by an Indian. In the compressive chill after the First World War, however, these communities stood little chance of being retained. The former Madras Army was worst affected: by the 1930s, all of its combat regiments had been demobilised.

10. In the smaller towns, the Recruitment Directorate used mobile cinema units to screen recruitment films, which could be patriotic (such as *Watan ki Pukaar* – The Country's Call), or more direct (*Taraqqi* – Promotion). Other arms of government were also on the job. Political agents soothed the Maharajas, jealous of their sovereignty, as recruitment drives nosed deeper into the princely states. Civil administration was co-opted to spread the word, tailored to regimental requirements. The chain from collectors to village *patwaris* (accountants) conveyed to specific neighbourhoods the need for exactly six Hindu Rajputs, or eighteen Jat Sikhs. Medical officers were instructed to admit recruits with knock-knees, goitres and varicose veins, blemishing the turn-out of the ranks. See *Recruiting for the Defence Services in India*, Combined Inter-Services Historical Section (India & Pakistan), Delhi, 1950.

11. Gerald Douds, 'Matters of Honour: Indian Troops in the North African and Italian Theatres', in *Time to Kill: The Soldier's Experience of War in the West, 1939–1945*, eds Deighton, Addison and Calder.

12. The Madras Presidency contributed 18.6 per cent of these new soldiers – nearly 600,000 of them – twice as many as the United Provinces, and second only to the Punjab, which raised 750,000. See *Recruiting for the Defence Services in India*, Combined Inter-Services Historical Section (India & Pakistan).

13. Some recruits joined regiments raised entirely from their communities. Others reinforced regiments that treasured their ethnic identity, and scorned new troops of other racial stock. Plenty of homesick eighteen-year-olds deserted, and repeated memos from GHQ pressed commanding officers to assure 'sympathetic treatment' to 'hitherto unenlisted classes' – even to the extent of expediting their promotion to the VCO ranks, making them 'thereby competent to watch their own interests'. Regimental officers organised entertainments, or *tamashas*, in the lines; they let it be known that the penalty for desertion would be limited if a boy was returned to the regiment by his parents, rather than the police. When this happened, the parents were thanked in person by COs.

14. Major I. A. Anderson, a Deputy Assistant Director of Hygiene in the War Office, quoted in *Recruiting for the Defence Services in India*, Combined Inter-Services Historical Section (India & Pakistan), p. 117.

15. For an explanation of the Viceroy's Commissioned Officers, see Appendix 2, Indian Ranks.

PART TWO: WEST
Chapter 9: Second Field

1. In 1914, Indian infantry formed the heart of the British invasion force of the Mesopotamian campaign. Mesopotamia was eventually taken from the Ottomans, and after the Great War, it passed into a British mandate, which yielded to an independent kingdom, Iraq, in 1932. Iraq remained a vassal state, led by a British-installed monarch and bound by treaties that guaranteed a military alliance. When the new war began, Iraq was under pressure to declare war as well, but its regent was prevented from doing so by a coup. The new prime minister, the nationalist Rashid Ali Gaylani, declared Iraq neutral. This threatened Britain's continued use of airfields and ports, the right of passage to imperial troops, and the security of British commercial interests in Iraq's oil wells. Moreover, the distinction between being neutral, nationalist and being pro-Axis was, as in parts of India, more and more an academic one. By the summer of 1941, it was plausible that Stalingrad might fall, and Gaylani might repay German favours by opening a fascist road to India. Churchill was not having it. In April, the 20th Indian Infantry Brigade, under sail for Malaya, was turned around and disembarked at Basra. After Gaylani precipitated a stand-off at the key RAF airbase at Habbaniya, the full invasion of southern Iraq by the Indian Army began.

2. Persia, rather than the modern name Iran, because 'Iran' was deemed too easy to confuse with 'Iraq' in communications – a problem not unknown to invading nations sixty years later.

3. The 2nd Field Company, along with 161st Indian Infantry Brigade, had reached Baghdad from the Qassassin camp on

the Suez coast, after covering a thousand miles of desert in nine days, in a convoy of vehicles that extended over three miles.

Chapter 10: The Jemadars' Story

1. Second Field Company was part of another immense transformation in the Indian Army – its mechanisation – another change bemoaned by its old establishment but forced by Auchinleck and the demands of war. In 1939, India still employed eighteen regiments of horsed cavalry. Between then and the summer of 1942, when Bobby enrolled, the Army scaled up from only 5,000 pieces of motor transport to over 60,000. By then the mules and chargers of the Bengal Sappers had been returned to the Remount Depot, and the NCOs ordered to hand over their spurs. The provision of motor transport was not as timely. The 70th Field Company, for instance, received their vehicles just a day before they departed Roorkee – giving the drivers a single night to practise driving them.

2. Like the Fifth Indian Division itself, the divisional sign was formed and deployed in haste. The original submission for it had been a boar's head, a play on the nickname of its general, Lewis 'Piggy' Heath. Unit commanders protested that Muslims would not fight well beneath the sign of a pig. The chief of staff, Frank Messervy, next considered the heads of other animals, but found they'd all been taken. He settled on a simple red circle against black, which in time came to symbolise a ball of fire.

3. Ninth Indian Infantry Brigade, with battalions of 3/5th Marathas, the 2nd West Yorkshires, and 3/12th Frontier Force Rifles, joined by a machine-gun company of the Sudan Defence Force.

4. Tenth Indian Infantry Brigade, with battalions of 2nd Battalion Highland Light Infantry, the 4/10th Baluch and the 2/4th Gurkha Rifles.

5. As the 4th Gurkhas' history records of that day: 'It was some time before we realised that no one who left our position ever did return.'

6. Captain M. L. Katju, MC, also recounted his experience with the Baluchi battalion in the Cauldron. He described how 'breakers of dust rose and fell with the blast of the shells … The gun teams, stripped to the waist, disappeared in fountains of sand, and whenever the dust broke, men would be seen bandaging each other.' Only five officers and 190 men of the 4/10th Baluch ultimately escaped the battle. From *Tiger Kills*, p 125.

7. The 161st had not been in Egypt two weeks, but it had to replace two battalions after fighting on the Ridge. The fighting to stop the Axis advance, later called the First Battle of El Alamein, cost the 5th Division alone 3,000 casualties. At the end of the battle, the brigade comprised the 4/7th Rajputs, the 1/1st Punjab Regiment and the 1st Argyll & Sutherland Highlanders, which would shortly be replaced by the 4th Battalion Queen's Own Royal West Kents.

Chapter 11: The Lieutenant's Story

1. The unit was the 31st Field Squadron, Bengal Sappers, attached to the 3rd Indian Motor Brigade which was destroyed at Bir Hakeim.

2. From the recollections of Lieutenant Ivory of the 2nd Field Company, in Cooper and Alexander, *The Bengal Sappers 1803–2003*; the date of this attack is recorded differently in other sources.

Chapter 12: Kings of Persia

1. The film partially described here is *The Road to Russia*, produced by Ministry of Information, Middle East, accessed at the Imperial War Museum, London, IWM/CVN232.

2. Troops in Baghdad were still spared the worst of it. In Andimeshk, Iran, at the end of the double pipeline from the Abadan refinery, it was said that most soldiers' hands were bandaged, burnt on parked vehicles or canteens left lying in the sun. They joked that men who died in Andimeshk went straight to hell and found the weather there nice and cool. South of that was Dizful, the city of the blind, where the natives allegedly lived in caves under ground, never emerging, and gradually losing their sight. The wealthy lived deepest of all, and it was an Arab saying that 'in Dizful, the robes of the rich rest on Noah's waters'.

3. Douglas Alexander Pringles, 5th Indian Divisional Signals, courtesy of Imperial War Museum, London, accession no. 7368.

4. At Habbaniya they worked at the base of the plateau from which Rashid Ali Gaylani's guns had ranged in on the RAF bastion in 1941, challenging the British military presence in Iraq, and providing justification for the invasion two years before.

5. 'The confusion reigning on that night can scarcely be imagined,' Rommel wrote of the attack on Mersa Matruh. 'It was impossible to see one's hand before one's eyes. The RAF bombed their own troops. German units fired on each other.' Quoted in Desmond Young's *Rommel: The Desert Fox*.

PART THREE: EAST
Chapter 13: Enter the Hurricane

1. See Friedman, 'Axis and Allied Propaganda to Indian Troops'.
2. 'In Their Jungle Home: IAF on the Eastern Front', *Illustrated Weekly of India*, 13 June 1943.
3. This story is found in multiple sources on No. 2 Squadron IAF, including Rana Chhina, *The Eagle Strikes: The Royal Indian Air Force, 1932–50*. However, the true identity of the two pilots is not established.

Chapter 14: No Heroes

1. Later in 1943, the tank caravan of General Von Arnim would be put on display in Delhi's Connaught Circus.
2. The full citation reads: 'For continuous courage and disregard of personal danger during the operation on the FALAJA PASS at AMBA ALAGI in April 1941, this officer was recommended for an immediate award of the I.O.M. for conspicuous gallantry at CHEREN, and was outstanding throughout the ERITREAN operations but has received no recognition.' Accessed at UK National Archives, reference WO/373/29.
3. Madras was, however, bombed in a single, mysterious Japanese sortie on 12 October 1943. Shrapnel from that attack is on display at the Fort St George Museum in the city.
4. Indivar Kamtekar, 'A Different War Dance', pp. 197–8.
5. US and British troops consigned to the rear echelon were encouraged to view their own passive lifestyle with a good sense of humour. The Americans called Delhi 'Per Diem Hill', and their spending there did in fact bring the first flush of commercial life to the recently built capital. The

number of American soldiers sauntering around had already, a year before, made Gandhi nervous that British domination might be succeeded by US control. But Gandhi was in jail now, and the 'Queensway commandos' were having the time of their lives. The SEAC composed a poem, 'Sticking It Out in Delhi', which nicely captured the mood on Per Diem Hill: 'Fighting the Nazis from Delhi,/ Fighting the Japs from Kashmir,/Exiled from England, we feel you should know,/The way we are taking it here./ Sticking it out at the Cecil,/Doing our bit for the War,/ Going through hell at the Maiden's Hotel,/Where they stop serving lunch at four,' cited in Christopher Bayly and Tim Harper, *Forgotten Armies: The Fall of British Asia 1941– 45*, p. 376.

6. The Germans and Japanese did also have one safe harbour on the west coast of India: at the ports of Goa, then a colony of neutral Portugal. One of the better-remembered events of India's Second World War, thanks to a Hollywood movie made about it, was the secret operation by British commandos to sink the MS *Ehrenfels* anchored in Mormugao Bay in May 1942. Over a year later, a more public event drew the world's attention to Mormugao: the exchange of 3,000 civilian prisoners between Japan and the USA.

7. *Japan Varuvaana?* ('Will the Japanese Come?') was a Tamil pamphlet written by the intellectual V. Ramaswamy Iyengar, who wrote as VaRaa. It was published in 1943 as part of the series Thamizh Sudar ('Tamil Flame'), which aimed to inform the Tamil-reading public on topics of current importance. The pamphlet surveyed Japan's rise and its imperial exploits since the Russo-Japanese war of 1905, and described its victories against Britain since 1941.

However, VaRaa assured his readers that there was nothing to fear: that given its engagement in the Pacific theatre and the daunting size of the Indian subcontinent, Japan remained unlikely to attack Madras.

Chapter 15: Fascines and Gabions

1. William Slim quoted in Philip Warner, *Auchinleck: The Lonely Soldier*, p. 183.
2. Quoted in Philip Warner, *Auchinleck: The Lonely Soldier*, p. 138.
3. This accusation was thrown at, and later recorded by, Lord Wavell, the previous C-in-C and now Viceroy of India.
4. Antony Brett-James, *The Ball of Fire: The Fifth Indian Division in the Second World War*, p. 259.
5. Fascines and gabions were devices of classical military engineering. A fascine was a bundle of wooden sticks bound together, used to ramp up light defences or to fill moats and ditches and aid crossing. Gabions, in military usage, were wicker cages that could be staked down and filled with rocks or soil to create defensive bulwarks, around field artillery for example. Shako hats were tall, cylindrical military hats with short visors, commonly used in the nineteenth century by European armies, including in the Corps of Royal Engineers.
6. The Army consumed 800 million tablets of mepacrine during the Second World War.
7. Naresh Fernandes, 'Goering Had Two (But Very Small)', on www.tajmahalfoxtrot.in
8. Bose was transported in a German U-boat to the Indian Ocean south-east of Madagascar, where on 27 April he was transferred to a Japanese submarine, a journey that is now legend. It is less known that Allied intelligence was

tracking his movement, and was aware of the identity of the passenger whom the crew called 'Indian Adolf'. The Free Indian Legion remained under German command, and would be deployed on the Dutch coast and finally, under command of the Waffen-SS, in France to resist the Allied landings.

9. Editorial in *Harijan*, 31 May 1942.

10. The provisional government of Azad Hind was immediately recognised by the governments of Japan, Germany, Italy, Croatia, the Philippines, Nanking China, Manchukuo, Burma and Siam.

Chapter 16: The Jungle Book

1. In December, the division received a visit from Lord Mountbatten; two platoons of 2nd Field Company paraded for the Supreme Allied Commander of South-East Asia, and he worked his magic on them all. 'A' platoon was called on to ferry the Admiral across the Pruma Chaung, after which crossing, he turned to John Wright and told him, 'Bloody good – try a bit harder, and you'll be almost as good as the Navy.'

2. William Slim, *Defeat Into Victory*, p. 260.

3. Julian Thompson, *The Imperial War Museum Book of the War in Burma 1942–1945*, London, 2012, p. 102.

4. Barkawi, 'Culture and Combat in the Colonies'.

5. *Elephant Bill*, quoted in foreword, Jilly Cooper, *Animals at War*, p. 110. The Corps of Indian Engineers even had a No. 1 Elephant Company, well occupied in the Kabaw Valley.

Chapter 17: Fight with Your Ghost

1. Fergal Keane, *Road of Bones*, p. 177.
2. The Anglo-American air group flew 758 sorties to transport the entire 5th Indian Division to Imphal and Kohima – one of the largest military airlifts until that date.
3. The cause of this costly vacillation was laid out by General Slim in his memoir: 'Kohima Ridge was an infinitely preferable defensive position to Dimapur, which it covered. If we had not enough troops to hold Kohima, we certainly had not enough to hold Dimapur and, as long as we clung to the ridge, we had some chance of concentrating our reinforcements as they arrived, without too much hostile interference.' Yet Slim had emphasised to Major-General Ranking, the rear-area commander in Assam, that their main task was to safeguard the vital Dimapur base. When Ranking heard 'reports and rumours of Japanese units within striking distance of Dimapur', he ordered the 161st Brigade back from Kohima into Dimapur's outskirts. The reports proved untrue. From William Slim's *Defeat Into Victory*, pp. 356–7.
4. See Arthur Campbell, *The Siege: A story from Kohima*, p167. Campbell quotes a conversation between Colonel Laverty, the commander of 4th Bn. Royal West Kents, and his adjutant about the single Rajput company attached to their battalion inside Kohima. 'Of course it must be hell for them, fighting among strangers who can't speak their language,' the adjutant said.

    'I don't reckon we're strangers,' Laverty replied. 'The men aren't, anyway. They talk to them like long-lost brothers – language or no.'

    During the siege, Captain Mitchell of the Rajput company was killed by a shell, leaving the command to his 53-year-old Subedar, Multan Singh.

Chapter 18: The Cremation Ground

1. The British-Indian administration had banned the import of
   barbed wire into the Naga Hills, as a gesture to the area's
   reserved status. The failure to provide barbed wire before
   the Japanese arrival was typical of the neglect and
   oversights on the Burma front.

Chapter 19: The Elephant

1. Officers, identifiable by their hip holsters, were special
   targets in the fighting, and a hint of its intimate nature is
   that one British brigade lost two brigadiers while fighting
   for Kohima.
2. From an account of Captain Dickie Davies of the 2nd
   Battalion, Royal Norfolk Regiment, FVB. Quoted in Julian
   Thompson, in association with the Imperial War Museum,
   *The Forgotten Voices of Burma: The Second World War's
   Forgotten Conflict*, p. 238.
3. In his war memoir, *Leaves from a War Reporter's Diary*, the
   Reuters journalist D. R. Mankekar gave a close account of
   his struggle to send any despatches about the situation at
   Kohima and Imphal. 'My own scoop on the Japanese
   invasion of Assam was just a reward for sheer patience with
   the censors and experimentation with phraseology, plus a
   very large element of luck,' he wrote. Having managed to
   peek at the censor order from New Delhi, which stated
   that no story could mention the Japanese invasion of India,
   he typed the following flash – 'Dateline Imphal: For first
   time in 120 years there is war on Indian soil' – then
   browbeat the officer-on-duty into clearing it.

   The censors were more rigorous about denying the news
   that nearly all of Kohima had fallen into Japanese hands.
   After the 2nd British Division had arrived to counter the

Japanese 31st Division, Mankekar wrote, 'I was in difficulties to explain to my readers why British troops were attacking a British-held town!'

4. 'Operation Chawal' was conducted specifically in the areas ceded on the Imphal Plain, between Bishenupur and Moirang, by the 70th Field Company Bengal Sappers and Miners.

5. William Slim, *Defeat Into Victory*, p. 414.

6. Jehan Dad, the jemadar of 'A' platoon, would receive the George Medal for his rescue.

Chapter 20: The Road Ahead

1. K. Sankaran Nair, *Inside IB and RAW: A Rolling Stone that Gathered Moss*, p. 46.

Afterword

1. Mark Tully, *Stand at East*, BBC Radio 4, accessed at Imperial War Museum, London, cat. 28317/9.

2. Indivar Kamtekar, 'A Different War Dance', p198.

3. The Corps of Indian Engineers would itself grow from a strength of 200 officers and less than 11,000 other ranks in September 1939 to 7,000 officers and a quarter of a million men. During the war it built 1600 miles of major new road within India, most of that in the North-East Frontier, as well as 34 miles of bridging. See *The Corps of Indian Engineers: 1939–1947* by Majors S. Verma and V. K. Anand, p. 107.

4. Auchinleck papers cited in Daniel Marston, *The Indian Army and the End of the Raj: Decolonising the Subcontinent*, p. 75.

5. '200,000 on the move', *The Times*, 19 Sept 1947 and 'AICC Report on the Disturbances in Punjab, March–April 1947', both quoted in Steven Wilkinson and Saumitra Jha,

'Does Combat Experience Foster Organizational Skill? Evidence from Ethnic Cleansing during the Partition of South Asia'.

6. Wilkinson and Jha's quantitative study (ibid.) demonstrated this correlation, between the fact and the duration of Indian battalions' combat experience and the outcomes in terms of lethal and non-lethal ethnic cleansing in their home districts. Combat in the war, they concluded, imbued veterans with 'organizational skill'. Such skill – 'at private organization of defense, offense and mobility' – was greatly visible in the ethnic violence that forced minority emigration, but also in fostering of 'co-ethnic immigration' in home districts during Partition. The effect was the opposite, naturally, in districts where it was the minority community that was recruited for combat roles, as was usually the case with Sikhs.

7. Madhushree Mukerjee, *Churchill's Secret War*, p. 36.

8. Donny Gluckstein, *A People's History of the Second World War: Resistance Versus Empire*, New York, 2012, p. 189.

9. 'Mr Nehru May Go to Java', *Times of India*, 29 October 1945.

10. The peak of that battle, on 10 November, is still commemorated in Indonesia as 'Heroes' Day'.

11. In the phrase of Arjun Appadurai, a leading scholar of post-colonial nationalism, reflecting on his experience growing up in the 1950s, after his father had been the Minister for Publicity and Propaganda in the provisional government of Azad Hind. From Arjun Appadurai's article 'Patriotism and its Futures', *Public Culture*, 1993, 5:411-429.

Appendix 1

Timeline

1939

Sept: Kosh and Manek marry in Madras

1 Sept: Germany invades Poland; Britain and France declare war

3 Sept: Viceroy Lord Linlithgow unilaterally commits India to Britain's declared war

14 Sept: Indian National Congress demands self-determination in exchange for cooperation in the war

29 Oct: Congress provincial ministries begin resigning in protest of India's entry into the war

1940

10 Jun: Italy declares war on Britain, and prepares to invade Egypt, Sudan, Kenya and British Somaliland

17 Jun: Government declares all units of Indian Army open to emergency commissioned Indian officers

23 Sept: Second Field Company arrives in Port Sudan to join the newly raised 5th Indian Infantry Division

1941

19 Jan: Subhas Chandra Bose escapes Calcutta to make for Germany

15 Mar: Fifth Indian Division begins the attack on Fort
Dologorodoc in Eritrea

27 Mar: The fall of Keren to British Indian forces

1 Apr: No 2 Squadron, Indian Air Force, is raised at
Peshawar

18 May: After the defeat at Amba Alagi, Italian forces in East
Africa surrender

Jun: Eighth Indian Division, followed by 10th Indian Division,
invade Iraq

1 Jun: Manek commissioned into No 2 Squadron, Indian Air
Force

22 Jun: Operation Barbarossa begins, as Axis troops invade the
Soviet Union

Sept: Manek posted to Kohat, prior to Miranshah

15 Nov: John Walker Wright commissioned into the Indian
Army

7–8 Dec: Japan bombs Pearl Harbor and invades Kota Bahru in
British Malaya, opening the war in Asia and the Pacific

1942

Feb: No 2 Squadron IAF returns to South India for Army
cooperation exercises

15 Feb: Surrender of Singapore

8 Mar: Fall of Rangoon

23 Mar: Japanese troops begin the occupation of India's
Andaman Islands

23 Mar: Stafford Cripps arrives in India

End Mar: Bobby graduates from College of Engineering,
Guindy

5–9 Apr: Japanese carrier aircraft bomb naval bases in Ceylon
and South India

13 Apr: Evacuation of Madras ordered

27 May: Battle of 'the Cauldron' begins, leading to the collapse
of the Eighth Army back to Egypt

5 Jun: Ganny commissioned into the Indian Medical Service

20 Jun: Surrender of the Tobruk fortress; 30,000 Allied
troops, mainly Indian and South African, captured

July: John Walker Wright joins 2nd Field Company at El
Alamein

4 Aug: Nugs and Ganny marry in Kohat

8 Aug: Quit India resolution passed in Bombay

20 Aug: Ganny reaches Officer Training School in Mhow

26 Aug: Legion Freies Indien formed by Bose in Berlin

23 Oct–11 Nov: Second Battle of El Alamein

28 Nov: Bobby commissioned into KGVO Bengal Sappers &
Miners

Dec: Manek flies to Ranchi to train at low-level flying in
Hurricane aircraft

10 Dec: Ganny dies of asthma bronchitis in Thal

1943

1 Jan: Nugs's daughter born in Madras

14 Feb: The first Chindit expedition crosses the Chinwin River
into Burma

21 Feb: General Paulus's army surrenders and siege of
Stalingrad is lifted

17 Mar: Bobby joins 2nd Field Company in Iraq

7 Apr: Six pilots of No 2 Squadron IAF fly to Imphal to aid the
Chindit campaign

27 Apr: Bose is transferred from a German to a Japanese
submarine to be taken to Tokyo

1 May: Second Field Company embarks from Basra for Bombay

13 May: Remains of Rommel's army defeated in Tunisia,
ending the war in North Africa

25 May: Manek killed in a plane crash in Burma

20 Jun: Auchinleck appointed Commander-in-Chief India for the second time

25 Aug: Admiral Lord Louis Mountbatten appointed Supreme Allied Commander for South-East Asia

Sept: Eighth Indian Division, followed later by the 4th and 10th, join the Italian campaign

Sept: Second Field Company assembles at Monghyr, Bihar, to begin training

Dec: Second Field Company arrives at Chittagong

20 Dec: Edul Dadabhoy, Manek's brother, joins No 7 Squadron, IAF

30 Dec: Fifth Indian Division begins 'Operation Jericho' in the Arakan, launching attack towards Razabil fortress

1944

Jan: Fifth Division conducts 'Operation Jonathan', the assault on Razabil

8 Feb: Siege of the 'Admin Box' in the Arakan

1 Apr: Edul Dadabhoy killed in a plane crash in Burma

6 Apr: Siege of Kohima begins

18 Apr: Siege of Kohima ends with reinforcement by 1/1st Punjab

6 Jun: 'D-Day' – Allied troops invade the beaches of Normandy

22 Jun: Imphal–Kohima road is opened, ending the three-month siege of Imphal

23 Aug: Liberation of Paris

9 Nov: Bobby's death recorded

End Nov: Fifth Indian Division airlifted from Kalemyo back to India

1945

2 May: Berlin falls to the Soviet Army. Within a week, the
war in Europe is over

6 Aug: The United States drops the atomic bomb on Hiroshima

15 Aug: Japanese surrender ends the war in Asia

10 Nov: Peak of the battle of Surabaya, fought between
Indonesian nationalists and the 5th Indian Division

Appendix 2

The Indian Army

The Army in India consisted of two separate services: the British Army in India, and the Indian Army. The units and personnel of the British Army in India were entirely British and were controlled by the Secretary of State for War at Whitehall. The Indian Army was led by a commander-in-chief, who reported to the Viceroy and thus to the Secretary of State for India. It did, however, include British troops. Its battalions were generally one third Indian, one third Gurkha and one third British, at first commanded exclusively by British officers, though Indian and Nepali officers slowly gained admission after 1919. Thus a typical Indian Army brigade consisted of one Indian battalion, one Gurkha battalion and one British battalion. These proportions tilted toward Indian units as the Second World War progressed.

The Army division, the formation generally considered for strategic planning, consisted of three infantry brigades, supported by ancillary arms. Divisional engineers included an independent bridging platoon, besides a field park company consisting of a stores platoon, a workshops platoon and a field platoon for non-infantry troop support. Each brigade was a basic formation containing 'all arms': three infantry battalions, supported by one regiment of artillery, a sapper field company, and units of Signals, Service, Ordnance, Medical and other support corps.

The Army at War:

Army
(commanded by a full general)
|
Corps
(commanded by a lieutenant general)
|
Division
(commanded by a major general)
|
Brigade
(brigadier)
|
Battalion
(lieutenant colonel)
|
Company
(major or captain)
|
Platoon
(lieutenant)
|
Sections
(VCOs)

At Gazala:

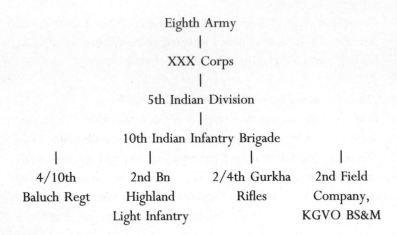

Eighth Army
|
XXX Corps
|
5th Indian Division
|
10th Indian Infantry Brigade

| 4/10th Baluch Regt | 2nd Bn Highland Light Infantry | 2/4th Gurkha Rifles | 2nd Field Company, KGVO BS&M |

On the Tiddim Road:

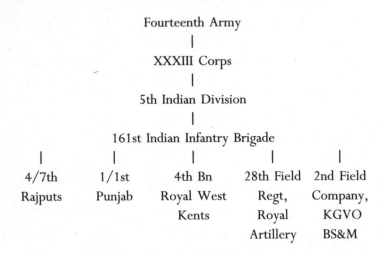

Fourteenth Army
|
XXXIII Corps
|
5th Indian Division
|
161st Indian Infantry Brigade

| 4/7th Rajputs | 1/1st Punjab | 4th Bn Royal West Kents | 28th Field Regt, Royal Artillery | 2nd Field Company, KGVO BS&M |

Indian ranks

Officers

The Indian Army officer corps comprised regular commissioned officers, as well as emergency or wartime commissioned officers, holding ranks identical to those in the British Army.

Viceroy's Commissioned Officers (VCOs)

Ever since the East India Company began to absorb Indian forces, three ranks were preserved to maintain the best native officers in charge: in ascending order, *jemadars*, *subedars* and *subedars-major*. (In the cavalry, the rank equivalent to *subedar* was *risaldar*.) These became the Viceroy's Commissioned Officers, the archangels of the British Indian Army, and intermediaries for the European *sahibs*. Promoted from the ranks, they were the best, most experienced soldiers in any unit, and the keystones of regimental order. Their authority was respected nearly as much by the British officers above as by the enlisted ranks below. As a second lieutenant, Bobby's rank was superior to the VCOs, although they were men often twice his age and with immeasurably greater service experience.

Non-Commissioned Officers (NCOs) and other ranks

havildar (sergeant)

naik (corporal)

lance-naik (lance corporal)

sepoy (private)

Engineering field companies

An engineering field company was typically commanded by a major, with a captain as second-in-command in charge of a headquarters group of about forty sappers. Three lieutenants commanded separate platoons of Hindus, Muslims and Sikhs, each comprising about seventy sappers. Other officers included an attached medical officer, British warrant officers and Indian VCOs.

Sapper platoon:

In the field, platoons were often self-contained, operating on their own sectors, and receiving orders from company headquarters. A platoon was led by a lieutenant, with a jemadar as second-in-command and a havildar as senior NCO. Each platoon typically received three non-enlisted personnel (a cook, a bhisti, and a sweeper) along with twelve trucks, two anti-tank projectors, four Bren guns, and ten Thompson sub-machine guns.

Sapper section:

A sapper platoon was divided as five sections of twelve men: four rifle sections and one driver section for the platoon's vehicles. Each section was led by a naik, a rank equivalent to the British rank of corporal. Naiks and their seconds, lance-naiks, carried Thompson SMGs. One team of two men worked a Bren gun, and the others carried rifles.

Second Field Company, KGVO BS&M in October 1944

1 (acting) major: Williams

4 lieutenants: Reid, Wright, Mantle, Rayner and Mugaseth

5 VCOs

1 warrant officer

12 havildars

14 naiks

237 lance-naiks and sappers

7 NCSEs (Non-combatant enrolled)

Select Bibliography

I was lucky to be able to reconstruct the journey of a field company, a miniscule unit in the scale of a world war. I detailed the career of 2nd Field Company by triangulating (or pentangulating) from five sources concerned with different levels of their formation: division, brigade, regiment, company and individual.

I relied enormously on the divisional history, *The Ball of Fire: The Fifth Indian Division in the Second World War*, by Antony Brett-James (London, 1951), as well as the history of a 161st Brigade infantry battalion: *Road of Bones, The Epic Siege of Kohima*, by Fergal Keane (London, 2010), which follows the 4th Battalion Royal West Kents. My description of the fighting in Kohima owes a great deal to his powerful and exhaustive account.

I also used the official history of the sapper regiment (*Brief History of the KGV's Own Bengal Sappers and Miners Group, August 1939–July 1946*), the war diary of the company (preserved at the Ministry of Defence History Division in New Delhi) and a personal account from inside the unit (interview with Lieutenant John Walker Wright at the Imperial War Museum, London).

Where Manek's air force squadron was concerned, the operations record books survive at the National Archives in London and the Ministry of Defence History Division in Delhi. The

Indian Air Force has been favoured with a devoted community of veterans and civilian experts, so its war history is relatively well documented. However the operations record books of No 2 Squadron are missing their pages between September 1942 and September 1943 – thus no official details of the Imphal detachment are recorded, and all we know of their experience is from press reports and anecdotes. On the IAF generally, I relied mainly on the *The Eagle Strikes* by Squadron Leader Rana Chhina, and the website Bharat Rakshak.

A few other books were integral to my account of the war in India's perspective. Foremost among these was the superb *Forgotten Armies: The Fall of British Asia 1941–45*, by Christopher Bayly and Tim Harper (London, 2004). The research of Indivar Kamtekar provided the social and economic vista of civilian India in 1942–43.

Bobby's family:

Khanduri, C. B., *Thimayya: An Amazing Life*, Delhi, 2006

'Remembering GP, the gentle colossus', *The Hindu*, 7 July 2012

Sahgal, Lakshmi, *A Revolutionary Life: Memoirs of a Political Activist*, New Delhi, 1999

Sankaran Nair, K., *Inside I. B. and R. A. W.: A Rolling Stone that Gathered Moss*, New Delhi, 2008

Sharada Prasad, H. Y., (ed), *GP, The Man and His Work: A Volume in Memory of G. Parthasarathi*, New Delhi, 1998

The Indian Air Force:

Chhina, Rana, *The Eagle Strikes: The Royal Indian Air Force, 1932–50*, New Delhi, 2006

'In Their Jungle Home: IAF on Eastern Front', *The Illustrated Weekly of India*, 13 June 1943

Lal, Air Chief Marshal P. C., *My Years with the IAF*, New Delhi, 2012

Lindqvist, Sven, *A History of Bombing*, London, 2002

Ramunny, Wing Commander Murkot, *The Sky was the Limit*, New Delhi, 1997

Sapru, Somnath, *Combat Lore, The Indian Air Force, 1930–45*, New Delhi, 2014

Singh, Jasjit, *The Icon: Marshal of the Indian Air Force, Arjan Singh, DFC*, New Delhi, 2009

———— *Defence from the Skies: 80 Years of the Indian Air Force*, New Delhi, 2013

Singh, Pushpindar, *The Battle Axes: No 7 Squadron IAF, 1942–92*, New Delhi, 1993

Omissi, David E., *Air Power and Colonial Control: The Royal Air Force 1919–39*, Manchester, 1990

The Indian Army:

Ahmad, Mustasad, *Heritage: The History of the Rajput Regiment 1778–1947*, Delhi, 1989

'Army in India Training Memoranda: War Series Omnibus', Simla, 1945

Barkawi, Tarak, 'Peoples, Homelands, and Wars? Ethnicity, the Military, and Battle among British Imperial Forces in the War against Japan', *Society for Comparative Study of Society and History*, 2004

———— 'Culture and Combat in the Colonies: The Indian Army in the Second World War' in *Journal of Contemporary History*; 41: 325 (2006)

Barua, Pradeep P., *Gentlemen of the Raj: The Indian Army Officer Corps 1817–1949*, Westport, 2003

Churchill, Winston, *The Story of the Malakand Field Force*, online at www.gutenberg.org

The Fighting Fifth: The History of the 5th Indian Division, New Delhi, 1948

Guy, Alan J., and Boyden, Peter B., *Soldiers of the Raj: The British Army 1600–1947*, London, 1997

Jeffreys, Alan, 'The Officer Corps and the Training of the Indian Army with Specific Reference to Lt Gen. Francis Tuker', in *History of Warfare*, Vol. 70 (2011)

Kaushik, Roy, (ed.), *The Indian Army in the Two World Wars*, Leiden, 2011

Kipling, Rudyard, 'Her Majesty's Servants' in *The Jungle Book*, London, (first published 1894), 2011

MacKenzie, Compton, *Eastern Epic, Vol. I, September 1939–March 1943*, London, 1951

Marston, Daniel, *The Indian Army and the End of the Raj: Decolonising the Subcontinent*, Cambridge, 2014

Prasad, Bisheshwar, (ed.), *Official History of the Indian Armed Forces in the Second World War*, New Delhi, 1953–60

Qureshi, Major Mohammed Ibrahim, *The History of the First Punjab Regiment: 1759–1956*, New Delhi, 1958

Recruiting for the Defence Services in India, Combined Inter-Services Historical Section (India & Pakistan), Delhi, 1950

Tully, Mark, 'Stand at East', BBC Radio 4, June 2005

Warner, Philip, *Auchinleck: The Lonely Soldier*, London, 1981

The Indian Medical Service:

Palit, D. K., *Saga of an Indian IMS Officer: The Life and Times of Lt Col. Anand Nath Palit, OBE,* New Delhi, 2006

Thapar, D. R., *The Morale Builders, Forty Years with the Indian Medical Services of India*, London, 1965

King George V's Own Bengal Sappers and Miners:

Brief History of the KGV's Own Bengal Sappers and Miners Group (August 1939–July 1946), Roorkee, 1947

Cooper, General Sir George, and Alexander, Major David, *The Bengal Sappers 1803–2003*, Chatham, 2003

Khanna, Colonel R. B., *God's Own Bengal Sappers*, New Delhi, 2003

Manual of Field Engineering, Vols I, II & III (RE), War Office, London 1936 (held at the Imperial War Museum, London, ref: WO 1208)

Verma, Major S., and Anand, V. K., *The Corps of Indian Engineers: 1939–1947*, Delhi, 1974

Africa and the Middle East:

Barnett, Correlli, *The Desert Generals*, London, 1983

Douds, Gerald, 'Matters of Honour: Indian Troops in the North African and Italian Theatres', in *Time to Kill: The Soldier's Experience of War in the West, 1939–1945*, eds Len Deighton, Paul Addison and Angus Calder, London, 1997

Paiforce: The Official Story of the Persia and Iraq Command, 1941–46, London, 1948

The Tiger Kills: The History of the Indian Divisions in the North Africa Campaign, with a foreword by Field-Marshal Claude Auchinleck, Her Majesty's Stationery Office, Government of India, Delhi, 1944.

Wrong, Michela, *I Didn't Do It For You: How the World Betrayed a Small African Nation*, New York, 2005

Young, Desmond, *Rommel*, London, 1956

Burma and the North-Eastern Frontier:

Cooper, Jilly, *Animals in War*, London, 1983

Frei, Henry, *Guns of February: Ordinary Japanese Soldiers' Views of the Malayan Campaign and the Fall of Singapore 1941–42*, Singapore, 2004

Friedman, Herbert A., 'Axis and Allied Propaganda to Indian Troops,' www.psywarrior.com/AxisPropIndia.html

Graham, Gordon, *The Trees Are All Young on Garrison Hill*, Buckinghamshire, 2005

India Command Joint Planning Staff Paper No 15: Defence of India I, 23 April 1942 (National Archives, AIR 23/1967)

India Command Joint Planning Staff Paper No 15: Defence of India II, May 1942 (National Archives, AIR 23/1967)

Kire, Easterine, *Mari*, New Delhi 2010

Lowry, Michael, *Fighting Through to Kohima*, Barnsley, 2003

Lyall-Grant, Ian, *Burma: The Turning Point*, West Sussex, 1993

Mankekar, D. R., *Leaves from a War Reporter's Diary*, Delhi, 1977

Masters, John, *The Road Past Mandalay*, London, 1973

Phillips, Lucas C. E., *Springboard to Victory*, London, 1966

Slim, Field Marshal Viscount, *Defeat into Victory*, London, 1999

Thompson, Julian, in association with the Imperial War Museum, *The Forgotten Voices of Burma: The Second World War's Forgotten Conflict*, London, 2010

———— *The Imperial War Museum Book of the War in Burma 1942–1945*, London, 2012

Civilian Life and the War at Home:

Fernandes, Naresh, *Taj Mahal Foxtrot*, New Delhi, 2012

Kamtekar, Indivar 'The Shiver of 1942', *Studies in History*, Vol. 18, No 81, 2002

———— 'A Different War Dance: State and Class in India 1939–1945', *Past and Present*, 176, No 1, 2002

Madras Musings, November 1–15, 1999

Mukerjee, Madhushree, 'Bengal Famine of 1943: An Appraisal of the Famine Inquiry Commission,' in *Economic and Political Weekly*, Vol, XLIX, No 11, 15 March 2014

————— *Churchill's Secret War*, Chennai, 2010

Murzban, M. M., *The Parsis: Being an Enlarged and Copiously Annotated up-to-date English Edition of Mlle. Delphine Menant's 'Les Parsis'*, Bombay, 1917

Nanavutty, Pilo, *The Parsis*, New Delhi, 1980

Reddy, O. Pulla, *Autumn Leaves*, Bombay, 1978

National Politics:

Habib, Irfan, 'Civil Disobedience 1930–31', *Social Scientist*, Vol. 25, No 9/10 Sept–Oct 1997, pp. 43–66

Herman, Arthur, *Gandhi and Churchill: The Epic Rivalry that Destroyed an Empire and Forged Our Age*, London, 2008

Pandey, Gyan, (ed.), *The Indian Nation in 1942*, Calcutta, 1989

Sarkar, Sumit, *Modern India, 1885–1947*, London, 1983

Subhas Bose and Axis-aligned Forces:

Bamber, Martin, and Neeven, Aad, *For Free India: Indian Soldiers in Germany and Italy during the Second World War*, Amsterdam, 2010

Chaudhuri, Nirad C., *Thy Hand, Great Anarch! India 1921–52*, London, 1987

Hauner, Milan, 'One Man Against the Empire', *Journal of Contemporary History*, Vol. 16, No. 1, (Jan 1981), pp. 183–212

Toye, Hugh, *The Springing Tiger: A Study of the Indian National Army and of Netaji Subhas Chandra Bose*, Bombay, 1959

Post-1945 Conflict:

Gluckstein, Donny, *A People's History of the Second World War*, London, 2012

Keay, John, *Last Post: The End of the Empire in the Far East*, London, 1997

Wilkinson, Steven, and Jha, Saumitra, 'Does Combat Experience Foster Organizational Skill? Evidence from Ethnic Cleansing during the Partition of South Asia', *American Political Science Review*, Vol. 106, No 4, Nov 2012

Index